# THEY ALL CAME TO BARNEYS

# THEY ALL CAME
# TO BARNEYS

A PERSONAL HISTORY OF
THE WORLD'S GREATEST STORE

GENE PRESSMAN

VIKING

VIKING
An imprint of Penguin Random House LLC
1745 Broadway, New York, NY 10019
penguinrandomhouse.com

Book design by Daniel Lagin

LIBRARY OF CONGRESS CONTROL NUMBER: 2025013741

ISBN 9780593654798 (hardcover)
ISBN 9780593654804 (ebook)

Printed in the United States of America
3rd Printing

The authorized representative in the EU for product safety and compliance is Penguin Random House Ireland, Morrison Chambers, 32 Nassau Street, Dublin D02 YH68, Ireland, https://eu-contact.penguin.ie.

*This book is for Fred Pressman,*
*who raised me, at home and at Barneys.*

# CONTENTS

# WE MADE SHIT HAPPEN

**THEY ALL CAME TO BARNEYS.** During the greatest, most exciting years in the world's greatest, most exciting city, it was the world's greatest, most exciting store. On any given day, you might see Susan Sontag getting her hair touched up in the downstairs salon, or Warren Beatty and Donald Sutherland buying Armani tuxes in the Grey Room on the second floor. Warhol would swing by for parties, multi-floor fashion shows where the models might be Madonna or your future wife (mine was). "Gee, Kid," Warhol would ask—he called me the "the Pressman kid"—"could I have a discount?" (I hated when people would ask that, but he was famously cheap, and he'd appeared in one of our ad campaigns—so sure.) Men would bring their wives, and their girlfriends—sometimes on the same day. We shut the store down for Elizabeth Taylor, for Michael Jackson, for the sultan of Brunei, who came with two busloads of wives and attendants and three body doubles, though not a soul was there but them. While the old department stores were gathering dust on Fifth Avenue, the action was all downtown.

Everyone shopped at Barneys: the glamorous and the difficult, the young and the old, celebrities and celebrities in their own minds—and our salespeople, many of whom thought they were celebrities, too.

Barneys wasn't a store—or not just. Yes, we sold suits—millions of them. Yes, we grew to incorporate clothes, and bags, and shoes, and makeup, and skincare, and gifts for the home, things you'd see there first and only. Armani before Armani was Armani, before the $2 billion global business and the one-name status; when we found him, he was a handsome guy called Giorgio with a rinky-dink office in Milan. Fornasetti, his illustrated faces beaming like the Mona Lisa off of Italian china. Isaia, the hottest young designer in '80s New York, who would saunter in and sell his stuff to delighted ladies right off the rack. More Japanese fashion than you could find anywhere outside Tokyo, geniuses like Yohji Yamamoto and Rei Kawakubo doing basic black before basic black was the official color of New York. It was a destination, an all-day, into-the-night entertainment, with a restaurant for mid-splurge sustenance. You'd run into friends, you'd run into exes, you'd run into enemies. Which was the most fun?

This is the story of Barneys: my business, my birthright. It's about the store that obsessed and defined three generations of the Pressman family, from my grandfather Barney, who founded it, to my father, Fred, who expanded it, to me and my brother, who modernized it. We grew up with the store and the store grew up with us, a downtown discounter that birthed a dynasty. It's a story about our family, who began as fledgling strivers on the Lower East Side and made our way to Park Avenue prosperity, a twentieth-century journey as American as apple blintz. And it's a story of New York as it grew to become the center of the universe, the most influential city in the most powerful nation on earth.

It's my story of life at the heart of it all, as the doldrums of the post-war '50s gave way to the electric abandon of the rock 'n' roll '60s, the

The Pressmans of Barneys: Bob, Fred, Barney,
and me in the original men's store, 1979.

party-mad '70s, the gold-plated '80s, and the hang-on '90s: the city during one of its most fertile and frantic eras. New York saw—New York was the epicenter of—the emergence of casual sex, drugs and delirious disco, the burgeoning gay rights movement, punk rock and new wave, gentrification and greed in the Wall Street boom. I was the luckiest person on the planet, born with a front-row seat to history. And I didn't waste a minute of it.

But I never meant to be there at all.

. . .

The best stores have always been more than stores. Their ambitions have always been bigger, their tactics grander. They're circuses, and arcades, and amusement parks. They can be meat markets and set pieces for meet-cutes, pickup joints par excellence: salespeople hitting on customers, customers hitting on salespeople, customers hitting on each other. There have been Barneys marriages and, I'm sure, more than a few Barneys divorces.

The fashion business has always been perceived as frivolous, a world of models and playboys, gay men and ladies who lunch. But it's showbiz. It's no accident that the guy who founded the National Association of Window Trimmers—the people that decorate shop windows—also created the Wizard of Oz. From the dawn of the modern department store in the early twentieth century—when Turkish bazaars, running fountains, and live birds enticed women in—to so-called "omnichannel," "retailtainment," and every other bullshit new coinage the so-called marketing geniuses invent today, it's always been the same. At Siegel-Cooper, the now-mostly-forgotten turn of the (twentieth) century "Big Store"—it included a bank, a barbershop, a post office, and its own orchestra—that stretched from Eighteenth to Nineteenth Streets on Sixth Avenue, Harry Siegel installed a searchlight on the building to project his advertising onto the clouds. (For the record, Barneys was always a specialty store—I hate when people call it a department store.)

It's an education business, too. You're exposing people to amazing things from all over the world that they might never experience otherwise, hoping to raise the bar. If you do it right, you elevate your customer and elevate the product, and you can power the creation of a whole new industry. The stores of New York helped to build the American fashion business as we know it, a homegrown alternative to Paris couture that began by knocking it off and then grew into its competitor—younger, cooler, more carefree. The stores were the tip of the spear of style, the wellspring from which the magazines drew and whose message they spread: The ambition of *Vogue*, wrote Edna Woolman Chase, who became its editor in 1914, was "to show the women in the rest of the U.S. what New York stores, dressmakers and milliners were offering and what the smart women of New York were buying." The twentieth century birthed a complete revolution in the business of clothes, an explosion of both creativity and commerce. These things don't just happen. You need visionaries to smell the change, find the innovators, teach and tempt new customers. It was a local, and then a global, mission, manifest destiny in a miniskirt. The stores, and most of all Barneys, were there.

I'm getting ahead of myself. It would be a long time—over fifty years—before women were shopping at Barneys, at least for themselves. (Women are, and always have been, major purchasers of menswear, for their husbands, sons, and boyfriends, though even early on, savvy women also knew that the best deals for themselves could be found in Barneys' boys department.) Barneys in its original iteration was for men and by a man, and that man was Barney. He crowned himself the "Cut-Rate King," dealt suits at a discount in the days when men wore nothing else, and bragged that there was nobody, and no body, he couldn't fit: He kept an army of tailors across the street and offered free alterations. (He also offered free parking, one of the many secrets to his success.) Even without the birds and fountains of the earlier stores, Barney figured out how to get his name out into the world. He was an advertising pioneer, buying up radio airtime until the store was one of the biggest advertisers in the New York market—and it was a little bit of tabloid genius on his part to run them during the constant coverage of the Lindbergh trial. Those radio ads—"Calling all men to Barneys!"—rang in the ears of generations.

Fred extended Barney's genius and enlarged his ambitions. Barneys began buying—and selling—full-price merchandise, and Fred's search for the best of the best took him to Europe. On family and business trips alike, Fred scoured Jermyn Street and Savile Row, the trade shows in Florence and Milan, the emerging men's ready-to-wear in Paris. In 1970, he opened the International House, offering Pierre Cardin and Yves Saint Laurent from Paris, Bruno Piattelli and Brioni from Rome, and, soon after, the greatest of them all, Giorgio Armani, who he introduced to America in 1975, with a new space in the store and, the following year, a TV commercial featuring Armani, with his movie-star looks, at home in Milan, sketching away at his drafting table. More show; more business.

If Barneys loomed large in my youth, it loomed in the background. Barneys was suits, and I was jeans. As a kid, I was proud of the store— everyone knew it—but I wasn't much interested in it. Mom would drag me down to buy stuff (or to take stuff), but I hated shopping. I was a classic hormonal hell-raiser, a bad boy of the suburbs, the one the teachers would aim for when they spun around at the blackboard and launched an eraser straight at the loudest loudmouth's head. I didn't mind the little bit of cred Barneys' success gave me—it was so well known by the time I came around that you only had to tell a taxi driver, "Take me to Seventh Avenue and Seventeenth Street," and he'd reel off the Barneys radio jingle as he drove you straight there.

But my youthful experience with Barneys was pretty limited. I was into girls and my guitar, often but not always in that order.

I may look like an heir apparent in retrospect, but I'd never thought I was destined for a life at the store. I was meant for the movies. I left home for college in 1968, an auteur in the making. It was a golden age of American cinema—in the four years I was at school, *2001, Rosemary's Baby, Midnight Cowboy, Easy Rider, The Godfather,* and my all-time favorite, *A Clockwork Orange,* all came out—and I was going to be one of the greats, too. When I graduated, in 1972, I went west to Hollywood, determined to make a name for myself. But my first gig doing gofer grunt work on the set of a Blaxploitation flick didn't seem like a sure path to glory, and my next interview turned out to be for on-screen talent in a porno film. No, thanks. I made my way home to New York, exasperated and uncertain, but open to anything. I needed a place to live, and got an offer I couldn't refuse: a marble-terraced duplex on Park Avenue, with a roommate—its owner, Barney. On Sixty-Seventh and Park, we were two peas in a gilded pod, Bachelor No. 1 and Bachelor No. 2: the seventy-seven-year-old widower, a buttoned-up gentleman born at the tail end of the nineteenth century, and me, twenty-two years old, a rock 'n' roll renegade forever in jeans.

I needed something to do, so with no expectations, I joined the family trade. Every morning, Barney and I would descend together to his chauffeured Caddy and make our way to the store: He to the offices and the top of the food chain, and me to the warehouse to start at the bottom. Barneys would become my canvas, my film. Show business *was* the family business. I just didn't know it then.

Over the twenty-five years I climbed the ladder, I brought Barneys to a new level as my father had. Fred raised Barneys up, with taste and discernment, and I took Barneys wide, opening its doors to women's wear, to sportswear, to cosmetics, to restaurants. I took it across the country and then around the world. With a team of the best, we made Barneys young, sexy, and essential. It reflected the culture, and it made the culture. At the store, Barney was "Mr. Barney," and Fred, "Mr. Pressman." But me? I was Gene. And would you believe we all shared a secretary, the sainted Miss Terry?

. . .

When people remember Barneys now—now that it's gone, a pale shadow of what we created is all that remains—sometimes they remember the stuff. The suit they graduated in, or got married in, or for those who go way back, got bar mitzvahed or confirmed in. They remember the Bonpoint baby gifts, and the Helmut Lang jeans (back when they were still made in Italy, scandalously), and the Prada bags in industrial-chic nylon. The stuff is great—we loved stuff, as long as it was the best, the finest, the rarest.

But Barneys was more than stuff. It was a relationship we had with people. It was pleasure; it could be like a drug. We knew we'd arrived not when we sold the most merchandise but when we became part of the vernacular. To this day, people still say, "That's very Barneys." When they encounter something precious and ever-so-slightly-off—ten degrees at most—that's very Barneys. And when they encounter something timeless and perfect, something trend-proof as all truly modern things are, that's very Barneys, too.

The thing that made Barneys Barneys—the thing that separated us from the rest—was the way we put it together. There's a magic, an alchemy, that comes from the right mix, shown the right way, advertised the right way. What Fred instilled in me, and in all of us, was that creative magic. "Merchandising" is a term that gets thrown around a lot in the industry, but few on the outside know what it means. Put plainly, merchandising is selecting the right stuff, and putting it together in the right place, the right time, the right color, the right size. It seems like it should be easy. It's never easy.

Fred lived in the details: the right tie to go with the shirt to go with the suit and the overcoat, down to the right buttonholes. He trained an army of buyers to go out and find the best and bring it back, and they did. They could extract the needles from the haystacks—and for the biggest labels, those were some big haystacks. Everything had to be quality: no dogs, no duds. (Or as Barney famously put it, "no bunk, no junk.") How many times did I swing through showrooms in Paris or Milan to oversee our team's "buy," the selection they'd make for the store from designers' full collections, and find them hard at it. On the other side of the table might be a stormtrooper disguised as a salesman. I'll never forget Kenzo Takada's business partner, Gilles, the bitter to Kenzo's sweet. He'd come around as we were writing orders, all supercilious charm, checking with the commercial staff to see how we were doing. Good, the sales guys would say. "Fine," he'd reply, then turn to us: "Now buy more."

You needed to stand up to guys like that—politely but firmly—to hold Barneys' ground. Our people could do that, and did. They wanted what they wanted, negotiated till they got it, and brought it back home. That's the reason people treasured what they got from Barneys, whispered it like a secret, kept it for years. They, we, were the substance of Barneys. It was always more than a label or an address or a name to drop.

It was a state of mind and a badge of honor. It wasn't about money—though we made a lot of it, and lost a lot of it—and it wasn't only for those with money. (I can't tell you how many women came in to buy a lipstick, just to get that black and silver shopping bag.) Going to Barneys meant pledging allegiance to the tribes of the stylish and the urbane, the ones who *knew*. It was downtown before downtown, a stalwart since Chelsea meant tenements and warehouses, guard-your-pocketbook territory, $250-a-month rents including all the rats you could catch. And then it was downtown as downtown emerged as the new cultural capital of New York, a land of thumping clubs, mush-rooming art galleries, and restaurants where the waiters were cooler, and having more fun, than you were. There was Barneys in the center of it all. Barneys *was* New York (even when it would eventually pop up around the country, in Tokyo, and beyond). It always had been, and in retrospect it seemed so obvious that we finally built it into the name: Barneys New York.

What follows is the history of what we created. Much of it I knew, and some of it I didn't—in the process of researching this book, speaking to more than a hundred people who worked with, in, and around Bar-neys, I got a clearer understanding of it than I ever had before, when I was too deep in the thick of it to see the big picture. Now more than ever, I'm amazed. The Barneys story really should be a movie—that's the right frame. There are multimillion-dollar deals and sex scenes and speed bumps. I feel—I've always felt—lucky to have been born into it all. Nobody had a more charmed life than I did. I wasn't per-fect. There were plenty of missteps along the way. But we created the greatest mousetrap ever to sell this stuff, and more than twenty-five years after we left the company, and even now, after its successor-owners steered it to its eventual demise, people tell me all the time: They miss it, and nothing has come along to replace it. Mostly they assume that there will never be another. But I believe—no, I know—that the spirit and authenticity of Barneys will always exist. That's what people are missing when they see something they love and say wistfully, wishfully, "That's very Barneys."

That was our store. This is our story.

# 1

# SELECT, DON'T SETTLE

## 1923-1963

The legend of Barneys' opening has all the trappings of a folktale—a particularly New York, Jewish kind. Young Barney, not yet thirty years old, pawns his wife's engagement ring for the down payment on a little shop on the east side of Seventh Avenue between Sixteenth and Seventeenth Streets: Barney's. (Many years later we dropped the apostrophe, and for simplicity's sake, throughout this book it'll always be "Barneys.") He opens his doors with two hundred craftily sourced suits (he was known to buy out the closets of the recently departed from widows in need of cash) and a sign proclaiming, "No Bunk, No Junk, No Imitations." The year is 1923. The Seventh Avenue subway was constructed barely five years before. The electric lights up and down the avenue weren't in place fifty years yet, and the telephones were still on the old exchanges—to call Barneys, you'd tell the operator, "Get me WAtkins 9-4600."

Barney and his wife, Bertha, were night and day: she was cultured, glamorous, a daughter of privilege with a taste for jewelry and a father who loved racehorses. Barney was a poor boy from the Lower East Side, about as tall as he was wide—size 40 portly short, the king of hard-to-fit, and his own perfect customer— with a lifelong stutter. But he wanted to make something of himself— he had plans. I think my grandmother loved that moxie, and may have recognized it, too: Like the Pressmans, the Gewirtzes, Bertha's family, had started out humbly on the Lower East Side. And even if luck had placed the Gewirtzes and the Pressmans on opposite sides of the tracks, fate had brought them to opposite sides of the street. When they married, at the Royal Lyceum on 114th Street on the first of June, 1919, he lived at 109 East Broadway, and she at 112.

Maybe being the daughter of a pony player gave Bertha a sixth sense about a good bet. Barney, and Barneys, was a winning ticket. Barney worked his short ass off. His innovation, and the thing that supplied the store in its earliest days, was a pipeline of retailers he established who would sell him their leftover merchandise at the end of the season: the unsold, the remaindered, and the returned, at, of course, a nice discount. Barney passed the savings along to his customers, though not before taking a healthy cut himself. By buying up other retailers' inventories, Barney managed to cut the producers out of the equation and end up with product even from those who flatly refused to sell to him—and that, along with the discounted prices he charged, made them crazy. But there wasn't much they could do about it, and the suits kept sailing in and then flying out. And when those companies continued to deny him business, he would work around them, setting up a network of stores, mostly in the South, that would sell him new merchandise if he promised to take out their label before reselling it. He'd mark them up short—that is, with very little difference between his cost and his customers' final price—so he'd make almost no money, but he'd have the labels that gave him greater and greater credibility, classic stalwarts like Hickey Freeman and Southwick.

In 1934, he expanded for the first time. In a photo of its opening-night sale, August 8, 1934, the room is packed with customers, bunting flying. In the '40s, Barney added boys' clothing, and generations of sulking sons were dragged by the ear to Barneys' Boystown for bar mitzvah suits. On Barney's birthday, enjoying the role of neighborhood grandee, he gifted five hundred needy boys warm coats for the winter. "Barney, born and reared on the Lower East Side, knows what it is to feel the pinch of poverty," the local paper reported. "He knows the bitter meaning of going without a coat in cold weather."

But Barney's cold-weather days were over. For decades, Barneys grew and grew—first out, taking over all the storefronts down to Sixteenth Street, and then down to the basement level, where Boystown would be, and finally up, taking over a second story. "Since World War II, Barneys' increase in volume has been almost six fold," his admen would brag when announcing the second level's opening in March of 1966.

For its first fifty years, Barneys was only menswear, and mostly suits: a sea of suits, a crammed ocean of sleeves as far as you could see. The Barneys' difference was volume. There was no one so tall, so short, so fat, or so thin that he couldn't find a suit at the store. That was a Barneys promise.

Bertha was never far. Barneys may have made Barney a wealthy man, but Bertha wasn't content to enjoy his largesse at home in Connecticut. No, she was in the middle of it all, in her big jewels and navy-blue sunglasses like something out of a Met costume exhibition, greeting customers as they came in, taking names and ushering them to the tacky Naugahyde bench seats in the cigarette smoke–choked waiting room. I thought it was hysterical—here's an elegant, sophisticated woman getting down and dirty. And she loved it. Fred, her son, basically grew up there; decades later, he'd recall tossing a ball around with the store staff out on Seventh Avenue. At night, Bertha went back to her rarefied world, their home in Stamford, where Gloria Vanderbilt lived across the street. But by day, she was as much a part of

Opening night at the expanded Barneys, 1934. Barney himself is right
behind the smallest of what looks like a trio of boy singers.

Barneys as Barney. Between the two of them, they made it a runaway success. This was the line Fred grew up to join, and by the time I was born, Barneys was selling more suits than anywhere on earth.

. . .

I came on the scene in 1950, smack in the middle of the baby boom, born to a couple of newlyweds starting out in the postwar afterglow. Fred Pressman had grown up, gone to Rutgers, and served his country in the military police during World War II. His new wife was a local girl from a wealthy suburb of Long Island, barely out of her teens.

Privileged though she was, Phyllis Epstein had had to fight for herself more or less her whole life. Her parents' divorce when she was eight left a lasting mark—she worshipped her handsome father, Mort, and struggled with her beautiful, vain mother, Dorothy, whom she blamed for breaking up the marriage, taking up with a Mr. Goodstein from across the street.

Sent to a girls' boarding school at eight while her parents settled their separation—in those days, many women divorcing set up camp in Reno, where the laws were more accommodating—Phyllis felt her isolation keenly, most especially from her beloved older brother, Euey, who was sent to a military school. She saw him twice a month, on the alternate weekends when her father would visit. Though she moved back with her mother and new stepfather after a year, she was never comfortable with them or her new stepsiblings. When World War II began, she felt all the privations of wartime, the stamp-book at the grocery store, the rations of everything from food to cloth to gasoline. (Her mother, she recalled, volunteered for jury duty just to get the extra two gallons of gas that she would be entitled to.) In high school, Phyllis would go down to the rail station to wave goodbye to the boys in her class who were off to war. Soon enough, that included Euey, who had begun college at Syracuse University but volunteered for the service.

Suddenly Euey, a nice Jewish kid from Long Island, was training in Fort Benning, Georgia, and Mineral Wells, Texas, where he was posted to the Christian Science Servicemen's Center. (At the top of one letter, on CSSC stationery, he crossed out "Christian Science" and made it "Jewish Servicemen's Center." Phyllis must've laughed.) Reading these letters now—Mom saved them like treasures—he sounds more than anything like a *kid*. "Dear Phil," he'd write. "Say, if you get in a good mood again, see if you can dig me up some homemade cookies—chocolate or vanilla. What gives on the home front—who's still around?"

He shipped out to Italy in January of 1945. In February, US newspapers carried word of a successful attack by American forces on Mt. Belvedere, in the Apennines north of Pistoia. What they didn't announce was the heavy American casualties—among them was Euey. It was only two and a half months before the end of the war. He was nineteen years old, a towheaded blond with his whole life ahead of him.

Mom was sixteen when she received the awful telephone call from the army, and had to wait the interminable hour until her mother got home to receive the news—despite her pleas, the officer on the other end of the line could only tell the news to a parent. For the rest of her life, she kept framed photos of young Euey, all blue eyes and not-yet-shed baby fat, in her home like a little shrine. She saved all his letters, the letters her father had sent to him—the last, in February returned unread, marked "deceased"—and the gut-wrenching letters his fellow infantrymen and officers wrote back to Mort's grieving inquiries.

"Late in February of 1945, our division attacked Mount Belvedere, Italy, one of the strongest and most heavily fortified German positions in the Apennine Mountains," a first lieutenant named John

Clayton wrote him. "Gene was in a foxhole with a Polish boy, whose name slips my mind at the moment though he was Gene's best friend and inseparable companion. The Germans started shelling and they made a direct hit with an 88mm shell on Gene's foxhole. The Polish boy was killed instantly and Gene was so severely wounded he lived only a few short moments. I crawled over to his foxhole and gave him a cigarette and a drink from my canteen and asked him how he felt. He said he felt OK except that he couldn't feel anything . . . that he was numb all over. One of his legs had been blown completely open and his other leg and stomach were ripped to shreds. I told him he'd be OK and that we'd be seeing him back in the States. He smiled, said, 'Take care of yourself, Lieutenant . . . get a Kraut for me.' With that smile still on his lips, he died in my arms there on Belvedere."

Phyllis wanted to get anywhere but where she was. Going to college was not a given for a girl in those days, but she found her way to Parsons College, a school in the farmlands of Iowa, where she was one of the only Jewish girls for miles around. She lasted two years. Two years of church services with farm-raised friends, two years of boyfriends on the football team. But home one summer, she was set up by a nosy friend of her mother's with a local boy, and that was that. Phyllis found her stability at last in Fred.

It was the summer of 1948, and she was all of nineteen. He was a well-to-do Stamford boy a few years older than her, with a swimming pool so big it had its own waterfall; she'd brought her own towel to their date, assuming he was taking her to the beach. But when he picked her up in his Jeep—the army was selling off its wartime fleet cheap—he brought her home, where she met his parents, strolled with them over the sprawling property, and got poison ivy for her trouble. Fred had been engaged to a Connecticut girl—a nice society WASP—but he fell for Phyllis's flirtatious charm, which covered, but never totally concealed, her steely independence.

The newlyweds, Phyllis and Fred, 1949.

The firstborn: Baby me, 1951, with Dad at
Barney and Bertha's Connecticut home.

Theirs was a fast courtship. Phyllis recorded it in her scrapbook, which still has the dried and pressed flower he got her for her twentieth birthday, the tickets to the Broadway show he took her to. (Henry Fonda in *Mr. Roberts*: "A perfect evening, excellent, wonderful!" she wrote. And Fred's comment: "But, honey, where can I park?") On March 27, 1949, they were married at Temple B'Nai Jeshrun, honeymooned for six weeks in Rio, and then moved into the Oliver Cromwell Hotel on Seventy-Second Street before Mort and his new wife, Ruth Roaman, who had her own high-end dress shop at 550 Madison Avenue, found them an apartment on upper Fifth Avenue. The next year, I was born. Phyllis named me in her brother's honor. One thing was sacred: He was Euey, but she couldn't bear giving away that nickname. My whole life, I'd always be Gene.

. . .

I was a little fireball from the first. A rambunctious, high-energy kid, I spent my earliest years terrorizing the playgrounds of Central Park. I couldn't sit still for a second. Mom brought me home with stitches after one particular swan dive from the playground slide (I thought I was Superman). That's not why Fred moved the family to Harrison, New York, just outside the city, when I was four—the arrival of my little brother, Bob, was more likely the reason for that—but it couldn't have hurt.

It seemed like from the get-go, Bob and I were polar opposites. He was quiet, blond and skinny, cautious where I was adventurous. I used to torture the kid, I regret to say—I never beat him up physically, but I was always going after him, though he got me back by running straight to my parents. The only time I ever remember my dad getting really mad at me was after some argument or other with Bob— who remembers over what. All I know is that I was probably eight or nine, and Bob four or five, and we got into it, like all brothers do.

Fred came into my room. He was an unassuming guy; he didn't take up a lot of space. At five feet ten inches, he stood a head taller than his father, but unlike Barney, who was a bullhorn, he rarely raised his voice. When he got mad, it was like a silence that could kill you; later on, his employees used to joke you'd see his head turn all the way around, like in *The Exorcist*. Fred had that look on his face and I knew I was fucked. He picked up a chair and smashed it into a million pieces on the ground. But all he said when he looked at me after that was, "Don't do that again." And he walked out. There's no way I did whatever that was again.

Besides that one time, I don't remember ever seeing Fred mad; it wasn't his way. Unlike my mother, to whom he left the bulk of discipline, he preferred to float above the fray—he had a confidence that things would turn out as they should if you didn't force them. He had light brown eyes and a bashful smile, and curly hair that he'd fuss with, a little self-conscious at its going thin. He dressed simply and elegantly, with an ease that could look almost disheveled. The collars of his end-on-end weave blue shirts (always blue, never white) were frayed from long wear. His suits fit him perfectly—nothing made him crazier than when the collar of an ill-fitted jacket stood away from the neck—and having been chubby in his youth, he was proud to be a perfect size 40 regular his whole adult life.

He may have had ironclad rules he followed—brown shoes, never black; inch-and-three-quarters cuffs on his trousers; no belts, no monograms—but he wasn't uptight. He was the only executive I ever knew who would wear casual corduroys if the mood struck him, or who kept wearing his felt fedora long after he'd worn a hole through the crown. He wore his trademark black knit tie every day, and scooped the same tuna salad onto lettuce for lunch.

I don't think Fred meant to go into the business. He was having a good time as a man-about-Manhattan, and didn't relate much to his father's discount shtick. But once he found his way in, he fell in love. Every night around the dinner table, there was one subject you could count on hearing about, and that was Barneys. Mom and Dad would sit at the two ends of the table, Bob and I in between. And Fred would just *talk*. Sometimes you'd think, God, I wish I could change this channel. But he spoke with such passion that you couldn't help but get interested.

It obsessed him. There's a reason that Fred is called the greatest merchant of his generation by nearly everyone in menswear. He soaked up every intricacy and every detail of every garment, from the fabrics they were made of to the stitches that held them together, to the invisible linings inside—the horsehair interlining that separates a great suit or jacket from a cheap, glued one. He was the opposite of what anyone might think of as a fashion person. But that's because Fred wasn't a fashion person. He loved *clothes*. One of his longest-serving deputies told me he'd never seen Fred happier than the day a big order of socks came in, beautifully made in Italy, and there was Fred arms-deep in them, inspecting every pair.

Fred was less interested in the discount business, though it remained for many years the engine of the store, and a huge driver of its bottom line. But thanks to the pile Barney had made in discounting, Fred had grown up with the finer things, and it was the finer things that attracted him. Barney's own motto might have been "No Bunk, No Junk," but Fred, who had been raised on the store's spoils, coined a new line: "Select, Don't Settle." All you need to know about the differences between the two men are in those two lines. "During the 1960s, I was convinced that the discount route was definitely not for us," Fred told an interviewer years after. That sent the store into what he acknowledged was "an identity crisis." But ultimately, he said, "I didn't want to sell low-end merchandise."

Fred tugged the business to a more refined place. When he realized the best things were made in Europe (outerwear in London, sweaters in Scotland and Ireland, suits and shirts in Naples, luggage in Paris), he began going there. And starting around the time I was thirteen, he took us with him. Those trips marked the true beginning of my education in culture. Once you've tried caviar, it's hard to eat Spam.

# 2

# BEING THERE

## 1963-1966

Call me biased—I happened to be a teenager at their height—
but the '60s created the blueprint for everything that came
afterward. The '50s, with very few exceptions, was a dull,
gray decade, a boring victory lap after the long hangover of
the Second World War. Americans had come home from the
war as saviors of the globe and now, indisputably, the United
States was the most powerful country on earth. These were
the years of the baby boom, picket fences, Norman Rockwell
on steroids. People lived safely sealed in little bubbles. These
years weren't safe or comfortable for everyone—not those who
shipped out to Korea in the early '50s, or the Black Americans fighting for the same seats at schools and lunch counters as their white neighbors—but for many newly prosperous
suburbanites, peace was a relief. It was also a bore.

By the early '60s, change was in the air. In 1960, Jack Kennedy became the youngest president elected in American
history, a Boston pretty boy who seemed effortlessly poised
to usher in a new Camelot—or at least that's how it played on

TV. (Most people have forgotten that he won in a squeaker, by less than one percent of the popular vote.) It didn't feel like the Democrat had beaten the Republican, sending sweaty Nixon packing. It felt like the two real political parties were the adults on one side and the kids on the other, who put up our middle fingers and said we've had enough of this shit. Our rallying cry was rock 'n' roll, the new, vital sound of protest. And it was getting louder. Dylan went electric in 1965, the same year Jefferson Airplane and Grateful Dead formed on the West Coast. And the perfect complement was the Black sound that had been coming out of Motown in Detroit. We bought albums—bands would put out albums every five or six months—like we were receiving direct transmissions from our own politicians. Harrison, New York, may have been the doldrums of suburbia, but a wider world was out there, and when you went into White Plains, you'd see kids lined up outside the record shops to get the good word.

When Kennedy was assassinated three years into his administration, it was like the death of the dream of progress. They say everyone remembers exactly where they were when Kennedy was shot, on November 22, 1963. I definitely do—it was the day before my bar mitzvah. Our family wasn't strictly religious—our faith was more like rooting for a hometown baseball team—but we were proud of our heritage, proud enough that Phyllis demanded I perform the rite. I'd been stuck for a year learning to sing a three-thousand-year-old language backward, from a beatnik rabbi from Brooklyn with long curly hair, a big curly beard, and his yarmulke hidden under a beret.

Finally the day came and there I was in my little Boystown suit at the Jewish Community Center of Harrison. Mom was hysterical because after all her planning, she was sure that the assassination meant no one would show up. That would've been fine with me. My parents had promised that the bar mitzvah would be a quiet affair, soon over— my lucky number has been 14 ever since, I was so desperate to get it out of the way. But they did show up, a cast of thousands on what was

At my bar mitzvah, 1963, barely into puberty and already
with my priorities firmly in order. After the Kennedy assassination
the day before, I was available to comfort any girls who needed it.

usually a quiet Friday night of prayer, to mourn. Adults and kids alike, no one could believe the golden boy had been shot, the photographs of glamorous Jackie covered in blood. And then, at my party after the Saturday morning service, they got trashed. The beatnik rabbi—an anomaly in Westchester to begin with, a guy who probably would've been happier following Dylan at Cafe Wha? in the Village than turning little Jewish boys into men—became a man unbound, running around sticking firecrackers into the centerpieces, lighting them with his cigar, and blowing the fake fruit to hell.

. . .

The next month, Fred took the family to Europe for the Christmas holidays. We flew into Venice on a 707, a transatlantic voyage in a thick cloud of neighboring passengers' Kent smoke. Once in Italy, we hired a car and drove through the mountains till we reached the tiny town of Cortina d'Ampezzo. Nestled in a valley in the southern Dolomites, Cortina d'Ampezzo was a skier's paradise, famous among the jet set and well known for having hosted the Winter Olympics in 1956.

We stayed at the Grand Hotel, which had been hosting dignitaries since the 1910s. Its Alpine wood-paneled rooms were filled with people, including a lot of kids my age, but no other Americans. All through the halls, you'd hear French, German, and of course Italian—I didn't have a clue what they were saying, but I loved the sound of it. I may not have understood the words (or even, when they spoke English, the accents), but it was clear that the Europeans knew how to live. The way they did things was just *different* from Americans. They sat back and enjoyed life for the beauty of it all. They certainly contributed to the beauty of it.

They were the greatest-dressed people I had ever seen. At the hotel, every day was an event to dress for. Men in jacket and tie—they cared as much as their wives about how they looked, maybe more. Women in furs. The kids in their prep-school best. Even their ski outfits on the mountain—those, too, trimmed in fur—were incredible. The way they tied their scarves, or tilted their hats—Americans in the '60s were decently dressed, but it wasn't the same. Between runs, they sat in mountainside cafes, relaxing, replenishing, big families all together, deep in conversation. The lunch was as important as the skiing. In the States, they'd be wolfing down a piece of pizza, maybe a hot dog or a sandwich on a greasy paper plate. Here they were eating the most incredible bowl of spaghetti Bolognese you ever had in your life. I thought, *This is what I've been missing*, and I loved every minute of it.

One night at the hotel, I befriended an English kid about my age, playing pool in the game room. I thought I was hot shit; we had a pool table at home in Harrison, which Fred had managed to buy from the pool hall where *The Hustler* with Paul Newman had been filmed. We started talking about music, and I was bragging about how great American music was: We had Elvis, the Beach Boys, and the beginnings of Motown, the Marvelettes doing "Please Mr. Postman" and Stevie Wonder when he was still Little Stevie. "Well," this kid says, "we have the Beatles."

I had no idea what he was talking about. I didn't know what the Beatles were. I never thought there was any kind of music *but* American music. And though the Beatles were already a sensation in the UK, America was slower to catch on. "You'll know soon enough," this kid told me. Momentum was building, and the day after Christmas, Capitol released "Please Please Me" in the States a few weeks ahead of schedule. When I got back after New Year's, the British invasion had already begun. The music was everywhere. "Please Please Me" hit number one by the middle of the month and they were talking about it all over school. By the time the Fab Four touched down at the newly renamed John F. Kennedy Airport in February for their famous appearance on the Ed Sullivan show, Beatlemania was official, ratified by four thousand screaming girls who met the plane right on the tarmac. And I had stumbled onto it earlier than the rest—if only by about a week.

I never forgot that. I happened to be at the right place at the right time. Part of my luck in life has been a luck in timing: I was just coming into my own for the revolution of the '60s, a revolution the Beatles effectively kicked off and whose wave they rode.

Things didn't change for the better overnight. But they didn't go back to the way they were, either. Bits of the old '50s culture persisted. Elvis hung on, a greasy shell of his former self, and by the mid-1960s, when the top of the Billboard chart was dominated by *Help!*, the Stones, and the *Goldfinger* soundtrack, it still made a little space for the hepcat big-band white jazz of Herb Alpert and his Tijuana Brass. (Tijuana Brass notwithstanding, Herb was a Jewish kid from LA.)

But the '60s were in full swing, and that swing started in London. London was "the swinging city," *Time* magazine announced. "In a decade dominated by youth, London has burst into bloom . . . it is the scene." "Right now, London has something that New York used to have," said the gallerist Robert Fraser, a baron of the scene who dealt in the work of artists like Peter Blake and Jim Dine. "Everybody wants to be there."

I wanted to be there, more than anything. Everything cool seemed to emanate from there, from the music—for that matter, all the arts—to the fashion, to the women. It was the era of Carnaby Street, where the mods would go for their striped suits, while their girlfriends flocked to Biba and hoped to get their hair styled at Vidal Sassoon. A few years later, Tommy Nutter would become the toast of Savile Row for his wild suits—it's no wonder Elton John became a major client, though the Beatles wore him on the cover of *Abbey Road*, too.

A more prominent English flavor was seeping into Barneys, starting where revolutions always start, among the young—in this case, in the boys' department. It was impossible not to notice by the mid-1960s that men's style was changing. The new generation was thrilled to be young, and the last thing they wanted was their father's haberdashery. They wanted a bit more flair. Fred understood that English style was the thing, and came up with the idea to rechristen part of Boystown "the Billy Baxter Room," which had a sort of Anglo-manqué ring to it, and sticking the Union Jack label on anything that was selling slowly. In 1966, he announced the new section with a full-page ad in the *Times*, introducing the fictitious Billy Baxter ("a swinging style-setter, he's very much part of the mod, mod world that's London today") who "wants you chaps to know you'll find the whole bloomin' bit at Barney's Billy Baxter Room." Fred hired a cool young American guy and shipped him off to London to find new lines to bring back.

Fred's emissary returned with jumpers and bell-bottom jeans, the first time jeans had been seen at Barneys. Boystown had been a little-kids place, but once cooler merchandise started coming in, it aged up. Even I used to shop down there, riding the train into the city and stopping on my way to or from Manny's, the music shop on West Forty-Eighth, and chatting up Richard, a sales guy who had a side hustle gracing the covers of smutty romance novels. (A few years later, the rest of the world would come to know Richard Roundtree as the ass-kicking *Shaft*.) Boystown wasn't fashion, exactly, not yet—fashion, in the way we understand it now, was still to come.

. . .

In the winter of 1964, at least partly inspired by my fervent Beatlemania—probably because I wouldn't shut up about it—Fred took the family to England for Christmas. He was passing on a family

Visiting the mods and rockers on Carnaby Street, mid-1960s.

tradition. He had been traveling to Europe ever since he was kid; Barney's success made a whole new world available to his son. He and Barney continued to travel to Europe for business—they were regularly going to Germany and to Holland to buy suits and outerwear for the store when Americans were still stonewalling them—but Fred loved England above all, and nowhere more than Harrods.

Founded in 1849, Harrods was an institution in Knightsbridge, a grande dame of department stores with nineteenth-century roots and twentieth-century bounty: fashion, shoes, furnishings, furniture, and Fred's favorite, a food hall packed with delicacies, a zillion rooms overflowing with every conceivable local and foreign specialty. You never saw anything like that in American stores, but it was a way of life for the English, and had been since the last century. He was equally drawn to smaller, historic shops like Asprey & Garrard, Turnbull & Asser, and Anderson & Sheppard. In all these stores, with their fine merchandise and beautiful service, Fred saw possibilities for Barneys.

We stayed at the Berkeley Hotel across from Hyde Park. The Beatles were playing their second annual series of Christmas concerts, three weeks of shows that had been sold out since the fall, after the wild success of the previous year's. Even so, Fred managed to get tickets somehow, and off we went to the Hammersmith Odeon, Dad, Mom, Bob, and me.

I'd never seen anything like it in my life. All these girls were screaming at the top of their lungs, going apeshit—and the band hadn't even gone onstage yet. Finally, after a bunch of corny comedy skits and the Yardbirds opening, they did. They played "Twist and Shout," "Can't Buy Me Love," "A Hard Day's Night." I only know that from after the fact. We couldn't hear one thing for an hour, just the Beatles shaking their heads and mouthing the words. The girls were screaming that loud, without a break. They'd run up to the stage, security would pull them off, and the entire thing would start again. Mom politely hated the whole thing. She preferred Sinatra, as she did for the rest of her life. My father couldn't have cared less. But Bob and I loved it. It would've been even better if we could've heard it.

From that moment, I decided to dedicate my life to rock 'n' roll. Soon, like every other kid in America, I had guitar-god dreams and a garage-band reality. Harrison wasn't exactly a crucible of rock, but neither was Long Branch, New Jersey, before Springsteen came along. I rounded up a couple of kids from the neighborhood and we did what generations of suburban kids do, practicing in finished basements, giggling through awkward, semi-stoned conversations with this one's or that one's dad. "Is everything copacetic?" Mr. Candee, our lead guitarist's father, came down to ask one day, trying out some over-heard slang already ten years out of date. *Yeah, man*, we managed to get out before losing it. *Copacetic!*

I played a Fender Precision bass to Glenn's lead and Mark's rhythm guitar, with Lupi Lupino on the drums. We noodled around with writing our own songs, but we were more interested in covering the rock stars we were sure we'd turn out to be. We'd play high school auditoriums, local battles of the bands, wherever we could find them. Glenn and co. all went to the local public school in Harrison, while I was already bristling at Hackley, a nearby prep school. I used to fake sick when we had a gig, getting Phyllis to bless my staying home then sneaking out of my attic room, jumping off the roof and racing to meet a local cab at the end of the block. I'd yank on my elevator-heeled Beatle boots in the backseat.

Fred and Phyllis never took my musical ambitions too seriously. I was young; there were about as many garage bands around as there were garages. I, on the other hand, was positive we had what it took. When we got good enough to draw a crowd, we decided to stage a real show. A blowout the whole neighborhood would be talking about. And some-how, with some combination of charm and bull, I got my parents to let us hold it in their basement. Just a few kids, I promised. What could be the harm?

But I always thought big. The sky wasn't limit enough for me. I always loved the thrill of the perfect show. It wasn't one element, not just the music, or the crowd, but all of it—the way we decorated Fred and Phyllis's basement rec room, the level of the lights, the flow of the set list, the onstage outfits. It was a full nightclub set we rigged up, as good as a professional operation, at least in our own minds. To prove it, we plunked twelve-year-old Bob at the door, to collect five bucks a head from anyone who wanted to come. If there was ever a less intimidating bouncer in the history of rock, I never met him.

How the word got out as far as it did, especially in those prehistoric days before social media, I'll never know. But kids started coming, and they didn't stop. Younger ones on foot, older ones pulling into the driveway. Tough kids, bookworms, jocks, teachers' pets . . .

Downstairs in the basement, we turned down the lights and turned up the amps, and launched into all our hits: the Animals' "House of the Rising Sun," "Help!" from the Beatles movie, "Hang On Sloopy" by the McCoys. The basement was full, and at $5 a pop, we were making a tidy profit. I always wanted to put on a show, and even before I knew how, I knew how.

But the kids kept coming. More cars in the driveway edging up onto the lawn, more stragglers on bikes and on foot, the line at the door growing by the minute, and poor Bob trying to keep a handle on things at the top of the stairs. We were at capacity, then over capacity. We dreamed it, we made it, and then we exceeded it. That pattern would repeat in our lives to come, the template for everything that followed: the Pressman way. I'd be the creative brains, setting the scene. Bob, nerdier and quicker with the numbers, would be running the books. And Fred and Phyllis on the sidelines, proud, nervous, probably fretting about their lawn and their driveway and their basement, but letting us do it anyway.

Did I know any of that then? Of course not. That in the decades that followed we'd put on a show that would draw bigger crowds, on bigger stages? That they'd make millions, and our names, and change everything? Couldn't have guessed, and never would've believed—much less that the stage would be Barneys. No, all I knew was that we'd pulled it off beyond our wildest dreams—the Pressman way—and then that we were in deep shit. Because as Sloopy was hanging on in the basement, a few more cars were pulling up outside, and our first greatest show was about to be broken up by the cops.

# 3

# LET THE GAMES BEGIN

## 1966–1970

In the 1960s, Cannes was the place to be. A thin strip of walkway, the mythic Croisette, is all that separates the beach from the five-star hotels, clubs, and cafes, and the party was constant. All day, the most gorgeous, sun-baked women strutted down La Croisette, goggled at by every man—it was a runway. All night, the clubs hummed, and the women traded their bikinis for dresses that covered not much more than their swimsuits. They danced the night away to what the French called "canned music," recorded tracks by froggy crooners like Johnny Hallyday and Jacques Brel. Only once in a while would they throw in a little good old American rock 'n' roll; the French government was so chauvinistic, they used to limit the number of rock 'n' roll songs and stations you could have on the radio.

I had squeaked through high school, and Fred and Phyllis rewarded me with a graduation trip. On the last night, that summer of 1968, I was with a gorgeous girl at the Playboy

Club. (No relationship to Hef or the magazine—but in the '60s, bunny or no bunny, everybody wanted to be a playboy.) This girl was a knockout. Dark hair, dark eyes; Brazilian, I think, or maybe Argentine. I can't remember—not her story, not her background, not even her name. What I do remember is the stares we got as we lounged at the beach, or slurped bouillabaisse at the terrace cafes. Every guy for a mile around doing full 360s, looking at her, looking at me, going *I don't get it—what's she doing with him?*

So I was feeling pretty good about myself that summer night. I didn't want to leave, but there were several more weeks of summer left in the city to think of, and then freshman year at Syracuse University in the fall. If this was to be my Riviera send-off, so be it. I was going to do it right, and return to America a new man.

At the Playboy Club, dates and little groupings of guys or girls sat at their own little tables, ordering up cold white wine and American-style cocktails. The guys were wearing tight, sharp-shouldered Pierre Cardin suits, not like the nine-to-five sack suits American men wore back home, and the women were in little summer dresses. There was some dancing, and a lot of flirting; the mood was one of hectic ebullience born of relief. That May, France had been wracked with protests that grew into riots in the streets of Paris—as in the United States, as in Britain, the students were rising up and saying *enough.* Kids not much older than I was were occupying their universities. Factory workers were striking. Police were cracking down, leading to brawls. De Gaulle, France's wartime hero and current president, briefly fled the country, until peace was finally restored with the promise of a new election. There was a heady sense in the air of crisis averted. Not that I knew any of that at the time. I was there to have a good time, and I was having one.

In the days before cell phones, it was an innovation that every table at the Playboy came with its own little landline telephone. Most European clubs were dark and sexy. Everyone had the same goal in mind, and that was to get laid—but this place was less subtle than most. If you liked the looks of the girl at the next table, you could call her up and try your luck. Since I was there with a date, I had no need to. But, feeling as I did like King Shit in a Lacoste polo and tight jeans, I can't pretend to have been too surprised when our table's phone began to ring. She was hot, she thought I was hot, life was hot. Of course someone wanted in.

I picked up the phone. *Hello?* The voice at the other end goes, "Gene?"

Now I was surprised.

"Turn around," says the voice through the phone, the club noisy in the background. "This is your mom."

The truth is, I had crashed their second honeymoon. My graduation trip was supposed to be to Israel and Turkey—Phyllis's choices. I think she wanted me to get a little Jewish culture. And there was Jewish culture I could really get behind—the women in Tel Aviv were gorgeous, with dark hair and green eyes.

After a stop in Istanbul, I was due to be shipped home to Westchester, but Mom surprised me. "Gene's been so good this trip," she said to my father, "why don't we let him come along with us to the South of France?" It was to have been a private holiday for the two of them, a little retreat. As much as I couldn't see them as anything but my parents, they were still young. Phyllis wasn't yet forty, and Fred was spry enough that, when we arrived in Cannes, threw on our swimsuits, and headed straight for the beach, the Argentine-or-Brazilian girl first made a beeline straight for him. Mom never lost her cool. "You don't want him," she said to the girl, and pointed to me. "You want *him.*" And then she and I were off, not to see my parents again till that night in the club when the telephone rang.

It didn't bother me to share the club with my folks. I'd never treated them much like parents—as much as I loved and respected them, it never occurred to me to be anything other than open and honest with them. When Phyllis asked me why I looked like shit (and felt like shit) on our little puddle-jumper flight to Eilat on that Israel trip, I told her the truth: I'd been up all night screwing. (When I smoked my first joint, at thirteen, I told her that, too.) *"Freddy!"* she yelped at my father, like she always did when she hoped he'd reprimand me. But that wasn't Fred's way—he'd just smile. We'd been doing this dance for years. "Was she Jewish, at least?" Phyllis asked, hopefully.

. . .

As we headed home from that trip, our lives were about to diverge. I was leaving the nest, and they were returning to it, one that was still very full: Bob had been joined by my little sister Liz in 1960, and Nancy, the baby, in 1963. Phyllis stayed home with them while Fred commuted every day to Manhattan to the store, where he had taken on more and more responsibility. They had both needed the vacation.

By the late '60s, Fred had been working with his father for twenty years, and Barney had been working the floors for more than forty. Through sheer force of will, Barney had turned a little discount shop into a megalith. Gone were the days when spies had to be sent out around the South to buy up unsold stock, and gone were the days when Barney's brusque bargain hunting made him enemies among manufacturers who weren't interested in selling their clothes at a discounter, or at a discount. The angriest among them even had sent in undercover Pinkerton detectives to cause a public scene at the store, screaming that Barneys was a "jib joint." For Barney, that was the price of doing business—if some people didn't like it, fuck 'em. He was a tough guy, raised in a tough neighborhood. I once saw him march up to a customer who was making a fuss, a guy probably twice his size, and tell him in his usual stuttering but certain terms, "Here's f-f-f-five dollars for a cab, get the f-f-f-fuck outta my store." Jimmy Cagney, Hollywood's go-to tough guy onscreen in the '30s, was Barney's childhood friend; he and Bertha used to go visit him on the set. At least once in the early days, Barneys was the scene for a plot like one Cagney might've played out onscreen: In 1937, the city papers all covered a holdup at Barneys by a machine-gun-toting band of crooks, one of whom was killed by the police after the gang made off with $45,000 from customers, clerks, and the store's safe.

Those days were pretty well behind Barneys by the '60s. Barney himself had mellowed a bit, and the business was changing, too. For one thing, it kept growing. The expansion made sense: The business was minting money. By the mid-1960s, Barneys was turning over between $11 and $12 million a year in merchandise, the vast majority of it in tailored clothing—the equivalent of more than $100 million today. The press called it "the biggest men's store in the world." The addition of a second floor in 1966 had doubled the selling area, and in 1968, it grew again, from two floors (plus a basement) to four.

Behind this expansion was Fred. "We're not a neighborhood store," Fred would say—sometimes multiple times in a single conversation, if he worried his audience wasn't getting the point. He was musing openly about acquiring neighboring properties, even expanding outside of New York City.

Stores reflect their owners, and though Barney was still president, Barneys was beginning to show Fred's influence. Fred had been a child of success, raised in silver-spoon Stamford, the happy result of Barney's ascension from the rough-and-tumble Lower East Side. Where Barney was loud and tough, Fred was soft-spoken and smooth. As he took on more and more authority at the store, he began steering it in a more elevated direction. Even the sales pitch you'd get on the shop floor reflected their differing styles. Nothing drove Barney nuts like seeing someone walking out of the store empty-handed, and he did everything he could so that he never had to, parking himself outside and frog-marching anyone who'd escaped back to their hapless (and now trembling) salesman.

It was Fred, with his connoisseur's taste, who presided over the transformation of Barneys into a higher-end, gentler kind of store. He couldn't afford to lose the bargain-hunting customers, but he began partitioning the space into individual "rooms" to separate them from their swankier counterparts. Higher-priced clothes went in the so-called Imperial Room, while the cheaper stuff went to the New Yorker Room. The more natural-shouldered, American styles were in the Madison Room, where he hoped, as the name suggests, to siphon off some of Brooks Brothers and Paul Stuart's faithful clients (those stores were, then as now, on Madison Avenue in the East Forties). Between the two of them, Brooks and Paul Stuart had the WASP-y New York businessmen's business sewn up.

This period of the late '60s saw the beginnings of a new world in fashion, first in women's wear, then in men's. Designer ready-to-wear as we know it—what the French call prêt-à-porter—which melded high design with accessible production and prices, was a new innovation. Yves Saint Laurent was first to the starting gate in 1966 with his Rive Gauche line. Saint Laurent had risen to instant fame a decade before, when he took over Christian Dior after Monsieur Dior's shocking and untimely death: Dior had been one of the great couturiers of his day, and here his shoes were being filled by a twenty-one-year-old kid from the provinces. (Saint Laurent was raised in Algeria, then a French colony.) In 1962, he had started his own collection, run by his partner, Pierre Bergé, and quickly rose to be the most influential designer on earth, casting a spell not only on Paris but the whole world. He wasn't the most natural figurehead of the youthquake; tall, bespectacled, and fussy, even friends described him as uptight. But as the '60s wore on, he loosened up—aided and abetted, as so many of us were, by drugs and sex—and his designs did, too. It didn't hurt that he was attended by a sort of clique-slash-harem of the coolest women in Paris, his muses and sounding boards. Between them, they set the tone for what the new generation wanted to wear. The Saint Laurent look was all over France when we were there.

The style uprising that was beginning in Paris in women's wear would soon bleed into a burgeoning men's style movement. Men's wardrobes were changing. "Men's clothing" had, since Barney's day, meant suits; "furnishings" were ties, cufflinks, hats, the stuff of the traditional haberdashers. But in the rage and rebellion of the '60s, those looked like his father's clothes. And while women's designers were on their way to becoming celebrities—Christian Dior had appeared on the cover of *Time* magazine in 1957—the idea of the "designer," the flamboyant, often tortured genius making your clothing, was more controversial in menswear. The whole designer idea seemed, to many guys, iffy and odd. When Bloomingdale's first started stocking Cardin suits in 1964, the idea of a designer label for men was still suspect enough that the store actually cut his label out of the suits. "It was not until the middle of that decade," *The New York Times* wrote later on, "that the idea of designer clothes for the American man seemed at all possible." When I wore my bought-at-Barneys Nehru jackets to school in the mid-1960s, my god, everyone ragged on me like I'd come to class in a Halloween costume.

But Fred was way ahead of the pack. He believed in the men's designer business, and put his weight behind it. In the 1966 expansion, he added a few designer boutiques to the themed rooms, and in 1968, he doubled down. "We are going to devote two floors to designer shops," he told an interviewer that year.

By then, Fred had replaced Barney as president, and though Barney himself still roamed the floors, the expansion plan was all Fred's. Barney found himself with less and less to do. He'd drift into Fred's office, where Fred would be going over samples with buyers, and give his

Fashion plates: Barney and Bertha, circa the '60s,
with her ever-present blue-tinted sunglasses.

The young Fred Pressman, apparently before
the advent of his signature black knit tie.

stuck-in-the-forties spiel. Fred would never embarrass his father, but I can only imagine what he was thinking when Barney would finger the samples and make old-world comments like, "Nice goods." "Goods" was pure garmento—a term Fred would never use. Europe's lavish but (relatively) discreet sophistication had made a deep mark on him. He began making plans for the International House, one of the major leaps forward for Barneys, a separate but connected building for the European-made suits he was importing. He bought the five-story building next door to the original shop to house it, and work began.

. . .

It wasn't only Fred who was taken with European style. In the '60s, a fever for European chic—or anything even approximating it—was sweeping New York. The coolest spots in town were the nightclubs in the East Sixties: Yellowfingers, Ondine, Arthur. (It was named in tribute to George's famous quip in *A Hard Day's Night*. "What would you call that hairstyle you're wearing?" "Arthur.") The Europeans had savoir-faire, or we thought they did. At these clubs (some of which were owned by Americans), anyone with even a hint of an accent could go from waiter to owner overnight, to say nothing of getting any girl he wanted. (That, no doubt, was one reason for the constant migration of young hustlers from the Continent.) Next to the Americans, the Europeans had panache: their suits were slimmer, their ties were bigger.

For a few years, fashion lagged behind nightlife—you could barely find European clothing, especially men's clothing, anywhere. There were little dribs and drabs of it here and there. A few Cardin suits shoved somewhere out of the way at Bonwit Teller, which had helped establish Fifth Avenue as an elegant shopping district thirty-five years before. (Donald Trump later razed the building, a crime against humanity, and put up Trump Tower in its stead.) But for any kind of selection, arranged with any kind of taste, you were out of luck. When Jean de Noyer, a young guy from Paris, arrived in New York in 1965 and got a job at Yellowfingers, so many people asked him where they could buy his suits—and tried to buy them off his back—that in 1968 he opened his own boutique on East Sixtieth Street. It was an instant success.

De Noyer stocked the things you wouldn't find in the American stores: Renoma suits, New Man velvet trousers in moss green and strawberry red, shirts tight enough to show off in. The *Times* covered his opening in 1968, writing up the shop practically before the paint had time to dry. "I was suffering for three and a half years—since I came here—having to fly over to Paris to get clothes I could wear," Jean told the reporter. I'd shop there, too—I knew him a little bit from Yellowfingers, never mind that I was in high school at the time. My trip to London in 1964 had cemented in my mind what I'd already been feeling: High school sucked, Westchester was a snooze, and a fast and glamorous world was waiting right outside. I was impatient to get out and join the party.

I wasn't the only member of the family to notice Jean. Soon after opening, he told me recently, Jean spotted Barney himself, whom he recognized from the newspapers, sniffing around the shop unannounced. De Noyer had hit on something big. As he put it, "On any given Saturday afternoon, people were lined up on the street to get into the store."

But de Noyer's was a small boutique. And Barneys, buoyed by the success and the capital of its thriving, decades-old discount business, would make a bigger splash. It would take a few years of planning and strategizing. Fred, as ever, was a canny marketer. He orchestrated a meeting with John Lindsay, New York's handsome young mayor, who represented the triumph of youth and excitement over the staid status quo. (The slogan for his 1966 campaign, borrowed from a local columnist's take, was, "He is fresh, and everyone else is tired.") Bringing along his adman, Jack Byrne, Fred arrived at Lindsay's office with a scale model of the International House. Byrne snapped a few photos, which became double-spread ads run in *The New York Times*. "A New York businessman and a New York mayor discuss the City's prospects for business growth," read the faux-headline across the top. It's a nice bit of spin that the New York businessman and the New York mayor are given equal weight. (If there was any question as to which of the Pressmans' influence was now dominant, the ad made it clear: The New York businessman pictured shoulder to shoulder with Lindsay is Fred, not Barney.)

As the arrival got closer, more ads piqued the public interest. The Pressmans commissioned Richard Avedon, one of the leading fashion photographers of the day, to shoot portraits of the designers the International House would carry, from the well known, like Givenchy, to the more obscure, like Gilbert Feruch, creator of the Nehru jacket. (Feruch told Jack Byrne, who spearheaded the ads, that one Barneys ad did more for him than he'd ever managed to do for himself.) Other campaigns played up Barneys' traditional wit. "Barneys is looking for a gardener," ran another, over an ink drawing of a wilting flower. "Help make new clothing establishment beautiful. Start September 30th. 7th Ave. & 17th St." The implication was clear: Big things were going to grow.

When it finally did open in 1970, the $3.5 million International House (and remember, those were 1970 dollars) was like a second Barneys grown by spore, and Barneys' dominion now stretched all the way down Seventh Avenue. (Eventually it would round the corner and wend its way east up the block, too.) The original building, with the addition of a new floor, became the America House, where American designs were still stocked. The interconnected International House had everything its American counterpart did: its own furnishings department on the main floor, designed by the great architect-designers

George Nelson and Gordon Chadwick, its own shoe department, a fur department with men's fur coats from France and Sweden. (It sounds crazy now, but in the '60s and '70s, furs for wealthy and famous men were what diamond chains and status-symbol watches are today. Joe Namath wore a fur. So did Fred, though more quietly—he had a zip-out fur lining made for his Burberry raincoat.) What's more, it had even more "designer dens" for the major names of European design. Saint Laurent, for one. Pierre Cardin and Dior, also from Paris, two more. Bruno Piattelli and Brioni from Rome. Hardy Amies from London. Not only was Fred bringing in the goods, but he was making shrewd deals to ensure you couldn't find them anywhere but Barneys.

The International House doubled Barneys' footprint to 100,000 square feet, making it, as the *Times* reported when the International House opened that September 30, "one of the largest units, if not the largest, in the United States," with yearly sales of over $22 million—more than $190 million today. The International House inaugurated a new focus for Barneys, one that had been quietly shifting for years. "Today the specialty store emphasizes its fashion leadership, rather than its original slogan of 'the cut-rate clothing king' although it still generally manages to keep its retail prices below those of its competitors for the same merchandise," the *Times* wrote. Men's clothing had been changing under everyone's noses, even if men's retailing had been slower to evolve, and now here was Fred to lead the way. "The showcasing of men's fashions hasn't moved ahead at the same speed as the new inputs of fashion for men," he said. "We didn't go into this expansion program just for volume alone, although we certainly expect to do more business with the added space. We did it to further the concept that New York City needs a large store of this sort to offer a fantastic variety of clothing to please everybody's taste."

It was a shift toward elegance. Lamps began replacing fluorescent lights. Carpeting went down, a few paintings went up. Before, Barneys made a point of being the biggest: rows and rows of seats, racks upon racks. Barney's pride was the double-height racks we called "rounders": Pulling out from the wall, they could spin all the way around, to reveal about a zillion more suits hanging on the back. They were arranged by size, marked out by circular plastic markers called "donuts." It felt like—it basically was—warehouse shopping. Fred sensed, correctly, that that wouldn't do for the new merchandise he was getting in. The rounders got replaced by single, or at most double, adjustable bars from which he'd hang just a few suits. The giant tables of pants, with a guy nearby hired to do nothing more than refold them as customers and salesmen grabbed them, splayed them, and tossed them back, began to disappear. More stock was squirreled away in small stock rooms on the floor, and even more in the literal warehouse across the street. Barney grumbled. As far as he was concerned, if you send the back stock across the street, you might as well send the sale out with it.

When the international suits came in they were ventless—the back panel of the jacket wasn't split at the bottom. (The conservative guys in the Madison Room went for single vents; Paul Stuart guys had double vents.) It sounds like small potatoes, but that registered as a major shift in slow-to-change menswear—we had to reeducate the customer in this wild new style. The shoulders were sharper, the American flap pocket gave way to a European besom pocket, a sleeker look: no flap, only a slit. The European merch had European sizes. It was all an adjustment for the midcentury man. But once he got on board, he was hooked.

At the International House's launch party, the world came to Barneys. Bobby Short tickled the keys in the Imperial Room and the crowd included many of the European designers Fred was making a home for: Hubert de Givenchy, Bruno Piattelli, Gilbert Feruch. Mayor Lindsay came to give the American endorsement. "Barneys is a New York

Fred with New York City mayor John Lindsay, showing off a model
of the new, expanded Barneys, now with the International House.
Not one to waste an opportunity, he ran this image as an ad campaign.

tradition, and this great expansion is important to our city," Lindsay said. "I highly recommend Barneys to any man who wants good-looking clothes. How's that?"

Not ones to miss or squander an opportunity, Fred and Jack Byrne recorded it as a soundbite for future radio ads.

# 4

# ONE GENERATION GOT OLD

## 1968-1972

With so much riding on the success of the International House, a multi-year project of construction and ambition, Fred had been too busy to notice that the start of my college career was not a major success.

I had arrived on campus in the fall of 1968. I was thrilled to be going to Syracuse University, but I was never going to be a star student. Already initiated into the lifestyle of New York, girls, cars, and clubs, I wasn't all that interested in a gray city halfway to Canada that gets more snow dumped on it than any big city in America every year. Most of the other kids seemed lame to me, and so did most of the professors—which is probably why I never bothered going to class, and bought the papers I turned in when I did. I was sure I was destined for greater things than Intro to Math, even if my math professor wasn't. Add to that that I pledged Sigma Alpha Mu—Sammy, as it was known to everyone—a fraternity of ladies' men and party boys, and you've got a recipe for disaster.

I got mostly C's and D's, and the school threatened to kick me out if I didn't take summer classes. It wasn't my dream summer vacation, but I wasn't about to get expelled. The Vietnam War was raging in the background—it was at Syracuse that President Johnson made his Tonkin Gulf Resolution speech a few years before, bringing the United States into the war—and the threat of the draft loomed large. College attendance earned you a deferral, the golden ticket I knew I had to cling to. The draft lottery would take place in December, and I'd be eligible, not *quite* young enough to skirt it. Vietnam, we all knew, was a war we shouldn't be fighting, and I had no interest in fighting it. And my mom, still grieving for her brother twenty-five years later, wasn't about to lose her second Eugene the same way she'd lost her first. Syracuse was a haven of safety for those of us who could afford it. It's a sad truth, but a truth nonetheless: Vietnam was a poor man's war, like every other war.

By August, I'd suffered through classes all summer, done well enough to pass (a B and a C, anyway), and figured I'd earned the right to party. Now, the summer of '69, if you were around and had a pulse, was Woodstock. That was the beginning, the middle, and the end of it. Held on a nondescript dairy farm in upstate New York over three days in August, the festival was one of those rare moments when you felt history happening not in retrospect, but as it happens. If the '60s were defined by the explosion of rock 'n' roll, Woodstock was rock's apotheosis, the moment when all of the strands of the decade came together, right before its end, in spectacular fashion.

Most of the biggest bands on earth, all of whom I was obsessed with, were there—Hendrix and Jefferson Airplane; The Who and the Grateful Dead; Janis Joplin, Creedence Clearwater Revival, and Crosby, Stills, Nash and Young; Sly and the Family Stone—and those that weren't, like the Beatles, Led Zeppelin, and the Stones, all lived to regret it. Advance tickets weren't cheap, at eighteen dollars for a three-day pass, the equivalent of about $150 today. But so many people showed up that the organizers had no choice but to take down the fences and make it free. For the 500,000 of us who went, it was a pilgrimage we couldn't miss. The little town that hosted the festival—sixty miles outside of Woodstock, New York, the originally planned location—was called Bethel. It might as well have been called Bethlehem.

I rounded up my girlfriend, Barbara, food for a few days, and drugs for a few more, and put a hitch on my Camaro. We hit the road, heading south to the Catskills.

The traffic to Woodstock was famously horrible, delaying acts who couldn't get their equipment in time and starting a domino effect that ended up pushing the festival's Sunday-night closing spot well into Monday morning. It was bumper-to-bumper from New York City on up. But coming from the north, we had smooth sailing. As we approached the town, you could see all the preparations that had been made for the festival, both legally and illegally. Roadside stands were set up selling trinkets, T-shirts, and gear to the gathering hordes, and others were set up right next to them selling every mood- and mind-altering substance in existence. Uppers, downers, pot, hash, loose joints, blotter acid . . . It was a total free-for-all, sold as openly as the gloves at Barneys' furnishings counter. State troopers were patrolling the roads right next to them, not quite oblivious but resigned. You knew if they busted one, three others would pop up to take his place. It must've been a long three days for them. They had to pace themselves.

Barbara and I were rolling toward the campground, feeling no pain. It was a gorgeous August day, the Camaro's top was down, and I was puffing a cigar, thinking I'm hot shit. All of a sudden, a huge Harley pulled up next to us. "Move over," said this behemoth on top of it. I wasn't about to let Barbara see me get pushed around, and I thought to myself, should I tell this guy to go fuck himself? What's the worst that could happen?

But something told me, sit this one out. I pulled over to the side, and I heard a dull roar from behind me. A hundred of this guy's best friends came screaming past me, each on his own bike, like a Hell's Angels family reunion. In those days, the Angels meant business—they weren't fucking around. I think choosing the path of peace was a good career move on my part. It was in the spirit of Woodstock, anyhow. For all the hundreds of thousands of people who came, it was a peaceful event, unlike Altamont, the "Woodstock West" that would take place a few months later and end in rioting and violence.

We arrived at the campsite and pitched our tent on the trailer hitched to the car. It was a nice setup, all told, and we were insanely close to the stage, basically pressed up against the giant speakers. The next day, those speakers yanked us awake at six o'clock in the morning as we heard a woman's voice belt, "Wake up, America!" It was Gracie Slick, the Jefferson Airplane's front woman, and her rallying cry might've spoken for all of us huddled on the farm, sick of the status quo, sick of the war, sick of the adults. With their guitars turned up to ear-splitting levels, the band launched into "Volunteers," its famous chorus our anti-battle battle cry: "Look what's happening out in the streets . . . One generation got old, one generation got soul . . ."

. . .

To be in college in the late '60s and early '70s was to be in a state of perpetual revolt. If the 1960s started the youthquake, and made clear the fault lines between them and us—our parents' generation and our own—college was all of us set free to run society in our image. Having left the house for the idyll of a college campus, utopia was ours for the making. We protested, we sang, we organized. We also did a ton of drugs.

Part of the rebellion of the day was a rebellion against the rules—if previous generations wanted us to get out and make something of ourselves, we were determined to turn on, tune in, drop out. By 1968, everything had started to get pretty trippy. LSD got popular on the West Coast, and like so much else, caravanned across the country. Its prophets were Timothy Leary and Ken Kesey, the guru and the Merry Prankster. Its theme song was "White Rabbit," which Grace Slick wrote after tripping, and its ambassadors were the Grateful Dead. (When I saw them play in the early '70s, they were so zonked, and noodled through their tunes for so long, that I ended up coming down before they finished.) With acid, you had to know what you were getting—you couldn't afford a bad trip, you might not come back from it. But I had a connection who got his acid through Kesey himself.

Besides music, the other thing acid opened up for me was movies. This was the beginning of Hollywood's second golden age, what the critics would end up calling New Hollywood, when—like everywhere else—a new guard was throwing out the rules and their parents' films. The dreck of the '50s was fading away before *Bonnie and Clyde, The Graduate*, and Stanley Kubrick's *2001: A Space Odyssey.* I went to see it that spring, which in Syracuse, felt more like deep winter, still under piles of snow in April.

It's no exaggeration—OK, maybe a *slight* exaggeration—to say that *2001* changed my life. Maybe it was the acid, maybe it was the time, maybe it was my seat on the floor in front of the front row, but this was the kind of film I wanted to make, a bold, unsparing look into the future and all it held. (I'd have this feeling again, even more, when I saw *A Clockwork Orange* four years later.) The creativity on display, the symphonic way the images, the music, the script, and the story all worked together, was mind-altering. Kubrick had distilled the fears and hopes and dreams of his moment and created something bigger than anything the medium had seen before. When I started making my own student films, he would be the master I emulated.

That was still to come. At that moment, I had my own Kubrickian drama to survive. I tumbled out of the theater into a snowstorm as dense and as lunar as anything I had seen on screen. I was still tripping my balls off, and the whole world was white. I didn't have a clue where I parked my car. I spent over an hour wandering around in a space-age daze before I stumbled across it. I was frozen nearly to the bone, but it all worked out in one way: by that time, I was sane enough to drive home.

Oh, and I went back and saw *2001* again the next day.

. . .

For all the eye-rolling from our parents about free love and flower children, the late '60s rebellion was a real one, with real consequences. Yes, we were stoned a lot, and yes, we saw a lot of movies. But the hazy memorials and the costume-party love beads that recall the '60s today often paper over the stakes at play. By 1968, the Vietnam War had been dragging on for years, chewing up and spitting out a generation of American boys, who came back, if they came back at all, spooked or hooked on smack. The pervading feeling was that even those in charge didn't know what the hell they were doing, and the game they were playing was with our lives.

Skirmishes between young people and the police became increasingly common. People were always busting the long-hairs, including the cops; "go take a bath," "go cut your hair," and "are you gay?" were all commonplace. Phyllis never commented on my long hair—except to say, "Are you gonna cut it?" As the decade wore on, these skirmishes turned with disturbing frequency into riots: in 1967 in Los Angeles, in 1968 at the Democratic National Convention in Chicago. All of the movements of the '60s were overlapping: antiwar efforts, civil rights. In 1968, both Martin Luther King Jr. and Bobby Kennedy were assassinated. By 1969, John and Yoko had taken to their bed to protest, begging "Give Peace a Chance."

On campus, students and administrators were figuring out how to work together, or not. The outgoing Syracuse University president had been just this side of fascist, squashing student activism; a new administration, in 1969, promised more openness. But that resolve was tested almost immediately. In March, dozens of Black students protested for, and eventually won, an African American studies program. Soon I was taking most of my classes in African American studies: Racism in America, Studies in African American History, and American History Since 1865. It gave me a front row seat into the divisions in the country, even the divisions between those on the same side—the upper-class international students from Africa could be brutal to the US-born Black students, whom they considered lower class.

As the '70s dawned, the war continued. In April of 1970, President Nixon announced an order to send troops into Cambodia, expanding the theater of war and spurring another round of protests nationwide.

Up till then, I hadn't been too active politically. Politics had never been a serious part of my education, and it wasn't much of my life at home—I don't remember Fred and Phyllis ever discussing it. Their attitude seemed to be, as it was about many things that weren't their immediate focus: *Let the people in charge figure it out, we've got our own things to do.* Fred tended to keep his own counsel; he wasn't going to run his mouth for the sake of running his mouth. And he had plenty to occupy him. The launch of the International House that fall was one of the major turning points in Barneys history, a huge undertaking—though he had his admen cast it in even greater terms, as "The Most Important Development Since the Beginning of Men's Fashion."

But the students of the nation were at work on their own American revolution. A national student strike was planned, and Syracuse was a tinderbox primed to explode. Plans were put in place for an enormous protest on May 4, which would gather three thousand people to Syracuse's main quad, where solidarity with the national strike was declared and three demands announced: an immediate end to American involvement in the war in South Asia, the release of Bobby Seale and peace with the Black Panthers, and an end to Syracuse's complicity with the military-industrial complex. It was in the middle of this protest that news broke of the Kent State shootings in Ohio, where National Guard members fired on protesting students, killing four of them.

On campus, I supported the strike cause in my own fashion. That spring, I was tooling around in my parents' old car, a racing-green Jaguar, with STRIKE signs posted in the windows—not exactly a VW bus. I showed up at one of the rallies that May at Hendricks Chapel on the center of campus. I was caught up in the spirit of the moment—I may have been a little cloudy from my usual indulgences (I had quit smoking cigarettes the fall before using an unusual method of my own devising: I smoked about twenty joints a day instead), but I still managed to make a little STRIKE sign for the band of my pageboy cap.

Inside Hendricks Chapel was a cast of thousands—the chapel seats a thousand, but many more seemed to be massing in the aisles and outside. The floor was open to speakers and the air was electric and, without knowing quite what I would say—and, to be honest, not entirely remembering now what I *did* say—I found my way to the podium. Even till the moment I spoke, I had no idea what was coming, but I was infected by the enthusiasm all around me. The words started coming out of my mouth. I realized that the one way to close down the university would be to shut down the telephone system, which in those days was still managed by an office full of telephone operators, like the ones we had at Barneys. In those pre–cell phone, pre–email days, if no one could call in or call out, you were as good as on Mars. I started preaching the idea. "Let's go over to the communications building! Let's shut it down!" And on and on. And to my surprise, the crowd starts going, "Right on!" In pictures from that day, you can see in my eyes that I didn't quite know what I was starting up—a deer in the headlights. Having said my piece, I got down from the podium and started walking out. But whether I liked it or not, people started following me. They lined up like foot soldiers, cheering and chanting, and surged out behind me.

This was more than I'd prepared for. I believed in the cause, but in those days, I never aspired to be a leader—I'd rather observe from the outside. Later in life, I'd lead the charge at Barneys, but that was still all ahead. I hurried along as the crowd grew to the back and the sides of me, swelling with enough people that no one noticed when at the next opportunity, I ducked behind a convenient bush and watched the throng move along ahead of me. This whole thing was getting serious, and I wasn't looking to be expelled for my antics, not with a war on.

They did shut down the communications, and for the next week, sit-ins and barricades blocked the normal functioning of classes. By some miracle, and with what he himself acknowledged as a "colossal bluff," John Corbally, the school's new chancellor, managed to bring things to a peaceful conclusion. Classes ultimately resumed, and commencement went on as scheduled later in the month. As I remember it, the school gave everyone A's that semester, though my transcript, revisited now in tranquility, says otherwise. That may have been a fantasy. Or a story I told my mother.

. . .

As my college years wore on, my attention drifted. For me, the first year at Syracuse was the most important—I made some friends, joined

Portrait of the artist as a young revolutionary:
Syracuse me, 1970, leading the strike (before ducking out).

the frat, made some connections that would shape my life in much more dramatic ways later on. But by my junior year, I had had enough of school. I'd bounced around departments and majors before finally landing at the film and television program, which in those days was mostly independent study. That was fine with me—I was confident I had it all figured out.

Music would have to play a big part in whatever I did. Some of the greatest bands of all time came through Syracuse in those days—in a single week in 1969, you could see Janis Joplin and Jimi Hendrix at the War Memorial—and ever since I was a teenager, I'd been going down to New York to check out the new clubs that were cropping up downtown, as I continued to do most summers during my school years. In probably less than a square mile were newly blossoming venues that would become legendary. It became my regular amble.

From Barneys, if you walked due east, you'd hit Max's Kansas City on Seventeenth and Park Avenue South, where the Velvet Underground played their first shows and Warhol was a permanent fixture. South of that, on St. Marks Place, junkie punk heaven, was the Electric Circus, during whose four-year lifespan you could see anybody from the Grateful Dead to Terry Riley (I saw Sly and the Family Stone). Below that was the Fillmore East, an old Yiddish theater that for a similarly short period in the late sixties and early seventies hosted Hendrix, Cream, Led Zeppelin, and Frank Zappa. It couldn't last—Electric Circus and the Fillmore were gone by 1971, as were Hendrix, Joplin, and Jim Morrison, each of whom died within months of each other at the cursed age of twenty-seven. But for a brief, perfect moment, it was all there for the taking.

I realized early that, though I was a decent guitar player, I probably wasn't cut out to be a full-time rock star. But those bands were my passion, and I figured film and TV were as good a way to celebrate that as any other. I worked up a documentary about the rock groups that were the decade's most fertile: the Yardbirds, which gave the world Eric Clapton, Jimmy Page, and Jeff Beck, and Buffalo Springfield, which introduced us to Neil Young and Stephen Stills before they broke up early and reformed as Crosby, Stills, Nash and Young. The school would lend you a passed-around Bolex camera to shoot with; I, naturally, sweet-talked Fred and Phyllis into buying me a top-of-the-line French-made Beaulieu. I made student films that were the definition of student films. A short about a blind guy angry at the world, with art-house shots of dust swirling around his cane. Tons of unusable vérité footage taken at the May Day march in Washington my junior year, when the world converged on DC to protest the never-ending Vietnam War. I was expecting genius in every frame. Of course, I was tripping on acid the whole time.

. . .

When I graduated in the spring of 1972, I packed my bags and headed for Los Angeles. LA was to be my second summer school—life was about to begin. My father had a friend, Natie Shapiro, who had some connections to the movie business. Natie was a tough bastard; his father had been Gurrah Shapiro, a notorious Jewish mobster in New York. (With Lepke Buchalter, Gurrah had formed a racket called Murder, Inc., which did contract killings for the Mafia and the Jewish mob. Lepke got the chair at Sing Sing; Gurrah died in prison.) Yeah, it turned out, Natie knew some guys. He got me an interview with Lou Perry.

Perry was a Hollywood producer, and a seedy little greaseball. That summer, he was riding high. Perry (real name Louis Peraino) was an associate of the Colombo crime family and one of the backers of *Deep Throat*, the first porno film to be a bona fide pop culture phenomenon. It was famous and infamous; in New York, Mayor Lindsay was waging a campaign to purge Times Square of massage parlors, porno houses, and other undesirables, and theaters showing *Deep Throat* were raided that August—after the film had been playing for twelve straight weeks. *Deep Throat* was a ridiculous movie with a sad backstory and a laughable plot, but it made history, and it certainly made Lou Perry. I explained to him that I went to school for motion pictures and I'd really like to get involved in the film industry. "Great," he says to me. "Get undressed and let's see the size of your dick."

That was the end of that interview. I wouldn't have been the first nice Jewish kid in porno—the leading man of *Deep Throat*, Harry Reems, was a pisher—but I preferred my sex to be of the off-screen variety. Perry took it well, all things considered. He had a long and sordid career ahead of him (he produced the Warhol Factory's *Flesh for Frankenstein*, as well as *The Adventures of Suzy Super Slut 3*), and it was no skin off his ass if I didn't come work for him. He put me in touch with somebody or other, and I ended up a gofer on a movie called *Black Gunn*.

*Black Gunn* was an unusual Blaxploitation film—not least because it was directed and produced by Brits, who were not, for obvious reasons, the likeliest contenders to understand the genre. But riding the wave of *Shaft* and *Sweet Sweetback's Baadasssss Song*, major studios were getting interested. The plot centered on a gang of Black militants—the BAG, or Black Action Group, a thinly veiled version of the Black Panthers—who rob a Mafia operation, leading to predictable violence on all sides. Gunn was played by Jim Brown, probably the best player in the history of Syracuse football, and one of the all-time great pro footballers, who'd retired from the Cleveland Browns a few years before. The Mafia capo, Capelli, was played by Martin Landau.

It wasn't a bad movie, really. It never found the audience of *Shaft*, which came out the year before, or *Super Fly*, a few years after. I rented a room in a residence hotel on Sunset Boulevard in West Hollywood and spent all day on set, with all the actors and the lighting and the cameras—which I loved. But I was doing bullshit stuff, hanging around, getting coffee.

Within a few weeks, it became clear that getting beyond a gofer was likely a pipe dream. The '70s were the real beginning of New Hollywood—all the movies I worshipped in college—but the town was very much still the old LA, clubby and cloistered. Fashion was just getting started; Rodeo Drive was still in its infancy, anchored by the slick Euro tailoring of Giorgio Beverly Hills. There were some good clubs—Whiskey a Go Go, where The Doors got their start as house band—but it was, even more than it is now, movies that ran the town. The big shots would take their meetings at Chasen's or the Polo Lounge at the Beverly Hills Hotel and compete to see who could be the most obnoxious. Wannabe actors and actresses would hang around the pool at the hotel, desperate to be noticed, and secretly call asking for themselves to be paged: "Telephone call for So-and-so!"

The town, I came to realize in a hurry, was full of unemployed twenty-one-year-old directors. Try as I might, I looked likely to become another one of them if I stuck around too long. By the end of the summer, tail ever so slightly between my legs, I flew back East. Back to my parents' house and my not-quite-childhood bedroom (they'd traded up since I'd last lived with them). Marooned in Westchester, I felt rattled, pissed, and aimless. Night after night on the fake-fur bedspread, I'd lay awake staring up at the silver, reflective ceiling and wonder: What the hell was I going to do next?

# 5

# WAR STORIES OF THE SHOPPING CLASS

## 1972-1973

Things were going nowhere as the fall of 1972 approached. I was living at home like a kid with Mommy and Daddy, my Hollywood era over before it even began. I'd been young and stupid to think that a few connections would send me to the top.

The reality set me straight. If I'd had different parents, maybe they would have raised more hell when I slunk back to Harrison, but it wasn't Fred and Phyllis's style to apply pressure; they left me alone to find my way. Bob, at eighteen, was about to escape the house for his first year at Boston University, but me? I was in Never-Never-Land, a twenty-one-year-old Peter Pan in arrested development with a bunch of Darling children hanging around (my sisters were twelve and nine at the time). The one good thing is that I was getting bored, and nothing has ever motivated me like boredom. I needed to get out of the house, and I needed to get on my way.

The answer was about to come to dinner. Sunday nights, Barney used to get driven up from the city to join us for a weekly meal. He was on his own now. After a short illness, glamorous Bertha, my wonderful grandmother, had died at the beginning of the year. She was one of the most tasteful people I've ever known, but for all her old-world charm, she was still a woman ahead of her time. (She palled around with gay men long before people talked about sexuality openly.) Barneys wouldn't have been Barneys without her, and not just because of the legend of the pawned engagement ring. She stayed on the floor till she could barely stand anymore, taking names and connecting customers with their salespeople. Barney wouldn't have been Barney without her, either. When she died, at seventy-four, they had been married for fifty-two years.

I think Barney must've been a little lonely, not that his tough-guy's pride would've let him admit it. Bertha was gone, as was their only daughter, Fred's sister, my aunt Elizabeth, who had passed away the year before. Barney was still working—he wouldn't officially retire for another three or four years—but he was taking a back seat to Fred. Barneys had ballooned into a major business, with some eleven hundred employees between the store and the offices, tailor shops, and warehouse across the street, and the guy was pushing eighty.

But with the two of them at the table, talk inevitably turned to the store. What was selling, what was tanking, who was a problem, who was a success. I'd been hearing Fred do the Barneys spiel for years without ever paying much attention. Now, at loose ends, I leaned in a little more than I had before. Things were changing in a way I liked. Barneys was going from a big-money player to something that was actually cool. The customer base was getting younger and hipper, and they were coming in from all over. It was starting to become fun.

Barney had none of Fred's delicacy—he didn't hesitate to ask me point-blank what it was I thought I was going to do. "I don't know," I told him. "At the very least, I'd like to move to New York."

He was living all alone in the palatial duplex he had shared with my grandmother on Park Avenue, with its wraparound terrace, the biggest I'd ever seen in New York. It was ornate, gilded to the hilt in rococo style. A twisting white marble staircase unfurled from the upper floor, where the bedrooms were, to the living room and dining room below. There were carved stone statues of cherubs and gorgeous, overflowing planters—many of which made their way eventually to Phyllis and Fred's in Southampton—and a hand-painted fresco Bertha had commissioned on the spiraling wall by the stairs, like in one of Marie Antoinette's palaces. And there was Barney amid the finery, whose most passionate cultural interest was the Jewish deli he had ordered in at all times, the little refrigerator up in his bedroom suite permanently stocked with Barney Greengrass for his midnight nosh. Of course he'd be a little lonely there—who wouldn't?—but even I was shocked when he cocked his head and said, "So why don't you come live with me?"

I swallowed hard. On one hand, I wasn't looking for a roommate, and if I had been, a guy who was born during Grover Cleveland's second administration wouldn't exactly have been my pick. On the other hand, New York was New York and my current prospects were looking slim. Fred and Phyllis didn't say a word.

"OK," I said. "When can I move in?"

· · ·

Every morning, a chauffeured Caddy would pull up to 650 Park Avenue. In went Barney and me. Maybe I'd slept the night before and maybe I hadn't, but either way, each morning, it was down to 106 Seventh Avenue, to make our way to the top and the bottom, respectively, of the food chain. Barney would head up to his office opposite the store. I, Barneys' newest employee, would start at the ground level.

I hadn't intended to go into the family business, but Barneys had a magnetic pull on everybody who entered its orbit. I wasn't even the only family member to join the store in a more official capacity in the early '70s. About the same time, my mother did, too. She was too smart to sit at home in Harrison all day, minding the kids, and by then even Nancy, the baby, was mostly out of her hair. Phyllis's marriage may have begun in the 1950s, but she was still a young woman in her forties when women's liberation began in earnest. Women were rushing into the workforce, though I don't think Phyllis found her way into Barneys to make a political point. If anything, it was self-protective. For decades, she'd been hearing every intricacy of the Barneys business at the dinner table, night in and night out. As the store became more successful, Fred spent more of his days and weekends on the floor or at the office, and at some point, she must have realized if she wanted to see her husband, she was going to have to be there. She started out offering a few suggestions on window displays—at the dinner table, or when she would come down to the store on the weekends—until eventually Fred told her, "If you know so much about it, why don't you come fix them?" So she did.

She was windows, I was warehouse. Now that Fred was pruning the sales floor, the warehouse, always a bit disorganized, was a chaotic mess. Merchandise that had once been crammed into Barneys was now crammed here, along with out-of-season clothing and shopworn suits that needed a breather from day-to-day action—nothing a quick steam or press couldn't fix, but not much to look at in its current condition. But with so much new merchandise coming in every day, so many boxes to be unpacked, things were arranged with little rhyme or reason. The warehouse was Barneys' storage closet, and it showed.

It was managed by Pete, a tough Italian who'd been there his whole life, or so it seemed to me—looking back now, he must've only been in his late forties. He was a big, strong guy, with a boxer's build and a zero-tolerance policy on taking shit. Warehouse work was itinerant labor for most of the people drudging away in there, and between the nonstop stream of deliveries coming in and a mostly transient staff of muscle floating in and out, Pete had to run a tight ship. On top of everything else, he had Barney dropping by to visit early and often; my grandfather couldn't keep away from seeing the new deliveries as they arrived. Still, even the tightest ship can use a little tune-up now and again. Pete cared about making sure everything got where it needed to be, when it needed to be there—and with big racks of clothes going to and from the store day in and day out, dodging cars speeding down Seventh Avenue, that was a big job. Once in a while some kid would tip over a rack by accident, jamming up traffic and strewing clothes all over the street.

But what Pete cared about less was the way it was organized and arranged; if it got where it needed to go at the end of the day, the store staff and merchants could handle the rest. The way they hung up all the out-of-season merchandise drove me crazy—they smashed it together, crushing the suit fronts. It was loosely organized by floor or "Room," but things got mixed up and rarely fixed. There was only so much raw manpower I could bring to the operation—I was one person—but I did have the Pressman eye. I got to work trying to organize and streamline a little bit. I wouldn't have called it that then—certainly not in the warehouse, where they would have laughed me out of the place—but I was boutique-building. I'd drift upstairs to see what was going on in the buying office, or across the street to the store. This was a bit of golden-boy privilege (I was the owner's kid, guilty), but I think they respected that I was also ready to roll up my sleeves and do the work.

Once a year, the warehouse was the star of the show, thanks to another recent innovation. With so much merch on hand—everything that would no longer be stored day-to-day in the store, plus the larger orders placed for the International House—and bills piling up from the massive expansion, someone had the bright idea to have a major sale. Not from the "new" Barneys, which Fred was working hard to upscale, but direct from the warehouse. The Warehouse Sale has since gone down in history, and any real New Yorker has stories of battling other shoppers for the best, heavily discounted stuff: the war stories of the shopping class. But initially, the idea was unusual; inviting customers into the warehouse to shop at huge discounts was like asking guests to a dinner party you were hosting in your bathroom, in your underwear. Fred took some convincing to bring on board.

The first Warehouse Sale was held in September of 1970, right after Labor Day. Readers of the *New York Daily News* opened their papers to massive ads: "Don't Go to Work Today," they read in all caps, promising "You'll save more money than you could make" at Barneys' five-day warehouse sale from September 8 through 12. From 9:00 a.m. to 9:30 p.m., customers flooded the scene, snapping up bargains of 50 percent off or more. Lines formed around the block; police set up stanchions and tried to manage crowd control. Luckily, Fred's team had pressured manufacturers to send new stuff specifically *for* the sale, to be sure that they had enough merchandise on hand, and for five days, the warehouse minted money—all of it in cash. The sale became an annual event, a favorite of shoppers, who looked forward to it all year, and of Barneys' staff and executives. Even Fred came around.

A few years in, the papers began covering the Warehouse Sale like a spectator sport, and few failed to notice that the warehouse and

Barneys across the street had grown in different directions. "With its plain pipe racks and uncarpeted floor, the warehouse probably looks more like the original hole-in-the-wall store opened by Barney Pressman . . . than the luxurious 100,000-square-foot fashion cornucopia his venture has become," *The New York Times* wrote in 1973. Seventh Avenue had parted the sea of sleeves, and the vast majority of them were now in the warehouse on the west side of the street, with "triple tiers of coat and suit racks and bins of slacks and shirts."

The *Times* reporter noticed a "mod 22-year-old" among the "braless write-up girls" and overwhelmed salesmen: me. I don't remember a thing about meeting this guy, but according to the paper, he asked me if I didn't want to follow in my grandfather's footsteps—meaning, apparently, not working for Barneys, but building my own business from scratch. "I'll stay here," I told him. I hadn't meant to come work for Barneys, but barely a year after I started, it was already home.

. . .

My days in the warehouse and nights on Park Avenue could only last for so long. I was young, hungry, and horny, a powerful and dangerous combination for a kid in the playground of New York. As much as I revered my grandfather, living with him was starting to cramp my style, and it wasn't necessarily in my interest to have my boss—really, my boss's boss's boss—know exactly when I was getting home every night, and with whom. "Cool it with the women!" Barney used to beg me. But that was never going to happen.

Within a couple of months, I knew I needed a place without a live-in grandparent. My old Harrison friend and Syracuse frat brother Jeff Klein was living on East Sixty-First Street, in the heart of Bloomingdale's Country. He knew of an apartment available in the building, and I jumped on it. 166 East Sixty-First Street became home.

Lines formed down the block for Barneys' Warehouse Sale,
both in real life and in our ads, like this one.

Though it seems hard to imagine now, the Upper East Side was one of the epicenters of New York cool in the early 1970s. From my perch on Sixty-First and Third Avenue, I was in the midst of everything. You could be as public or as private as you wanted. You could hide out at Isle of Capri, the red-sauce Italian joint next door, or you could go out to see and be seen. Yellowfingers was still such a hotspot, now with a new disco in the basement, that in 1971, *Life* magazine had run a fashion story on its cover called "The View from Yellowfingers." Sixties joints like Maxwell's Plum on Sixty-Fourth and First—the ur-singles-bar, a combination restaurant/movie musical—were still going strong. And Bloomingdale's, though I was loath to admit it, was at the height of its cool, with sexed-up window displays and more young, hip labels than any of the other department stores.

My new building was an anonymous-looking brick co-op; surrounded though it was by lovely townhouses on all sides, 166 East Sixty-First Street itself wasn't much to look at. But as a combination launch pad/ crash pad/after-hours club, it was perfect. I wasn't the only one who used it as a home base. I heard Barbra Streisand had a place in the building; so did Lou Reed, who lived in the apartment below mine. I used to see his girlfriend and muse, Rachel, coming in and out of the lobby, but Lou himself was never to be seen. He *was* to be heard. He'd rattle my floorboards with his god-awful guitar till five or six o'clock in the morning, until finally I got so fed up that I'd go to war with him. I tipped my own giant speaker towers face down and blasted my music right back at him.

Not long after I traded up to my own place, I left the warehouse. I think Fred knew that it wouldn't hold me forever, and he quietly encouraged my sniffing around the buying office upstairs. Before long, I had made the leap.

It was Barney, not Fred, who first started taking me out into the market. He was less and less involved in the big picture of running the store, but Barney wasn't ready to call it quits. Unexpectedly for a guy in his late seventies, he had a youthful heart and a genuine interest in what the "kids" were doing. As Fred cleaned up the tailoring that was Barneys' bread and butter, Barney himself gravitated toward the younger section, where the action was. Jeans were the thing, and when Barney went to the denim trade show at the McAlpin Hotel in Herald Square, he took me with him.

At the McAlpin, jeans brands booked individual rooms and suites, setting up racks of their wares and smooth-talking the buyers like carnival barkers. Jeans were more than ever the American uniform—denim shops had cropped up all over the city, even in Bloomingdale's Country, places like The Different Drummer, where I used to shop. The big stores were no longer content to cede the market to thrift shops and secondhand stores. Barney was the oldest person at the trade show by double, but that didn't embarrass me a bit—he was the emperor. And he was there to buy: The Billy Baxter Room had been rechristened the Underground, after the London Tube, and was stocking more young lines than ever. But it helped him to have me, a flesh-and-blood twenty-two-year-old, around as a focus group of one and a divining rod.

Barney and I had split up—he'd gotten buttonholed by one of his many admirers, or maybe just a wholesaler who smelled a potential sale. I was browsing around, doing my own thing, when someone waved me into a room featuring a brand called UFO. UFO would go on to some fame in the following decades for its plasticky nylon cargo pants, but at the time, it was a relatively new company, the brainchild of a former army-surplus entrepreneur who realized he could adapt the styles of military surplus to a new jeans collection.

The guy waving me in looked like a hipster pirate who'd gotten lost among the secondhand shops downtown. He stood about my height, but he had a giant mop of unruly dark hair that gave him an outsized presence—it was big enough that he looked like he'd put a wig on backward. (He let me give it a pull—all real.) He favored funky looks I never would've attempted; it turned out he lived above Granny Takes a Trip, the dandified, acid-fried frock shop imported a few years before from the Kings Road in London to Sixty-Second Street, and from the way he dressed, it seemed like he had a private entrance directly from his apartment. He used to wear a big silver chain with a fake stone locket I wouldn't have been caught dead in, but he got away with it. His name, he told me, was Michael Schreier.

He was a Long Island kid a couple of years older than me. We got to talking, and hit it off immediately. He had a laissez-faire attitude to life, love, and work that resonated with me—this guy was on permanent cruise control. He was there to sell, but he wasn't going to get ruffled doing it. It took about two seconds for our talk to wend away from business, anyway. UFO had a model on hand to try on jeans, a blond chick with a big smile. "She's hot, isn't she?" Michael said to me. She is, I agreed. "Why don't the three of us go into the bathroom and smoke a joint?" he asked, with a glimmer in his eye.

We locked the door, and lit up a joint—you probably could've smelled it the next hotel over. And, as they often did in New York in the early '70s, when the hippie ethic of free love flourished in a world where STIs were for sailors and AIDS hadn't yet appeared, things progressed from there. Me, the pirate I'd known for all of five minutes, and the jeans chick made what we used to call a scene, as the halls around us buzzed with browsing buyers. I knew then that Michael was cut from the same cloth as me. He had the moves. He was slick, he could talk, he could hang, and he could do it all sober or stoned.

I had just climbed out of the warehouse, and barely started to get involved with the store's buys. Still, getting slightly ahead of myself, I decided the first thing I needed was a buyer to work for me, and that was Michael. He was ready to trade in his VW Beetle full of jeans, and

I was ready to have an assistant I wouldn't mind spending full days, and what turned out to be many, many nights, with. I introduced him to my father, who looked at him kind of cross-eyed, but blessed the hire.

. . .

Once we met, Michael's live-in girlfriend didn't last long. Michael was as straight as they come—so was I—but we found that we were each other's best wingmen, and getting each other laid became first a game, and then a competition.

By day, Michael and I would hit up the showrooms of New York, figuring out how to buy as we went. Michael had style but no structure—he was very thrift shop, not surprising, given his last job was selling jeans out of the trunk of his Bug. I was a bit green myself, but I found that, like Michael, I had taste and plenty of opinions. Schmoozing salesmen at the showrooms along Seventh Avenue, I could talk the talk, but also pretty quickly cut through the bullshit. What we really had on our side was youth. We knew how people our age wanted to dress, in ways that the buyers who had worked for my grandfather for decades didn't know, and didn't care to. If we wanted to bring the young, horny energy of Bloomingdale's down to Barneys, it wasn't going to come from selling more of the same old suits.

By night, we went straight from the office to dinner and then out to the clubs. The disco era, still in its infancy, was just getting started in New York. I was a denizen of the rock clubs—like the Bottom Line, which opened that year—but many of them were closed or on their last legs by the early '70s. The Electric Circus and Fillmore East were gone. The dance scene, on the other hand, was heating up.

The club of the moment was Le Jardin, in the Hotel Diplomat on Sixth Avenue and Forty-Third Street. The fashion industry swarmed to it basically the second it opened. With its cavernous back ballroom, it was perfect for fashion shows and other off-hours events as well as dancing, and in 1973, people were always flocking there for something or other—a Frederick's of Hollywood show, which was a joke, or a Pierre Cardin show, which wasn't. Right around this time, we were buying a ton of Cardin suits for Barneys, and I was getting to know Nick De Marco, Cardin's US representative. Movie-star handsome, with a chiseled jaw and gym-toned muscles before there was a gym on every corner, Nicky worked out of a big showroom building nearby on Sixth Avenue. He was recently divorced—let's call it newly single—and despite a couple of kids, he was ready to shake off his red-sauce Brooklyn-Italian upbringing and find a good time.

We didn't hit it off—at least not initially, when I strolled into the Cardin showroom, put my cowboy-boot-clad feet on the table, and asked him point blank, "What is this shit?" Fred might have had that thought privately—he wasn't much of a Cardin man, and neither was I—but he'd never say so out loud. But I didn't hesitate to bust Nicky's balls. I brought the same shtick to the showroom that I brought out to the clubs at night. Michael and I could tell in a second he was one of us. Along with a few friends from the old days, like Jeff Klein, and an old Hackley friend called Steve Hanson, we became an inseparable posse, sampling the best New York had to offer.

That meant places like Le Jardin. Technically speaking, it was a gay club, or was conceived to be, but the party was too good—the social types discovered it immediately. The mix was one of the things that made it electric; you never knew who you were going to find there. Even if it had been strictly a gay club, that would've been a plus as far as I was concerned. We loved going to the gay clubs, for one good reason: No competition. Women loved going dancing with their gay friends, who were feeling more comfortable being themselves than ever before and wanted to celebrate it—remember, this was just a few years after the Stonewall Rebellion showed that there was only so far into the closet New York's gay men and lesbians were going to be pushed before they said fuck it and fought back.

Out among them at the clubs, we had our pick of the hottest chicks there, and the guys played the best music to boot. (The one thing I couldn't stand was their mustaches. They all looked like policemen to me which, in retrospect, was probably the point.) Le Jardin and 12 West, another gay disco on the side street Little West Twelfth in the Meatpacking District, were our regular haunts. And while I'm not sure I even realized at the time that it was all essentially market research—gay guys were, and still are, at the cutting edge of men's fashion, way before their straight compatriots—we were soaking up what was newest in men's style direct from the dance floor.

New York was partying hard. The city had a wild new energy—thanks in no small part to the free flow of drugs in every dark and not-so-dark corner, bathroom, or tabletop. But beneath the disco balls, all was not as bright or shiny as it seemed. The city was floundering financially. Mayor Lindsay, it turned out, had been kicking the can down the road, with all sorts of shady accounting, borrowing wildly and deferring payments. Term-limited out of the mayoralty at the end of 1973, he gave way to his comptroller, a squat accountant and lifelong Brooklyn pol named Abe Beame. When our new mayor took office in January of 1974, he was facing a $1.5 billion deficit, one he loudly blamed on his handsome, profligate predecessor, though as comptroller, Beame had signed off on the budgets, too. Was the party ending? Some drew a firm line between the headwinds on the horizon and the packed clubs. "There is a feeling of fiddling while New York burns, a feeling that you have to live it up while you still can," an anonymous disco denizen told the *Times*.

# 6

# KIDS IN A CANDY STORE

## 1973-1974

At five feet six or so, Ed Glantz was a miniature fixture of Barneys. He was the furnishings and accessories buyer for the International House, where the department had pride of place on the ground floor. Only a few years my senior, Eddie seemed a lifetime older. I'd known him since my first times sneaking out of the warehouse and into the showroom upstairs, where he'd be sitting with my father looking through huge orders of ties. Usually he'd have laid out his selections already, but one day, I decided I liked them another way, and started rearranging them for him. I don't know what gave me the guts. He can't have been very pleased about it. But Fred noticed, and rather than reprimand me, he suggested I accompany Ed on one of his buying trips to Europe. I think he was trying to lure me in deeper, though he'd never have said so; his style was to lay in wait and let you come to him. Years later, I found out that Barney himself had taken Ed aside and told him, "Take care of Gene, introduce him around."

That first trip, in the fall of 1973, was a revelation. We touched down in Milan, the heart of the Italian fashion industry. Milan doesn't have the gaudy splendor of Rome or the winding little medieval side streets of Florence. It's a grayer, more concrete city, befitting its industrial importance to the nation, as well as the fact that it was decimated by Allied bombs during World War II. Some of the city's greatest landmarks, treasures of the world, suffered unbelievable damage: La Scala, one of the world's premier opera houses, sat exposed to the elements, and the Galleria Vittorio Emanuele II, the nineteenth-century shopping center with its elaborate glass dome, needed extensive repairs. In the postwar aftermath, Milan was rebuilt in a darker, more concrete "modern" style, and yet it remains one of Italy's most wonderful cities, whose blocky buildings and high walls conceal beautiful gardens and sprawling apartments. And it's colonized by the most extravagant peacocks the world has ever known: Italian guys.

Ed brought me along to an appointment in the center of Milan, where we looked through shirts by a company called Punch, all cut in fabrics by Solbiati, a producer who had been making them in Italy since the 1870s. They didn't look like Brooks Brothers, or even anything we had at Barneys. These linens came in beautiful pastel colors whose wrinkles were an essential feature, not a headache to be ironed out. Americans at the time used linen only for napkins, and proper shirts— except for hideous floral sports shirts for the Ralph Kramdens of the world—*never* came in colors like these.

Watching Ed pick fabrics for our orders, I saw how creative it could be. I loved that part of Barneys—building your own expression from the cloth up, smuggling that interpretation of European style back to the home front. And privately, I had a feeling that I could do it as well as he could.

In the following seasons, I'd go back often with my dad and the buyers, searching out (and sometimes competing jealously with other store owners for) the best stuff. We'd refuel on homemade pasta at the Barneys unofficial cafeteria, BiCE, with Mamma Bice (short for Beatrice) seated by the cash register nodding us toward our table next to her post. Then we'd take the train from Milan three hours southeast to Florence and do it all again at Pitti Uomo, the Florentine menswear show where Fred would walk the aisles like the Pope, fussed over by every manufacturer. That was cool, but I wanted more freedom to make my own mark, to grow out of Fred's shadow. I began nursing an inkling that I was going to need my own niche at Barneys, and started thinking about what it should be.

. . .

By this point, international merchandise was integral to Barneys. And in menswear, the initial conduit between Europe and America was the license business. Unlike today, when the major European fashion brands all have businesses in every major territory around the world and handle production and often distribution themselves, in the 1960s and '70s, companies were nowhere near as international. They had neither the resources nor much interest in hovering over every detail, and for cash-rich, taste-poor (in their opinion) markets like America, they were all too happy to outsource to licensees on contract. They'd sell the rights to use their name to manufacturers who would create product tailored—figuratively and literally, since American guys tend to be bigger than Europeans—to the US market and earn a percentage royalty on top. Nominally, the designers whose names were featured on the label—Saint Laurent, Cardin, and so on— would approve the designs, but in practice, as long as the checks came in, they were generally content to live and let live. When readers of *GQ* opened their magazines in the early '70s to see a gabardine suit by Piattelli or a panné velvet evening suit by Feruch being promoted as a "fashion find" at Barneys' International House, the names on the label may have been the designers', but the man behind them, likely as not, was Fred.

The license and manufacturing business made millions for those who were well positioned, either by savvy, connections, or family factories, to take advantage of it. These people, little known outside the trade papers of the industry, were often characters in their own right. People like Maurice Bidermann, for a time the most important men's manufacturer in Europe. Born Maurice Zylberberg to Polish-Jewish émigrés in Belgium, he was hidden during the Holocaust by a family in Marseilles, and after the war, ran off to join the Israeli army. Upon his return to France, Bidermann joined his uncle's menswear company and began buying up larger and larger factories, first making suits for the Soviet Union and then the United States. When France's couturiers decided to try their hand at the men's market, Bidermann was there to handle production.

Companies like Bidermann employed their own designers, anonymous workhorses who were tasked with making these name-brand collections palatable for their individual markets. Barneys bought plenty from these licensees. They were affordable—a three-piece suit by Yves Saint Laurent might go for $149.99 at Barneys—and we sold them by the truckload. But Fred realized that Barneys could do its own licensing and effectively cut out the middleman. Most of the license suits we carried were either made in America—the stuff you'd get in the Madison Room, like Oxxford and Hickey Freeman—or wherever it was cheapest; despite the French name on the label, a Saint Laurent suit might've been stitched in Colombia. By that point, Fred's enthusiasm had endeared him to the men who made the best products in the world. He began making his own handshake deals to license their names for Barneys—sometimes for a fee, and sometimes, unbelievably, for the handshake alone: That's how much these men believed in Fred and how valuable they thought international exposure at Barneys could be for their businesses. He repaid that trust with lifelong devotion and respect, as well as with occasional gestures that went far beyond the typical retailer relationship: When Bruno Piattelli's daughter was kidnapped during the terrifying wave of ransom plots that gripped Italy a few years later, it was Fred who fronted him the money to save her.

What Fred and his deputies realized early on was that they could be the ones who adapted what factories and designers were making for the needs of American men. It was vanishingly rare to find an Italian-made suit in New York in the 1970s—the ultra-high end suits from Brioni were about it. But there was a gap between the $1,000 Brioni suit and the $149.99 Saint Laurent one, and a lot of customers who fell into it. No one was making European-tailored suits for these guys—and Fred could. In the '70s, his lieutenants made their way to Europe regularly, sometimes as often as every six weeks. One of them once told me that when his son drew a picture of him, it was waving good-bye from the window of a TWA plane.

Much of Barneys' later success was built on the private-label business that Fred made. No one knew his customer better than Fred, who seemed to never be off the sales floor; he was so delighted to be there, he was known to sometimes break into a little soft-shoe number among the racks. (He was also known to lock the doors of the managers' offices so they'd have to be on the floor, too, like it or not.) Fred also realized that private-label let you name your own price. If no one else in town had a line, then no one else in town could undercut you on it, and when you set your own price, you set your own margins. He was savvy enough to realize that not everyone in Italy was walking around in a Brioni suit—Italy was, at that time, a pretty modest country. The suits they were wearing had to come from somewhere, though. When he sent his people out to investigate, they found dozens of factories making beautiful suits, but very few had the connections to get them to the United States, or most anywhere else. Manufacturers who would go on to international prominence—like Belvest, who ended up making the tailored clothing for Burberry, then for Armani, Hermès, and Prada—were unknown in America at that time. Barneys began developing what were effectively private labels from these manufacturers, exclusive to us, and pricing them right between the entry-level options and the highest end. Doing so made a ton of money for the store, and not just for the store. In 1970, Italy was exporting only about 500 million lire worth of textiles and clothing. By 1980, it was 3.7 billion.

Private label would become a major focus of the subsequent years, and Fred was never happier than when he was working on the collections. By the late '70s, the store was ordering five thousand to ten thousand pieces at a time. Fred would sit for hours in his office, surrounded by rolling racks, trying on the garments, thinking up how to market them, putting together a business plan. Peter Rizzo, who joined Barneys as a men's merchant in 1978 and worked as closely with Fred as just about anyone in the company's history, described him as being like a kid in a candy store. Fred noticed everything—Peter believes to this day that it was the hand-stitched, working buttonholes on the suit he wore to his interview that got Fred to hire him—and nothing happened in tailored clothing for many, many years without Fred being involved.

. . .

By the mid-1970s, a revolution was brewing in menswear, and a parallel one was in the offing at Barneys. The store celebrated its fiftieth anniversary in 1973 with a block party that took over Seventh Avenue, and the distance it had come was huge. A television ad from this period, with faux-newsreel of a young "Barney," looked mistily back at the beginnings: "He opened that store with a grand total of forty suits," an announcer's voice said. "He worked long, and he worked hard." But by the mid-1970s, the tiny original shopfront had grown to take up an entire city block, and those first forty suits had become tens of thousands. "Barneys has changed a lot in fifty years," the announcer intoned, meaning perhaps more than the marketers intended, "but Barney hasn't." The ad closed on an elderly Barney, pinching the cheek of a harassed-looking kid in a Boystown suit.

But his time at the store was coming to a close. Fred was by now indisputably in charge, and the whole tenor of the place was changing. Though Fred loved and deeply respected his father, Barney was a man of an earlier era. The hard sell of yore had been replaced by a softer one; around this time, one ad agency or another, sensing the shift, suggested we print up metal buttons—the same kind they used to use for admission at the Met—that read "Just Looking," for customers not in the mood to be harried.

Within a year or so, Barneys had an entirely different feeling and with it, a different clientele—younger, more sophisticated. It wasn't like the flip of a switch. We still had a New Yorker Room, where wiseguy types with manicured nails shopped for bargains, but now we also had an English Room, complete with a real-life English manager, offering Burberry and Aquascutum along with Kilgour, French & Stanbury, which Fred nominally imported from Savile Row, but in actuality, licensed and essentially designed himself. The service got better, too—fewer alterations came back late or slightly off, less merchandise mysteriously walked off the floor. Barney accepted that Fred's vision was the one that would take us forward. He met and married a Canadian widow named Isabelle, and in 1975, retired down to Florida to sit and schvitz and relax—though, being Barney, "relax" was a relative state for him, and he still called in at the end of every day (collect) to hear the store's sales figures.

Men's styles were changing in the 1970s, and men themselves were, too: Barneys' world of a proper suit and tie, topped off with a hat, was giving way to a more modern conception. A new guard of men's designers were busily working to create the future. Stylistically, the early '70s arrived as a bit of a mess. The Carnaby Street styles of the '60s were still hanging on, joined by flower-power hippie chic. The American businessman still largely wore his sack suit from Brooks Brothers, though Cardin and Saint Laurent were pushing a more "Continental" style: stiff, tight, and square-shouldered.

Into the break rode men like Walter Albini. Though he's clearly what we would now call a designer, at the time he was known as a "stylist." The very idea of a "designer" as we know it today wasn't even in circulation at the time. An Italian journalist, writing in the *Corriere della Serra* in the early '70s, posed the question, "So who are these famous fashion designers?" and answered that they were "mad mindless hobgoblins" who existed to drive Italy's clothing manufacturers nuts. Freelance "stylists," who might work with a number of manufacturers, could have a handful of contracts, or more: Men like Albini, a wild dandy who designed for Italian boutiques and labels like Krizia, Basile, and Cadette in the 1970s and 1980s, and men who would later become headline-famous in their own right, like Gianni Versace and Karl Lagerfeld. These designers at first went uncredited, but the press soon got wise, and it became a parlor game to guess whose hand was behind which show. Soon companies were leaking the names of these designers to goose interest.

These were the beginnings of what would come to be known as designer sportswear—not in the Nike and Adidas sense of gym clothes, but a more casual, still elegant category of individual pieces to be mixed and matched like women's wear was. The uniform of an earlier generation (a suit, a tie, an overcoat) was splintering into a freer conception of what could be. You might have an overcoat, or you might have a blouson (a short jacket with a whiff of sophistication about it). Instead of a suit, you could have trousers and a beautiful sweater. You didn't have to take the dictates of one label, one company, as gospel; a modern man no longer had to be a Paul Stuart man or a Hart Schaffner Marx man head to toe. Designer sportswear brought with it the possibility of individual style, both for stores, whose buyers could pick and choose what to offer, and for customers, who'd snap up the pieces that best expressed their own taste.

Designer sportswear would become my first fiefdom at Barneys, my own little corner of the world. It made sense—I hadn't worn a suit in years, my own uniform consisting of jeans and Lacoste polo shirts. I corralled a little budget from Fred, and a section of the third floor to call my own, right next to the cafe where Fred would have his tuna salad lunches. So, like my father before me, I headed for Europe. And with a little intel from Nick De Marco, who knew France from working with Bidermann and Cardin, Michael and I hit London and Paris like a couple of vagabonds.

There were no men's fashion shows in those days, or barely—a very few Italian brands had eked out little shows of their own in the early '60s, but nothing existed for men like the twice-a-year runway pageants they stage today. In London, we homed in on specialty stores with their own labels, like Browns, the specialty store run by the grande dame Joan "Mrs. B" Burstein, and convinced them to sell to Barneys. (Our sales guy there was a floppy-haired young lad from the East Midlands who did a bit of design himself, Paul Smith.) We hunted out classic flannels and English woolens from Margaret Howell, who was just beginning to make inroads in the UK and US, and didn't even have her own shop yet.

In Paris, we went to the menswear trade show at the convention center by the new Charles de Gaulle Airport, and to small shops like Marcel Lassance, who made tailored clothes that seemed less stuffy than their stiff predecessors. Many of the brands we picked up don't mean much to people today, names like Christian Aujard, Daniel Cremeux, and Daniel Hechter, French labels with huge businesses through the '70s and into the '80s. And many of today's more familiar names were still to come. We blew through our first budget, until, in short order, we no longer had one. Fred didn't care. He actually said to us, "Boys, I don't mind being stuck with beautiful merchandise."

Sportswear marked an inflection point for American men. As international designers (and licenses) made designer suits a reality, sportswear applied the same principles to weekend wear. Men are as susceptible as women to conspicuous consumption—maybe more so—and with the right coaxing, were plenty capable of seeing the appeal of better-looking, better-made clothes than their fathers ever had. Fred had the clothing rooms of Barneys under his watchful eye, but sportswear was an area where Michael and I could have our own way. The timing was right. It quickly proved profitable, and brought in not only dollars but new customers as well, including celebrities, Hollywood types, entertainment people and artists. Yul Brynner, one of the great leading men of the '60s, came in one day and fell in love with a blousy shirt and a pair of tight black cotton pants. He's declaiming like he's onstage, "I want to buy them all in white, and all in black!"

Meanwhile, I was still out almost every night. I didn't consider myself an ambassador for Barneys, per se, though I certainly didn't mind if a certain amount of Barneys fame shined my aura a little brighter and opened every velvet rope in town. But being everywhere and visibly so, I was getting the word out without having to shout it—very Fred-like, in fact. I was only a few years out of college, my Hollywood era still a recent memory, but things were beginning to fall into place at Barneys. The bug had bitten. I was seeing how Barneys could be more than a sea of suits. Who needed the movies? Life was a movie, and commerce could be an art form all its own. Warhol was our durable patron saint—Warhol, who I used to see at Max's Kansas City a few blocks from Barneys—and as he would put it in his *Philosophy of Andy Warhol*, published the next year, "Making money is art, and working is art and good business is the best art." Who was I to disagree?

Dipping a toe into the industry in the early '70s at a men's
fashion show in Milan. Bob Beauchamp of *GQ* is left. John Jones,
the men's buyer of Ultimo in Chicago, center.

. . .

I was settling into my midtwenties, a myopic era in a young man's life. The world went on churning. Nixon, exhausted and abandoned after the scandal of Watergate, resigned in August of 1974, and before the whole thing was through dozens of his collaborators would be indicted or jailed. New York's finances were shot to hell. But to be honest, none of that broke through to me. The world as far as I was concerned was Barneys downtown, East Sixty-First Street uptown, and the clubs and discos in between.

Culturally, we were stuck in an old gear. The art of the time seemed to look more backward than forward. Retro was the flavor of the moment, as if we needed a break from the turbulence of the '60s and early '70s. Everyone seemed to be obsessed with the twenties and thirties, which, at our forty-years' vantage, seemed both novel and untainted by the modern blech. At the box office, people lined up to see '30s-set neo-noir, like *Murder on the Orient Express* or Jack Nicholson in *Chinatown*, and Robert Redford in *The Great Gatsby,* which featured costumes by a still-rising menswear designer named Ralph Lauren. Art collectors were snapping up deco pieces like they hadn't since its own day, not least of them, Warhol, Mr. Modernity himself, who could—and did— set a trend with his purchases as much as with his paintings. Timeless schmaltz like "The Way We Were" ruled the radio, and the ferment and fury of the '60s seemed oddly far away.

Even Barneys fell prey to the period-piece mania. Two years earlier, in 1972, Fred and his admen had created one of the great TV spots of all time, called "Men of Destiny," which featured a little Barney (a kid actor), bullshitting on a Brooklyn stoop with little Humphrey Bogart, little Louis Armstrong, little Fiorello LaGuardia, and little Casey Stengel. All the other kids had big dreams—to play baseball, to be in the pictures, to blow the horn, to be the mayor of New York—but little Barney had humbler aspirations. "You'll all need clothes," was his tagline. The old style worked—the ad won awards and a permanent place in Barneys' heart and lore—and in 1974, the ad guys repeated the trick, with sepia-toned TV ads of the old Barneys of the '30s presided over by a "young" (although not *that* young) Barney.

A change was on its way. Fashion's '60s greats were now growing a little stale in their fusty middle age, and some of the greatest innovators in design were just around the bend. I was about to discover them. As I tiptoed into the fashion world in Europe, I still had one foot in my New York clubhouse. Within a year or two, I had moved from my first studio apartment into a one-bedroom on the seventh floor, with a direct sightline into Bloomingdale's from the bathroom. I used to fantasize every time I took a leak that I was pissing down onto it. Honestly, I was envious. Michael and I would spend weekends there, roaming the racks, checking out the girls, seething that they still had cooler stuff than Barneys, and women who wanted to shop it. Women brought energy and excitement to a store, the way they looked through every piece, shopped in pairs and packs, made a day of it . . . Men got in and out as quickly as possible. Why couldn't we have that?

My old friend Jeff was still installed in his penthouse apartment upstairs. Jeff had the place to himself and turned it into our own personal den of iniquity. Twenty-four hours a day, it seemed, people were going or coming. A poker game was on at all hours in one of the bedrooms. Drug dealers would be passing out a little pot or hash in the kitchen. I'd bring a date, or come home there from a bad one. I'd stay until we ordered up breakfast from the Greek diner, the Argonauts, downstairs—Jeff never had more on hand than a box of Mallomars in the freezer. Then to Barneys to get back, a little groggily, to work. No one had it better than I did in those days—no price was too high, no bridge too far. As Jeff likes to remind me to this day, when I wasn't there, I'd call in long-distance from Paris or wherever to have him do play-by-play of the Knicks playoffs over the phone.

# 7

# DRUM ROLL, GIORGIO

## 1975-1976

The man who really moved the needle for the International House was a young northern Italian designer. When Fred maneuvered to steer him into Barneys, with a ten-year exclusive contract to license his menswear, he was a startup—not quite a nobody but a long way from the top.

The first time I ever even heard of the guy was in the family house in Harrison around 1975. Sitting around the TV in Dad's wood-paneled library, rain beating off the lead-glass windows, he and I were glued to the Knicks playoff game. It was a great time to be a New York fan and I wasn't going to miss a minute.

Fred, ever the multitasker, was parked in his Eames lounger in his corduroys, one eye on the game and one on a thick imported copy of *L'Uomo Vogue*, the Italian men's magazine that was miles ahead of its American counterparts. It was there that he came across an editorial and, in his typically laconic way, held it out to me. "This is a really beautiful coat," he said, sweeping his index finger over the page as if he could feel the fabric; really, he almost fondled it. He paused and chewed it over to himself. "I think this guy is really talented," he murmured.

I was, with all due respect, more engaged with the game at that moment; I hardly paid attention. At that point, there wasn't much to pay attention *to*. Yeah, yeah, I told him. Sure, you should try to talk to him. Right, maybe we can get an exclusive. Truth be told, at that moment, I half wished he'd leave me alone and let me watch. But he was a bloodhound when he sniffed greatness. He could make something of this Giorgio Armani.

At that time, he barely had a label to speak of; he'd founded Giorgio Armani S.p.A. out of a two-room office on Corso Venezia that year. It was basically a two-man operation: Giorgio, a former window-dresser with steely blue eyes and a fierce determination to succeed, and his boyfriend and business partner, Sergio Galeotti, a former architect eleven years his junior who gave up stability and certainty to bet big on Armani's future. Giorgio was the creative, Sergio the business—not that Sergio even knew all that much about business at the time.

Armani had put in his time behind the scenes. He was forty-one years old. For ten years, he had been working for Nino Cerruti, one of the great men of Italian tailoring and textiles. Not content to merely make some of the finest fabrics in Italy at the third-generation family mill in Biella, Cerruti had founded his own label, Hitman, in the late '50s, and would go on to create another in his own name.

Cerruti and Hitman would be Armani's true education in fashion. He had dithered in medical school and served time in the army but, to his parents' chagrin, was drawn to fashion. He worked first in displays at La Rinascente, one of Milan's grand department stores, and then for Signor Cerruti, where he learned, stitch by stitch, what goes into making a garment. Cerruti made beautiful but more traditional men's suits, and it was there that Armani began to be known—his name started to appear in company ads at the time as a stylist (in much smaller print than they ever would again).

From Cerruti, he began working for a variety of Italian manufacturers, building his perfect wardrobe out of their facilities and on their dime. The so-called designer revolution hadn't hit Italy yet; it was manufacturers, not individuals, who had the power, and Armani used them as his training grounds and laboratories. Sicons leathers, Hilton suits, Montedoro raincoats . . . he designed for them all. On one of his many trips to Italy, Eddie Glantz brought back a Montedoro raincoat by Armani for his new wife, a tough, elegant translator named Gabriella Forte, who worked for the Italian Trade Commission in New York.

That fateful page in *L'Uomo Vogue* convinced Fred he had to get Giorgio Armani to Barneys. Finding him was the first step. Via Eddie, Fred asked Gabriella to track down the man behind this perfect raincoat, the guy from the magazine. She didn't know him from Adam, but she gamely pulled down the Italian phone book and one call later she was on with Galeotti. (Forgetting what country she was calling from and the time difference between the two, she ended up ringing them around 11:00 p.m.)

She talked Galeotti into making a visit to the United States; Armani, then as now, more reserved, even reclusive, and less interested in the glad-handing and kibitzing of the fashion industry, stayed behind. Sergio was his perfect complement: gregarious, mischievous, a little wicked. Armani had the chilly bearing and silver hair of an icy, superior god, but Galeotti, with his pencil mustache and impish charm, was more like a gentlemanly devil.

Through Eddie, Gabriella knew Barneys well, and adored both Fred and Barney. All three of us had been at their wedding at the St. Regis—that was how important Ed was to Fred and to Barneys. (At the wedding, Barney, with his usual rough charm, went right up to Gabriella's redheaded mother-in-law and barked, "Is it yours or from a bottle?") She took Galeotti uptown and down, to all the major stores, over the course of a day that stretched well past business hours—Gabriella, dazzled by Galeotti's elegance and wit, remembered calling Eddie at home and telling him, "I'm going to be late, I've met the man of my dreams." She helped steer him, and Armani, to Barneys.

Over dinner with Galeotti, Eddie and Fred—with Gabriella as translator—began hashing out the details of a partnership they would finalize in Milan the following year. Barneys would invest heavily in Armani, promising tens of thousands of dollars in business each season, and in return, would get the exclusive license to manufacture an Armani men's collection specifically for American businessmen, in addition to carrying Armani's more high-fashion couture line. For the next ten years, Armani's and Barneys' fates would be tightly linked. "Barneys was an important platform for me in every way," Giorgio says today. "Their enthusiasm was unconditional, and they immediately decided to give me visibility. We developed a very close relationship that went beyond work."

Galeotti, savvy marketer that he was, suggested to Fred that Barneys' windows and displays could be more modern to bring them up to Armani's (yet-to-be-earned) standards. Fred probably would've taken more offense if Phyllis hadn't been telling him the same thing at the dinner table. And Galeotti was ready to think big. He had stars in his eyes and a star, in his opinion, back on Corso Venezia. Fred agreed. He was already envisioning an incredible, bigger than life TV commercial of Giorgio in his design studio in Milan.

It didn't hurt that Armani was still movie-star handsome; with his piercing stare, trim frame, and graying hair, he looked a bit like an older Italian Alain Delon. (He appeared in some of his own ads in the late '70s, including one shirtless and hunky on the beach.) In 1976, Ally & Gargano, Barneys' ad agency at the time, sent a team to shoot Armani in his Milan atelier, panning down on him from above in his gilded palace. He had traded up by then to a separate office on Via Santa Cecilia, closer to Milan's bustling center and nearby Via Monte Napoleone, which would soon become a Milanese Madison Avenue.

"Many people consider this man the world's finest fashion designer," a voiceover intones. "When he goes shopping for stores, he looks for the same things you should. In New York, with all the fine stores, there's only one he's chosen to represent his men's couture collection: Barneys New York."

Sketching away at his drafting table, the epitome of perfect simplicity in white shirtsleeves, tanned to a Forte dei Marmi bronze, Armani looks directly into the camera as the voice announces, "His name: Giorgio Armani. You see, even though Barneys may not understand his Italian, they fully understand his fashion."

If Armani helped to make Barneys into an institution of fashion, Barneys helped to make Armani an institution, too. When his first collection for the store arrived on Seventh Avenue in the fall of 1976, it's no exaggeration to say that men's fashion would never be the same. Fred and his new discovery Giorgio would see to it.

. . .

For all that it seems like a foregone conclusion now, the Armani revolution wasn't immediate. Despite the fanfare with which we launched

Giorgio, despite the TV commercial with the matinee-idol designer, the first few seasons mainly sat on the rack and went nowhere.

Men and fashion were a work in progress. Sportswear was picking up steam, but even the word "fashion" was still faintly suspect where men, and especially corporate, office-working men, were concerned. Fashion was for wives or girlfriends (or gay men, who understood Armani much more immediately). Even with the Saint Laurent and Cardin wave of the late 1960s and early 1970s, the suit in America was still seen as more of a tool than an expression of anything. A man wore a suit because his father wore a suit, and because his boss wore a suit.

Fred might've had the connoisseur's eye that made examining stitching and linings a passion, but he was the outlier. Suits for most customers were a commodity to be bought by the armful and run through like handkerchiefs, at which point they'd be cleaned, hanged, and the cycle would start again. Especially for American designs—the famous Madison Avenue "sack suit"—well, the name says it all. A suit was a sack a guy crawled into. Even at Barneys, where the merchandise was of a higher caliber, the sea of sleeves didn't encourage preciousness. Armani's suits, especially Armani's suits of the men's couture collection, the line that he designed himself out of Milan, were like something from another planet.

Armani had consulted on the buying at La Rinascente, where he had customers eager to spend and a hard time finding clothing special enough for them. "As a buyer, I found it difficult," he said later. "The clothing had very little detail and made all the men look the same. I wanted clothing that could bring out a man's personality."

It's amazing, in retrospect, to realize that Fred, an ocean away, was thinking the same thing. In 1975, Barneys ran a whole TV ad about precisely that. "Don't you have something with a little different look?"

a hopeful customer asks at some other men's store, where every suit looks exactly the same. "Sir, this *is* the look," a grim salesman replies. "At Barneys, we think you're big enough to dress yourself," a voiceover announces. The hopeful customer comes to Barneys instead, where he tries on jackets and suits of several different styles. "What do you think?" he asks his Barneys salesperson. "What do *you* think?" the salesperson replies. The answer, of course, is "Terrific." We won a Clio Award for that ad.

Giorgio had an eye for every tiny detail, one honed over ten years at Cerruti and Hitman. The fabrics were works of art unto themselves. Years in and around the lanificio had made him a connoisseur himself. The American man wore gray or navy. Giorgio loved his browns and greens, colors that could've been dull or swampy if not for the expert weaving that gave them depth and texture.

But his real innovation was in cut. He made the lapel notch wider. He moved the waist higher. He moved the button stance lower, which gave his jackets a louche drape. As time went on, Giorgio became famous for "unstuffing" the suit, taking out linings, making everything lighter and easier. His jackets swung; they hung like sweaters, rather than standing at attention like armor. Some people poked fun at this deboning. Even a few years later, wags were making jokes about cosmopolitan New Yorkers—the ones shopping for avocados at Balducci's and riding Japanese ten-speed bikes—in their Armani suits. A humor writer for *The New Yorker* had a whole bit about a date with a woman of the '70s: "She asked if it had been raining in my part of the city. I said no, the suit was supposed to look that way, it was an unbacked Giorgio Armani." But fashion types recognized a seismic shift, in construction but also in attitude. "A revolution had begun," *GQ* declared. Today, Armani still speaks of Fred's respect and profound understanding of his work, even from the earliest. "Fred appreciated the cut, tailoring, and craftsmanship of a suit, and that was what he loved in my clothes," he told me recently. "He knew my world inside out."

Depth and texture were not what the typical office drone was looking for in his nine-to-five uniform. And this is where Fred's genius met Giorgio's. Though he had the rare clarity to see in Armani a promising future for American menswear, Fred also had the sense to accurately size up American menswear's present. The customer wasn't ready—not on the scale he would need to be for Armani to be a major success.

Fred was able to translate Armani's vision into a Giorgio Armani for Barneys collection that bridged the gap. As he would do often in the course of his career, Fred shared his own industry contacts and favorite factories with brands that he loved and trusted, most especially his beloved Belvest in the Veneto, who made (and make) some of the best suit jackets in the world. Armani was one of the first we midwifed in this way, though Fred took care not to tell the manufacturers who they were working with. Kind as he was, he was still a competitive businessman. He just referred to it as his "young line"—though Armani's signature was soon so distinctive that they had to have figured it out pretty quickly. And Giorgio trusted Fred—"one of the great men of our métier," he called him years later, after Fred died.

Fred managed Armani's tailoring line, with Ed Glantz as his go-between when he couldn't get to Milan himself. Giorgio would put together sheets and boards with beautiful fabric swatches pinned to them, to give a sense of the feeling for the season, and Fred would assess it all and make quiet suggestions in his inimitable, soft-sell way. Michael and I were involved from the first, too, taking ownership of the sportswear. We were so young—in our midtwenties—but then, so was much of the company: Sergio was barely into his thirties, and Armani's sales director, Adriano, who used to translate for all of us, was about the same. We'd have lunch in the showroom, prepared by a chef they kept on call, then go through racks and racks. I remember Giorgio had just done a story for *L'Uomo Vogue* designing his interpretation of military uniforms, which were, of course, the most stylish

Barneys sent a team to Milan to film Armani on his home turf.
"Even though Barneys may not understand his Italian,"
the voiceover said, "they fully understand his fashion."

standard-issue rations a soldier could ever hope to get. When I admired one—shawl collared, khaki green, with a chocolate-brown leather closure—he smiled. "Ecco," he said, and handed it to me. "Take it." I wore that jacket to death, and I would still—if my wife hadn't appropriated it from my wardrobe a few years ago.

While it didn't happen overnight, as time went on, the real fashion-oriented customer got wise to Armani, and that it was only at Barneys. You started seeing a different class of customer coming to the store: People like the kids from *Saturday Night Live*, which debuted in 1975. Armani—and Armani for Barneys—helped bring American men and American menswear forward. Within a few years, Steven Spielberg and George Lucas were coming in to buy it by the armload. It had been the definition of a loss leader, and it soon became a leader. In 1978, we brought him to town for a co-ed fashion show—his first in America—under a circus big top in the Barneys parking lot. "It seemed that the whole world came to watch," the press said. And it was all ours. As an ad we ran in the late '70s put it, underneath a photo of two handsome suited guys and their gorgeous blond date fending off the attentions of camera-wielding paparazzi: "The Giorgio Armani Couture Collection. Unavailable to everyone but Barneys."

· · ·

It wasn't all work and no play. We stayed busy—me, Michael, Jeff, Nicky De Marco, and a few others, a roving pack who assembled around nine or ten in the evening and disbanded around four or five in the morning. Dinner at Un Deux Trois, a brasserie in Times Square, or Moon's, a townhouse joint in my neighborhood where the owner set up a barbecue in the backyard and grilled enormous steaks he called "carpetbagger's steak," butterflied and filled with clams. Then out. Yes, we had jobs, and we did them. Did them well, even. But there was too much to do, too many scenes to check out, too many girls to call. The groovy psychedelics of the 1960s were giving way to cocaine, super-charging the city like never before. Everyone associates coke with the Wall Street '80s, but by that time it was old hat and I'd given it up. In the '70s, we were on turbo.

It was 1975 when I met the woman who first pinned me down, at least for a while. Michael and I were out at a model party somewhere, one of my favorite kinds of parties. After a few years of glad-handing for Barneys up and down Seventh Avenue, and now in Europe, too, I knew most of the top agents, including Eileen and Jerry Ford, the respectable mom and pop of the industry, who had been running their agency since the 1940s. Eileen was a tough old broad, with a strict insistence on what she considered propriety; the girls used to call her "Madame." She'd scout out young models and then move them into her townhouse in the East Seventies, where she'd rule the roost like the house matron at a girl's dormitory. "Gene," she used to say to me with a hint of threat in her voice when I'd come pick up a girl for a date, "you know better." I did—but what fun was that?

The upstart on the scene was Johnny Casablancas, a handsome rogue and a bit of a sleaze, who founded Elite Models in Paris in 1972. The agency had been open for a year when he met a seventeen-year-old coat check girl in Sweden and gave her his usual line: "You know, you could be a model." She'd thought he was bullshitting—another pickup line, nothing unusual for a tall, gorgeous Swede with bright green eyes and a knockout figure—but when she convinced her father to let her give it a try and go to Paris, she got work immediately.

When I met her, she was a new arrival in New York, a little older (though not much) and a lot wiser, a seasoned cover girl. Even in a room full of models, Lena Kansbod was the most beautiful one. Lena had no makeup on, and an old men's bomber jacket; it was like she was hiding her beauty under a bushel, which only made her more beautiful. Michael tried first, going right up to her like the cocky big shot he thought he was, with one of the worst pickup lines in creation—his specialty.

She obviously thought so, too. She brushed him off like a fly—first ignoring him, then physically swatting him away. He slunk back over to me with his tail between his legs. That was all the encouragement I needed. I strolled over and turned on the Pressman charm. Our first date was at Maxwell's Plum, *the* singles bar of the '60s, then getting a little shopworn but still a scene, where the impression you could make walking past that long bar was way more important than the mediocre food. It was one of the first restaurants-as-showbiz—Warner LeRoy, its impresario, was a descendent of the actual Warner Brothers—and Lena was a star. Within about a month, she had moved into the East Sixty-First Street apartment with me and I was, officially at least, settled down.

If it didn't feel much like a traditional shack-up, that's partly because Lena was never there. She was working constantly. Fashion liked her—Scavullo shot her for the cover of *Cosmopolitan*—but so did red-meat-and-potatoes America: While we were together, she made the cover of *Playboy* and the cover of *Sports Illustrated*'s Swimsuit Issue in back-to-back months.

When we lived together, Dino De Laurentiis's son used to call the apartment all the time looking for her, begging her to be in their new film project. De Laurentiis was a major producer at that point. He'd worked with Fellini on some of his early films, like *La Strada,* and, despite some difficulties with his own studio in the '70s, still managed to produce some of the greats, from *Serpico* to *Barbarella*. Lena was interested, but I talked her out of it. Models in movies—it was a little tacky. Besides, she was in talks to get a major Revlon campaign. That was the better move, I told her, and she went on to be the face of its Natural Wonder line for years, shot by Arthur Elgort.

So Dino came up empty on that one. He made his picture anyway, a King Kong remake for Paramount. Truth be told, I might've been wrong in this case. Though it isn't much watched today, *King Kong*, starring Jeff Bridges, became the fourth-highest grossing movie of 1976, selling more tickets than *All the President's Men, Taxi Driver*, and *Carrie*. The Lena part went instead to another up-and-coming New York model in her first film role. Her name was Jessica Lange.

. . .

When Lena wasn't out of town working, we were out every night. Le Jardin, in the Diplomat Hotel. 12 West. The Meatpacking District, long before the condos and the high-end fashion stores took it over, when it was still blood and guts and mostly gay guys. And Infinity, the new club owned by Maurice Brahms, the disco kingpin, which opened to a two-thousand-strong crowd, on Bleecker and Broadway in November of that year.

SoHo and the area around it—where Infinity was—was still pretty desolate. The name, short for "South of Houston," had been coined about a decade before (London's Soho was far better known than New York's at that time) and even into the '70s, when its cast-iron buildings earned it landmark status, newspapers had to explain to their readers what and where it was. To everybody, that is, but artists, who knew very well: It was the only place left in town to get affordable studio space, and in 1971, the city rezoned about a thousand formerly industrial lofts in SoHo for residential use by artists. Hundreds of artists had been living illegally in those studio lofts by then anyway.

As we left Infinity one very early morning, the streets were deserted and creepy. All night, guys had been swarming around Lena like piranhas. I looked for a taxi in vain—cabdrivers were as nervous as anyone else about this part of town. Lena suddenly went white. "Let's go, let's go," she told me, urgently.

Out of a little two-seater convertible Mercedes parked a little way down the block came a screaming lunatic. I realized, with a start, that he was screaming at Lena, calling her every name in the book: "You bitch, you whore, you piece of shit." I wasn't about to let him talk to her that way, and shouted at him to get back in the car or else.

Out of nowhere, a cab appeared behind us and Lena, thinking quick, flagged it down, opened the door, shoved me in and jumped in behind me. The guy, she told me, had been one of several bothering her that night while I'd been getting us drinks. She told him flatly that she wasn't interested, but this guy wasn't prepared to take no for an answer and Lena, all hundred-and-change pounds of her, had pushed him to the floor. This guy had no shame and now apparently he was back for revenge. If that cab hadn't shown up right at that moment, who knows what would've happened. Coke cranked a lot of partygoers way up.

These were edgy years in the city, and dangerous ones. Going out, it felt like each street could be your last. Crime had been rising precipitously through the '60s, and continued into the '70s; in 1975, it hit a ten-year high. I had a friend who made folding metal security gates for stores, and business was booming. Police patrolled the subway cars with German shepherds, and even still, graffiti covered every inch of them. It was no secret to anyone that these weren't streets you wanted to hang out on after dark. If you saw the movie *The Warriors* a few years later, you get the picture. You could be mugged, jumped, or worse.

The ongoing financial crisis in the city had only exacerbated the situation. For much of the year, Mayor Beame had been trying and failing to stabilize the city's ledgers, but he proved unequal to the task. First too slowly, then too quickly, he laid off tens of thousands of city employees, the ones who made the streets safe, clean, and walkable—cops, firefighters, garbagemen. None of that helped crime, or the threat of it; before the layoffs, the police union printed up brochures reading "Welcome to Fear City" and handed them out at the airports, Port Authority bus terminal, and Grand Central.

The budget was a mess, and by the middle of 1975, the city's credit rating had been suspended, meaning it was no longer able to generate cash by selling bonds. New York City was careening toward bankruptcy, and just as bad, had become a laughingstock or a lost cause to the rest of the country. On TV, Johnny Carson—who had filmed his *Tonight Show* in Midtown before decamping to LA—made cracks about aliens touching down in Central Park and immediately getting mugged. In Washington, President Ford wasn't overly interested in cleaning up New York's mess. In October, the *Daily News* memorialized what seemed to be the national opinion with a huge headline splashed across its cover: FORD TO CITY: DROP DEAD. "Will Congress Save Us?" the cover of *New York* magazine wondered in November. "Don't Bet on It."

But as for me, I was young and energized, with money in my pocket and a Swedish model on my arm. What's more, bad times for budgeters were good times for Barneys. Even as we were steering the store to higher-end, European merchandise, we still did a huge trade in discount suits, and the time was right for bargains. The year before, we'd run an ad promising "a terrific solution for the shrinking dollar": wash-and-wear suits. High fashion they were not, but as the ad copy ran, "at these prices ($59 for the suits, $49 for the jackets), you can eat hot dogs for lunch. And dine on Beef Wellington for dinner."

# 8

# WINGING IT

## 1976

In the early '70s, we ran a holiday ad that made me crazy. "Once a year, Barneys becomes the world's largest women's store," it read. A large photo showed a half dozen chic women, in mega furs (one is even wearing a turban), shopping—for their husbands. "We make sure that a woman won't run out of ideas before she runs out of men on her list," it went on, teasing shirts "from Gant to Givenchy," "Dior bathrobes," and "exquisite silk crepe de chine ties by Piattelli." (The Piattelli tie pictured looked practically big enough to be a tablecloth.)

If not the largest, I thought Barneys could be the *best* women's store, and not once a year, either. I wanted the buzz that women could bring to a store, and it was no secret that the women's market was a huge one. In a way, it was the most logical avenue left to explore—we were already the biggest men's store anywhere, so the only place to grow was outward. Women's wear and men's tailoring are two very different businesses, but women's wear and men's sportswear is another story. The sportswear we'd been buying was seasonal, fashion-driven, and could be bought, edited, mixed, and matched in any number of different ways. Women's was just the same.

After we'd been buying men's sportswear for a little while, I decided to try women's wear, too. I went to see a friend of mine, Marion Greenberg, a nice Jewish girl from New York who turned out to have great instincts about fashion. (Later on, she was an early supporter and collaborator of Comme des Garçons and Jil Sander.) At the time, she was working at Henri Bendel, the only store uptown I thought had any taste at all. Bendel's was small enough to be discerning; it represented the best. Under the watchful eye of its president, Gerry Stutz—one of the few women to run a major store, as she had since the late '50s—Bendel's was where truly chic women shopped, walking up and down its ground-floor "Street of Shops," which Stutz had modeled on the retail thoroughfares of Paris and Milan.

Marion had been at Bendel's since the early '70s, buying for their "Fancy" department. (At the time, it was mostly evening wear, and the store was still enough of a socialite magnet that they closed down the floor for the summer, when their clientele went to their country and beach homes and the parties migrated there with them. Can you imagine?) I asked Marion how to get started in women's and, at no small risk to herself, she filled me in—though Barneys was a men's store, Stutz was incredibly competitive, and she would not have looked kindly on Marion sharing anything with me at all.

Twice a year, she told me, Paris gives a big ready-to-wear trade show in this huge fairground near the airport. They have a zillion designers there and you should go and look. I said, "Michael, you're coming with me," and off we went. Neither of us had any clue of what to do. We had no budget or what's known as an "open to buy"—what retailers call the plan they set out at the beginning of a season to make sure they've got the right amount of stuff. We figured we'd just go there and pick out a few things.

But "a few things" has never been my specialty. We combed the entire show, morning to night. We raced around, grabbing everything; after the second day of the show, half these companies would put up signs on their booths reading, "Sold Out." There wasn't a second to waste—we literally ran through the show and joked it would've been easier on roller skates. But we found so much great stuff. We scooped up women's collections from the same sportswear designers we had bought for men's: Christian Aujard, Daniel Hechter. We discovered new designers who are legendary today, like Issey Miyake. I bought more than I probably should have; I didn't want to leave anybody behind, like the Marines. If I found something I liked I had to buy it. Many of them had businesses already with department stores and were worried about selling to New York competitors. "Don't worry," I told them, "we're downtown." The ones who knew Barneys were excited that we were now in women's. I didn't tell them we weren't yet.

. . .

We had to start smart. We couldn't afford to be timid. If we were going to go into women's, we had big competition out there, in our customers' own neighborhoods uptown.

That competition broke down into two categories. One was the big stores, like Saks or Neiman's, as well as a number of big names of the midcentury who faded away: Lord & Taylor, Bonwit Teller, and B. Altman, the stores you'd see advertising several times a week in *The New York Times*. By the mid-1970s, most of them were stale and dusty, catering mainly to the middle of the road or the carriage trade. The exception was Bloomingdale's. Under Marvin Traub, Bloomingdale's in the '60s and '70s had reinvented itself as a hip destination, a kind of fabulous madhouse, overrun every weekend.

Bloomingdale's made a huge impression on me. Its big-store competitors had noticed, too. In the 1970s, Saks, Bonwit's, Bergdorf's, Lord & Taylor, and Macy's all undertook major renovations to modernize, in response to the elephant in the room. "No one wants to mention the competition, but Bloomingdale's is behind a lot of the change," an anonymous executive told the *Times*, which noted that, for stores, 1976 was "the Year of the Face-Lift." Nobody wanted to put their name to that admission, of course, except maybe Bonwit Teller's president, Kal Ruttenstein, who told the reporter that during Bonwit's construction, the combination of tighter quarters and construction noise gave it the exciting energy of "Bloomingdale's on a Saturday." You've gotta laugh. Would you be shocked to hear he later went to work for Bloomingdale's?

Barneys was a big store, for menswear, at least—in the men's world, we easily competed with Saks and the like. But for women's, there was no way we were going to start so big. And we didn't want to. Bloomingdale's was the exception in the '70s, as a sizable store that still seemed cool. The real energy, and the second source of our competition for women's, was coming from boutiques.

Small boutiques, which had been popping up for several years on Madison Avenue, the Upper East Side, and even the Upper West Side, could have a much more defined point of view than the big guys. They could be braver, more cutting edge. "By any definition, the boutique is the most important thing to hit retailing since discounting began 15 years ago," one newspaper wrote.

In the '60s, a new wave of boutiques became social hubs in New York. Charivari—a family affair like Barneys, owned by Selma Weiser and eventually her kids, Barbara and Jon—opened on the Upper West Side in 1967 with a go-go dancer gyrating in the window. We'd go on to compete with them for designers and exclusives as they got cooler in the '80s. At Serendipity, on Sixtieth Street, you could buy little jean skirts, T-shirts, *and* order a hot dog and a tall glass of "frozen hot chocolate." (That hot chocolate became famous—they still sell it by mail order all these years later.) Paraphernalia, on Sixty-Seventh and Madison, played rock 'n' roll—the Velvet Underground did a gig there—and employed a young designer named Betsey Johnson, who made flouncy sportswear girls loved. That store flamed out, but Betsey went on to cofound her own boutique, Betsey Bunky Nini on East Fifty-Third, which itself became a sensation. They had identified a real gap in the market. "Customers had just begun to do their own thing," she said, "and department stores didn't cater to it."

And customers *wanted* to do their own thing. At the very least, they didn't want to be dictated to by Seventh Avenue manufacturers or distant, old-guy designers. When the fashion industry tried to create a fad for midi skirts in the early '70s, women revolted. They created mock coalitions like POOFF (Preservation of Our Femininity and Finances) and declared "We're not going to let them pull the wool over our legs as well as our eyes." The gals of GAMS (Girls Against More Skirt) held demonstrations with signs reading "Legs! Legs! Legs!"

They didn't want what their mothers had worn; they wanted new stuff, like "hot pants"—a term *Women's Wear Daily* popularized in the early '70s for the shortest shorts imaginable, the kind designers like Betsey were making. "They seem right now," she told the paper. "They're a zillion times better looking than short skirts." Soon, hot-pant mania was sweeping the world. The revolutions of the late '60s—all the women who had burned their bras, inspired by the feminist Miss America protest in 1968, or chopped off their hair, wowed by Vidal Sassoon's famous pixie cut for Mia Farrow in *Rosemary's Baby*—had paved the way for these styles to go big in the '70s. The *Times* found a psychiatrist to opine that hot pants were "an expression of the female's new freedom, and they mean she's no longer willing to be submissive to convention. They also show that she is on a serious mission to relate to other people—especially men." The Italians worked themselves up into a lather when a pop group wore hot pants for an audience with the Pope.

What's more, the coolest boutiques were for men and women both. That's not to say there weren't some great small men's shops—like the classic-but-cool San Francisco on Lexington Avenue, still kinda seedy—but by the late '60s, the cutting edge was going co-ed. "It's called unisex . . . a way of life that's invaded fashion," *Women's Wear Daily* informed its readers in 1969, when you still had to explain this kind of stuff. The little downtown jean shops and army/navy surplus places were all unisex, or were treated as such, and the uptowners wanted in on the action, too. The Different Drummer, which opened on Lex in 1967, had men's and women's clothes, and men and women customers, and by 1969, *Vogue* was pushing it as "one of the best ways to give yourself a costume that's sassy snappy."

But the era's most defining, see-and-be-seen his-and-hers boutique had to be Fiorucci, which opened in 1976 on East Fifty-Ninth Street. Elio Fiorucci had opened his first jeans shop in his native Milan a few years earlier. But it was in New York that he became a global sensation. At Fiorucci, the salespeople were punks, or peacocks. (Joey Arias, a.k.a. Joey Fiorucci, went on to become a performance artist; David Bowie plucked him to sing backup on *Saturday Night Live*.) The music was blasting; the windows might be filled with, instead of mannequins, people dancing. "Once you get inside a Fiorucci store, you feel just wonderful," the writer Eve Babitz wrote in appreciation a few years later. "Two minutes after stepping into a Fiorucci, it dawned on me that Saks—with its atmosphere of leisured, muffled plush—was invented to make you feel old, or at least experienced. In Saks you're supposed to feel as if you've been around the block a couple of times and you know the good stuff from the bad, and of course you haven't got time for the bad. But in Fiorucci, oh, in Fiorucci you feel the world is your oyster. You're young again, and full of energy and life and that driving rock beat."

That was the energy I wanted for Barneys. Women already shopped there, remember, even before we officially had clothes for them—even *Life* magazine noticed that women were "invading stores like Barneys in New York in search of men's vests, neckties, Cardin pinstripes and low-priced three-piece suits." Why not bring them in properly? We might not ever be fully "unisex" but we could have the best of everything, the sparks that flew when you had men's and women's wear together. That was the energy the girls I dated wanted, and the type of place they wanted to shop—believe me, Lena and her friends were not going to Saks. And with a small section of women's in Barneys, we could have that boutique spirit—in the mega-sized men's store with its tens of thousands of suits. Thanks to sportswear, it was already beginning to happen in the men's department—at least on the third floor. "And all of a sudden on Saturday at three o'clock, the store was packed," Michael remembers. "Andy Warhol would come every Saturday with some of his friends, looking at the clothes and just hanging." But the real charge would come from getting women in, too. Barneys' men's store gave us the capital to go big, but women's wouldn't be about huge collections and something in every size and price point. It was all about a narrow focus, bringing in the absolute newest and best fashions in the world.

. . .

In the fall of 1976, we opened the first dedicated women's space at Barneys. "We've given women the floor—or at least part of one," we announced to the press. It was on the third floor—where the men's sportswear had been—near the refurbished cafe, which had been transformed from the roast-beef-slicing pub of yore to a place where you could get soups, salads, and Perrier for lunch, and boeuf bourguignon and a fifty-cent glass of wine for dinner. (Remember: We were open until 9:00 p.m.) There was open access between the America House and the International House on every floor: On three, the Women's Shop and international sportswear were to the north, the

International House side, while the New Yorker Room and the Special Sizes Shop, stalwarts of the original Barneys, were to the south, on the America House side.

When my first women's buy from Paris arrived in 1976, I realized something. Why hadn't I gone to Italy? How can you be in the women's business if you don't go to Italy? So, the next trip, we went to both France and Italy. And there, too, I found great things: Krizia, a label by the Italian designer Mariuccia Mandelli and her CEO husband, Aldo Pinto. (Bergdorf pressured Pinto to keep me from getting it, hot air that led nowhere.) We carried a line called Basile for men, so I went to see the company's other collections, like Callaghan, Complice, and Genny, which were being designed at that time by a young, then-unknown designer in his twenties named Gianni Versace.

Not everyone would sell to us. Missoni said no; they had big businesses with Bloomingdale's and Saks. Sonia Rykiel in Paris said no; she had Bendel's and Bloomingdale's, and didn't want to jeopardize that. But I had a feeling that there was something about me that she liked—when I went to her showroom, I kept catching her looking at me. Not directly, but I'd look up at the big mirror in the showroom and meet her eyes. She wasn't young—twenty years older than me, and pushing fifty—but she was an eternal coquette. She used to whisper my name when she said hello to me, pronouncing it with that jagged zee sound peculiar to the French—I was Zheen, like "zhuzh." That was better than what some of the other French fashion people were calling me. Over at Agnès B., a young Jean Touitou—he would go on to found the label A.P.C. years later—called me Press Man, because, he told me many years later, of how tightly my Levi's squeezed my balls.

We were winging it. I think that was part of our charm for the industry lifers we were meeting. The department store executives were like

Not averse to a little flirting if it helps close the deal.
Sonia Rykiel and moi, probably 1980s.

corporate drones. We were young, maybe a little bit wild. Michael and I first met a young English designer named Paul Smith—then still working for Browns, the best specialty store in London—when he showed up at our hotel room with a couple of shirts he was hoping to sell. "Sure, we'll take a look," I told him—but I was doing my push-up routine and didn't care to stop. Poor Paul looked ashen, but Michael just laughed. "Take out your shirts," he told Paul, "and stick 'em under his nose while he's up." So that's what Paul did, switching out each for the next in the split second before I went nose-first into them. But we bought those shirts, and eventually we did quite well with them—Paul was a Barneys man for a long, long time after that. He remembers having to show us his collection while dodging left hooks when I got into boxing years later.

When I developed a taste for something, I didn't want a little, I wanted a *lot*. I became this fashion addict. I had to have everything. As the orders began to come in, I quickly realized I bought too much. They were taking over the whole floor, and weren't likely to stop at just one. Women's might have started small. But it was never going to stay that way.

Nor was I living moderately after business hours. I was partying hard, and the line between the two wasn't always perfectly clear. Work hard and play hard is the old adage, until it all becomes a blur. I'd never have copped to a drug *problem*—I was having too much fun being young and stupid—but things weren't always so pretty. Go out three days in a row, barely sleeping, you can start to hallucinate. And in the late '70s, it wasn't all that unusual. Miss Terry would cover for me when I needed her to, and never asked too many questions about where I was or what I was doing, except one: "What do I tell your father?" she'd wail, ringing me at my apartment when I didn't show up. It didn't help matters much that Bob, who graduated from B.U. in 1976, joined Barneys' operations and finance department straight after and was playing bright eyed and bushy tailed to my bleary and bushed. "Tell him I'm not feeling well," I'd say, trying to throw a little charm on it through a crushing hangover. "Tell him I had a long night." I don't think anyone was buying it. And it would get worse before it got better.

# 9

# SEEDY AND LOVING IT

## 1977–1978

"Now is the summer of our discotheques," punned a night-life columnist in June 1977. That April, the most famous of them all, Studio 54 (just "Studio" to those who knew) opened, beginning what would be a short, never-to-be-replicated three-year run. I was there on opening night—and onward.

Studio came to define the disco era, as much as Donna Summer or disco balls ever would. Its set pieces have become the stuff of legend—the crescent moon descending from the ceiling with a coke-spoon beneath its nose, Bianca Jagger riding into her birthday party that May on a coke-white horse—and its regulars are enshrined forever in the party pantheon. Everyone and their mother has stories of going, or having been, or, for the most honest, trying to go. Many entered, few were chosen at the velvet rope sweepstakes at the door.

Studio was the brainchild of two of my old frat brothers, Steve Rubell and Ian Schrager, native Brooklynites who'd hung around post-graduation while I was still coasting through my degree. Rubell—Little Stevie, as he'd come to be known in the press, though never to me—was a sweet, odd guy who'd always stuck up for me when the Sammies at Syracuse were hazing me to hell. Small, with thinning hair and a goofy smile, he wasn't what you might expect of a major nightclub impresario. And until Studio, he really hadn't been. He'd picked up a few extra degrees at Syracuse after graduating and eventually found his way to making a little cash in the market trading penny stocks—though not so much that he didn't still need his parents' savings to back up his first business, a chain of restaurants called the Steak Loft in Connecticut and Long Island. The Steak Lofts gave him enough income to hire Schrager, who'd gotten a law degree, as his lawyer.

Like everyone else, Rubell came to the city to socialize, and he seemed to have spent the past few years surveying the landscape with a professional interest. At Le Jardin, he insinuated himself into the scene to such an extent that people assumed he worked there—he'd be at the door with the bouncer. The club made a real impression on him. Le Jardin's anything-goes mix—gay, straight, partiers, socialites—informed his clubs ever after. Housed in a former CBS television studio—hence the name—at the rhyming address of 254 West Fifty-Fourth Street, Studio was a sensation from the very beginning. It was soon both famous and infamous: Within a month, it had both hosted the Bianca bash and been briefly shut down by the state liquor authority.

In spite of troubles like that, or more likely because of them, Studio quickly became a magnet for the biggest stars in the world. Andy Warhol was a permanent fixture, his wig off-kilter, doing his whole gee-whiz thing. So was Halston, white as a ghost, with his earthier Venezuelan boyfriend, Victor Hugo, and all of their favorite models, dubbed the Halstonettes: Pat Cleveland, Beverly Johnson, Alva Chinn. Liz Taylor, Liza Minnelli, New York socialite types like Diane von Furstenberg and her German-prince husband, Egon. There were paparazzi, flashbulbs going off every second, but that was half the point. When celebrities really wanted to hide, they'd go down to the lower level, which functioned like a private club within a club, where they could do their drugs in relative peace. Steve was never far from that.

For the few years it was really going strong, Studio was *the* place. The legends are all true—whatever you think it was like, it was, only way worse. Paul Smith joked that while he did go to Studio, he avoided going with me, because he was married—and he's *still* married, he said, probably because of that decision. If you were in New York at the time, you had to be there, which is why I decided to take my parents one night. I danced with my mother, who loved it. My father was his usual quietly amused self. He wouldn't have dressed for the disco. I have no doubt he was wearing his standard-issue uniform, his black knit tie, carrying his old raincoat over his arm. Steve buzzed over to say hello to the two of them. He'd known my parents for years.

The key to Studio was the mix. More than the music, more than anything else, the mix was the whole point. Studio never segregated the celebrities from the rest—they sat on the couches that surrounded the dance floor, right up front. If Steve picked up the idea of mingling gay and straight crowds from Le Jardin, Studio managed to mix gay, straight, famous, anonymous, old, young—the sidewalk outside was always jammed with masses of people who had been refused at the door, but those few who did get in might be anyone from anywhere, as long as they looked good. There was a seventy-seven-year-old lady who came every night with her granddaughter, and Isaac Mizrahi used to come in from Brooklyn as a teenager, skipping curfew.

Fashion was a huge part of deciding who was worthy and who was not. Disco brought out the peacock in men—they were becoming as bad as women. The disco moment helped bring men into fashion—the designer look was as inextricably part of the scene as the zoot suit had been to the jitterbug era of the '30s and '40s. Think of the disco anthem "He's the Greatest Dancer," which came out near the end of Studio's reign: "He wears the finest clothes, the best designers, heaven knows / Ooh, from his head down to his toes / Halston, Gucci, Fiorucci. . . ." In his own book, Nile Rodgers, who wrote that song for Sister Sledge with his Chic bandmate Bernard Edwards, remembered that "only the hippest folks knew who those three fantastic names were and what it meant to use them as lyrics at that time." People would show up for Studio every night like it was Halloween, overdressed within an inch of their lives.

Studio's door was guarded by an unflappable kid named Marc Benecke. He was all of about nineteen years old, but he held the keys to the kingdom. "I wouldn't let my best friend in if he looked like an East Side singles guy," Marc used to say, and I saw it in action. "I don't like the way you're dressed," he told one kid. "I want you to go to Barneys and buy a nice outfit and come back tomorrow and I'll let you in."

Now, Barneys *was* a place where you could dress for going out. We started doing a brisk business catering to these guys. Michael could be found on the floor like a de facto disco stylist, steering them toward our new merchandise. A printed silk shirt, leather pants . . . we had *never* sold leather pants at Barneys before. Sure, you'd bake like a potato in them at Studio, but people didn't care. It was all about looking good. Guys would buy them even if it took a shoehorn to get them on. That wasn't my style. I wore whatever I usually did, my same old jeans and a white button-down or a tight T-shirt, showing up at Studio sometimes several nights a week.

It's tempting to revise history and call those nights work. There's no question that Studio seeped into our consciousness, and the styles we saw there informed the new things Michael and I were bringing into the store. You would definitely run into fashion people there (I even did an impromptu interview with a future Barneys hire there once). Fashion types were such a fixture of Studio that Halston gave the toast at its anniversary party, crowing on about how much it had done for New York, and Issey Miyake decorated the club for the event, staging a fashion show there for four thousand gathered guests. You'd regularly read the who's who of any given night at Studio in the next day's *Women's Wear Daily*, and all the European designers coming through New York stopped in. (It was the one thing nemeses Yves Saint Laurent and Karl Lagerfeld could agree on.) Fashion shows became a regular occurrence—the sportswear designer Bill Kaiserman of Raphael threw one even before the club opened—and some out-of-town fashion buyers joked they'd never even have seen the inside of Studio if not for a fashion show they were invited to there.

But, to be honest, I wasn't making deals at Studio, or courting designers. I was there to get laid.

. . .

I was single again. Lena and I had been drifting, and we officially split, with no hard feelings, in 1977. I was a man unleashed.

New York was in its red-light era. Others have written that the brief period right around 1977 was the golden age of consequence-free sex in the city: After the introduction of the Pill, and before the outbreak of AIDS, the kids of the postwar generation were out on their own, with a little money in their pockets and their parents' home in Harrison (or Levittown, or Great Neck, or wherever else). It was a wild time to be out and about in Manhattan. It was also, frankly, a little gross.

We were high on our own license. The drug of the moment was Quaaludes—disco biscuits—which had been circulating since the early

'70s. A prescription sedative with the added bonus of making you horny, ludes were everywhere—in part because they were *legal*. It took about two seconds to find a doctor to write you a scrip, and you could fill it at any pharmacy, either for the orange ones we called sopers or the white 714s. Not that anyone bothered with a prescription, really. Dealers were everywhere. Unlike other downers, Tuinal or Seconal, there was no hangover. Take half a pill and in twenty minutes you'd be buzzing and tingling. Twenty minutes more and you'd start to slur. But you never lost consciousness or lost control—you'd just kind of float. Ludes made sex incredible. It never occurred to me that people might sneak them to their dates, in part because I never had to. It wasn't hard to find a girl looking to split a lude with you. And if you did, everyone's intentions were crystal clear.

Sex, sex, sex. It was on the big screen for the first time, at grungy theaters in Times Square where guys would go in raincoats to jerk off—except now, joining them, were intellectuals and party people, thrilling to the badness of it all and wanting to see what all the fuss was about. *Deep Throat* had been a sensation a few years before, the rare porno movie that filled theaters with ordinary people, not only scattered single guys. Soon it was joined by intellectual equals like *The Devil in Miss Jones* and *Debbie Does Dallas*. Mainstream filmmakers expressed their appreciation, and even critics gave the thumbs up—Ebert gave *The Devil in Miss Jones* three stars! And the "serious" films that followed in the late '70s clearly took advantage of the new freedom to push the boundaries further in legitimate films than ever before. Bernardo Bertolucci was definitely taking notes for *Last Tango in Paris*. And don't forget Bob Guccione's *Caligula*, with Helen Mirren and Malcolm McDowell.

Sex was on TV, too. Public access cable was a cheap, available medium, and after dark, the limits on what you could show were a little more flexible. Wander into a dark alley at night and you might find "Ugly George," a saggy-assed schmuck barely wrapped in a shiny, one-piece Tarzan getup with a camera strapped to his back, whose whole act was pressing women to strip for his camera or, worse, come back with him to his apartment. This passed for quality content. Or Al Goldstein of *Screw* magazine—one of the most unattractive people who ever lived—who hosted *Midnight Blue*, with naked women, some professional and some amateur, and for the most part, as unattractive as he was. These were buttressed by ads for phone sex lines, and Goldstein's own enthusiastic review of Plato's Retreat, the uptown swingers club that opened in 1977 in the basement of the turn-of-the-century Ansonia Hotel on West Seventy-Third and Broadway.

In the spirit of the times, I went to Plato's once to see what it was all about, and contrary to what you might hear, it was *disgusting*. At the marquee, you were greeted by a character right out of *Superfly*, but not as cool. There were signs everywhere, house rules of the ridiculous. *No single men on the mat. Only women or couples.* Inside, down the stairs, you descended to a cavernous basement below, where a wet pile of human spaghetti was tangled on the filthy floor, doing god knows what to each other, with a buffet to one side serving what looked like week-old tuna salad left over from someone's wake. I brought a date and tried my hardest to get into the mood, in a small side room far away from the central mat—we were here, why not try it?—but after gallantly setting down my leather jacket so her knees wouldn't touch the floor, we still couldn't shake the images we'd seen and gave up after about five minutes. Plato himself would've run screaming in less.

Needless to say, sex was also happening at Studio—flagrantly, in whatever dark corner two (or more) willing participants could find. It was hard not to pity the poor bathroom attendants who had to stand and listen, and then pass around hand towels.

The balcony was even worse, a sea of asses pumping up and down. I tried it once, I confess. A few minutes in, I got the eerie feeling someone's watching and sure enough, some creep was lurking over my shoulder. "Can I help you, buddy?" I asked him. "Did you lose something?" He just grinned. Miss Jones or Dallas Debbie might've appreciated an audience, but I collected my date and went the hell home.

. . .

It wasn't only me who was driving in the fast lane. In the late '70s, drugs seemed to be everywhere, widely accessible and barely stigmatized. The basement of Studio was rife with them—often straight from Steve himself—and they weren't too hard to find anywhere else, either. Especially in fashion. The designers who crowded Studio, from Calvin to Halston, were forever buzzing. I used to run into Calvin in the club's bathroom, taking advantage of whatever opportunities were being offered, and we had lots of laughs. While writing this book, I asked him what he was doing in that bathroom—I mean, who remembers by now? "What do you *think* we were doing in the bathroom?" he asked with a chuckle.

That year, for Halloween, I rented JFK's yacht, the Honey Fitz, for a hundred-person bash. It was a seated dinner, although the usual dinner-party rules didn't apply—of one hundred people, I think seventy-five of them were models, and the other twenty-five were guys. My friend Joey Hunter, the head of Ford Models, brought what seemed like half his roster—including his girlfriend, Debbie Dickinson, Janice's (hotter) sister.

Debauchery didn't begin to cover it. I was young, single, and rich—I invited several girls I was seeing all at the same time and brought what must've been a gallon-sized bag of Quaaludes and an ounce of cocaine. Everyone was getting wasted—or at least the people that had managed to navigate through or around the West Village Halloween Parade to get to the dock in the first place.

Soon we were on the high seas—a hundred feet from the dock in the Hudson River—and all bets were off. Everyone was having a great time, wasted off their asses as we puttered around the tip of the island and back. It was a mix of the gorgeous and the riffraff; even the photos from that night aren't in focus. Friends like Johnny Calvani, Jack Nicholson's best friend, who used to joke to me he was the only person who volunteered for service during the Vietnam War rather than be drafted—because he'd heard the Vietnamese had the best weed. He brought along *his* friend Alan Finkelstein, who had a name like a synagogue cantor and a profession like a mafioso—he was arrested a few years later with pounds and pounds of drugs in one of the biggest busts of the decade. People were *flying*.

At one point, the boat's captain, a Gorton's fisherman type, came up to me, livid. "You have to tell everybody to stop doing drugs right now!" he yelled. "If not, I'm pulling this boat around and heading back to shore!" It sounded like something Fred would've yelled at me and Bob in the backseat during a family trip somewhere.

"No, you're fucking not," I told him, in my best asshole voice. "This is my boat, and we're partying."

That's what a hearty handful of coke will do to your personality, especially if you're a silver-spoon kid with wrong-side-of-the-tracks aspirations to whom life hasn't yet delivered its inevitable beat-down.

The party went on.

.  .  .

Meanwhile, I kept forging ahead in women's wear. After a season or two buying women's on our own, I realized that if we were to be contenders, I'd need to bring on someone with know-how. Michael and I had taste and balls, but that would only take us so far. We needed expertise and long experience, someone who knew the ins and outs of the showrooms and trade shows where business was still largely being done. Before long, I found her.

Louise Ohm was about as unlike me as a woman could possibly be. I was all of twenty-six or twenty-seven years old; she was closing in on sixty. I was a New Yorker born and bred; she came from Millbank, South Dakota, population 3,544. She was a department-store lifer, having started her career at Dayton's in Minneapolis—one of the finest stores of the time—and slowly moving her way east, to Halle Brothers in Cleveland and Garfinckel's in DC. By the time she got to my office, she'd been in the industry almost forty years.

She was an elegant lady. She favored tight pencil skirts—she had great legs and she knew it—and dressy blouses. I never once saw her in pants. She was always perfectly coiffed and immaculately made up, but beneath the makeup, she was a tough cookie—as you had to be in those days to make it as a female executive in a still-overwhelmingly male world. We had an interview in the winter of 1977. It was cold that year, and Louise walked in wearing a long mink coat. She reminded me of Bertha a little bit, and I offered to take her fur. "Don't bother," she goes, and tosses it right onto the floor like it was a $20 raincoat. I thought, *I love this chick.* She got the job then and there. (I later learned from another Garfinckel's alum that she was famous there too for dragging that mink behind her in the office like a high-end raccoon tail.)

Louise came on the next Europe trip and the doors kept opening. She had a great reputation, and a take-no-prisoners attitude, and having her on board signaled that Barneys meant business: we were now in women's for real. We may have looked a little like Harold and Maude, but Louise and I were great partners in crime. She liked my energy, and I liked her drive—we had a kind of mother/son thing going for the few years she was there. I had the sense I could learn something from her. And that's not a sense I got from too many people.

French fashion was hot. Rumors circulated that all wasn't well with Yves Saint Laurent—he'd gone druggy and reclusive by the late '70s—but then he'd pop back up with a collection the press couldn't get enough of, Grace Jones stomping down the runway as the opening look of a show that could last two and a half hours. (Today's runway shows generally clock in at around eight to ten minutes.)

Saint Laurent's key competitor was Karl Lagerfeld, a starchy Teuton now as famous in fashion as Santa Claus, a caricature of himself with his powdered ponytail and bitchy, German-accented pronouncements. Now he's more associated with Chanel, where he worked from 1983 until his death in 2019, but at the time, he was designing some of Paris' best ready-to-wear at Chloé. Fred loved Chloé—whenever business took him to Paris, he would shop for my mom there, at the boutique on rue de Gribeauval on the Left Bank—and when we started women's, his constant question to me was, "Did you get Chloé yet?"

And then there was Kenzo, who'd come to Paris from Tokyo in the '60s and by the mid-1970s was doing millions in business. He was an enigma: A sweet but superquiet guy whose big, bold, colorful designs were everything he personally wasn't. His show was the highlight of the Paris season, and his boutiques—first on rue Vivienne and then on Place des Victoires, the circular plaza near the stock market, with a big statue of Louis XIV smack in the center—were always packed. (He'd originally called his shop "Jungle Jap," but the early PC police weren't crazy about that.) For his show, he'd erect a giant circus tent over the whole Place, with Louis XIV right in the middle of it, and send the models marching out from the shop.

Like so much else that happened in my life, all this seemed to be falling into place at the perfect time. Women's fashion was at the dawn

With Barneys' first women's buyer, Louise Ohm, the Maude to my Harold.
We were crazy about each other (platonically).

of a major talent boom. The designers acknowledged as masters today were just starting out. There was new heat in America—these were the early days of Calvin Klein, Ralph Lauren, and Donna Karan, more on them in a minute—but that heat was matched by their counterparts in Paris, who were creeping out of manufacturer anonymity and setting up shop on their own.

Azzedine Alaïa was working away in his little apartment/atelier on the rue de Bellechasse; I'd come to know him soon enough. Thierry Mugler, his former employer, had started a few years before. Claude Montana, the king of leather, would soon be out on his own, but for the moment, he was still designing for the MacDouglas label—a leather house, run by a little Algerian Jewish guy called Poncho, who we knew well. How? My father and even my grandfather had been buying men's leathers and shearlings from him for years.

Paris was lit up with a new energy. The French are fundamentally conservative and slow to change—despite what people say, it's the Italians who like to move the needle. But Paris was shaking things up. There were few better symbols of it than the Centre Pompidou, the modern-art museum that opened in 1977. It was a museum inside out, its facade snaking with all the mechanicals usually concealed inside: brightly colored pipes and tubes supplying circulation, electricity, and plumbing to the building. The design had been chosen by a jury of some of the greatest architects on the planet, but that didn't mean it was an instant hit. It was as radical as anything the city had ever seen. Though it's now considered a modern classic, the French at first were aghast. "Paris has its own monster," wrote *Le Figaro*, one of its top newspapers. (In its defense, the French didn't like the Eiffel Tower at first, either.)

I loved it at once—which isn't to say I was spending much time there. From the moment I touched down in France, it was go, go, go: I'd drop off my bags at L'Hotel, our hotel by the École des Beaux-Arts—always room #26, on the top floor, whose terrace offered sweeping views of Paris—and then off I went. If it wasn't shows, it was appointments, if it wasn't appointments, it was showrooms, if it wasn't showrooms, it was coffee at Café de Flore or La Coupole, drinks and then dinner at L'Ami Louis in the 7th (there were two Louises, actually, the chef and the maitre d'). Or Caviar Kaspia on the Place de la Madeleine, for omelets heaped with caviar at the little restaurant upstairs or great heaping tubs of it to take away from the épicerie on the ground floor, with glass cases like a Jewish deli, but with beluga instead of Barney's favorite whitefish salad.

Then, the clubs. A few of the classics hung on: Régine's was still going, and Maxim's, the stuffy, velvet-swaddled supper club that had been a celebrity hotspot for decades, was still drawing crowds but going a bit threadbare if you looked hard enough. (Dark as it was in there, it wasn't easy to look.) Michael and I were regulars at the hotel club of the Élysées Matignon across from the Plaza Athénée, where all the Swedish girls modeling in Paris would go. But in the late '70s, Paris opened up its own answers to Studio. Le Palace opened in March 1978, a mega-club that quickly became a fashion favorite. On opening night, there was Grace Jones again, on hand to sing "La Vie en Rose" at 4:00 a.m. And at the end of the year, Les Bains Douches joined it. Les Bains Douches took its name, and much of its decor, from its former life as a nineteenth-century public bath—they even left the bath tile up on the walls. A young Philippe Starck did the design, including the checkerboard dance floor.

The whole fashion world converged there, from the designers with their entourages, to every model on earth—in those days, models starting out from all over Europe would go to Milan or Paris first to build up their portfolios with all the photographers who were based there. On any given night you'd see Saint Laurent and Karl (generally at opposite ends of the room), Kenzo, Loulou de la Falaise, Jerry Hall. At the door, a gorgeous young Algerian girl called Farida was the one you had to impress to make it inside—she was barely out of her teens but was the de facto decision maker of Paris. Before long, she'd become a major model and one of Azzedine's enduring muses.

# 10

# HELL ON WHEELS

## 1978-1979

I used to walk Fred through the deliveries as they arrived, trying to woo him with the merchandise—I knew the way to his heart. "Dad, look at this stuff," I would say, unpacking an international shipment of puff-sleeved Kenzo blouses. "They're going crazy for it." One day, over lunch at the Barneys cafe—tuna salad on lettuce leaves—I pleaded my case. We needed more space, I told him—which was true, at the rate we were buying. It had quickly become clear that the little area we'd carved out on the third floor wasn't going to cut it. Deliveries kept arriving and arriving and arriving, and our section was getting fuller and fuller. Women were starting to notice what we were doing. Ladies shopping with their husbands, and ladies shopping for their husbands, suddenly found themselves diverted to their own section.

Fred considered it, poker face intact. In most stores, the women's business dwarfs the men's, but at Barneys, with more than fifty years in menswear behind us, it was still a drop in the bucket: less than 1 percent of the overall sales. I think Fred was, at least at the beginning, a little intimidated by the women's market: the Bergdorfs and Bendels of the world had a huge head start, and women's fashion was (and is) light-years away from men's. Men shop for uniforms; women shop for art. It's like speaking two different languages.

In his Fred way, he thought it over in silence. There was a faraway look in his eyes. And then, with a nod, he gave his blessing. With that, no one could touch us. Not the numbers-watchers, not the buyers, nobody. The only question I remember him asking was about Chloé. It was back to the merchandise, back to the sales floor, as always. But then, Fred loved Chloé in those days.

I went to Gordon Chadwick, who had designed the ground floor of the International House, and with a million-dollar budget, began sketching out a plan for a larger women's space, two floors of it on six and seven, at the top of the store. The Penthouse was to be an aspirational space for aspirational merchandise. Did we know it would set the tone for the store for decades to come? We did not. We just had a hunch: If you build it, they will come.

By early 1978, the women's section was taking over three, filling up with Louise's and my collections, a mostly European mix of influential designers. Armani. Versace's Complice and Genny. The first collections by Gianfranco Ferré, the heavyset don of Milan. (He later took over Dior.) Here and there were a few lower-priced lines, like Kenzo and Agnès b. "We're running it like a special boutique," Fred told a reporter. "The Penthouse is a good business decision. We don't expect profit the first year. But we didn't go into the ladies' business just to have a beautiful room."

When the Penthouse opened in the summer of 1978, it was another one of those sea-change moments at Barneys. You could see it even in the attendees of the opening party. "On a hot Wednesday evening, invited guests were ushered past the shirt salesmen and cheap leather goods and delivered to the Penthouse in a private elevator," *Daily News Record*, the menswear industry's trade paper reported. "The minute the doors closed, disco music blared to the top . . . a mix of Fred's friends and Gene's freaks made the retail evening one of the best." Fred and Phyllis "managed the evening in their conservative style," the reporter added. "Gene, who gets around more than any other buyer on this circuit, was glowing from his recent Ibiza suntan and commenting on how much better and sicker this island is than the Pines."

. . .

Like all of Fred's nudges toward a more upscale store, the Penthouse was a calculated risk. "There are those who say the store cannot lose its 'downtown' image," newspapers sniffed, back when "downtown" was a synonym for "grubby." (Old Barneys ads used to run the tagline, "You go out of your way to get here. We've got to pay you back.") "Some contend that Barneys cannot effectively lure men and women who have been buying the same expensive clothes in uptown stores such as Bergdorf Goodman, Bloomingdale's and Saks Fifth Avenue and in Madison Avenue shops such as Paul Stuart." But Fred was uncowed. "No, we're not going to satisfy somebody who wants a $100 suit," he shrugged. The bar had been raised—at least a little. Barneys still had a wide variety of merchandise. You could get a $150 suit, Fred made sure to note.

For all the move toward the finer things, Barneys has never been solely about luxury. If there's one word I hate, it's that one: overused, abused, nearly meaningless at this point, applied to everything from beautifully made Hermès bags to single-ply toilet paper. Fashion has never been only about luxury. It takes no taste at all to spend a fortune and get good stuff; it takes real skill to find half-buried gems at the thrift shop and look like a million bucks for twenty. Long after we left Barneys, people complained that it was too expensive, too fancy, too much—most of whom had probably never been inside. There were plenty of expensive collections at Barneys. There were also plenty that weren't.

There had to be. When I used to sneak into Bloomingdale's in the early '70s and envy the mix and the energy inside, it wasn't only high fashion that was drawing the crowds and making the place such a scene. It was the cute girls flitting around the Young East Sider section. Young East Sider had been the old Juniors section, but had grown into the epicenter of the developing contemporary market, "contemporary" being fashionese for younger, more affordable, easier-to-wear clothes.

A generation before, "contemporary" had barely existed. Young women had to content themselves with "Juniors"—which catered to teenagers, mostly, high school girls up till college—and the dreaded "Missy" section, which sized down the dowdy clothes your mother (or, really, your grandmother) would wear. Something new was needed. Women were entering the workforce in greater numbers than ever before—a trend that would continue steadily through the nineties—and no one was offering them clothes they wanted to wear.

The Juniors market had been big in the '60s. The youthquake had created an appetite for the trendiest, most disposable clothes: fast fashion before fast fashion. It was filled with guys like Bernie Ozer, a squat schlub with a taste for loud hats and junk food, who made a killing scouring the streets for faddish items like pegged jeans and jelly sandals, which he famously spotted on the beaches of Dubrovnik. (His obituary, many years later, proudly called him the "World's Oldest Junior.") He and the other buyers would send their finds off to Hong Kong to be knocked off on the cheap, then set up huge showrooms where department stores would come buy them up: trend-spotting with zero sweat.

This kind of knockoff culture wasn't exclusive to guys like Bernie. Seventh Avenue manufacturers, homegrown "adaptation" artists, used to love shopping Barneys for ideas to bring back to their pattern-makers. One of our buyers told me about a Seventh Avenue guy who was particularly shameless, coming up to her on the floor and asking what her bestselling blouse was. At the time, it was a Kenzo top, big puff sleeves and bright colors, buttons all up the arm, and he happily snapped it up. When she saw him years later, he beelined right for her. "Thanks," he said, "that blouse put my kids through college."

But we wanted better stuff, better made, and some of the younger lines coming in from Europe filled the bill: Kenzo's bright, cheerful patterned blouses and dresses. The easy cotton separates from a French shop-turned-label called Dorothée Bis. Their corduroy jeans, knit minidresses, and hot pants were perfect, one fashion writer wrote, for "the young, swinging crowd who prefer to change their style every season, if not oftener."

It was all about the mix. The clothes weren't separated into individual designers, or categories like dresses versus coats versus whatever. It was all put together, "a more freewheeling concept" as one store buyer told *Women's Wear Daily* in the late '70s, one that would have been completely clear to any of its twenty-something customers from their own closets, if anyone had bothered to ask one.

I had a pretty big focus group of this kind of girl—all of the models I was dating my way through in the late '70s would've qualified. They didn't want to wear Armani Couture and Basile when they weren't on the job. They wanted to throw on jeans and little Agnès b. striped tops. We had to get this stuff, too. God love Louise, but I didn't think the matron of the Midwest, with her furs and her couture buys, was going to be the person to bring it in. So in 1979, I found someone who could: a young woman named Debbie Bernstein, who'd spent the better part of the decade making Young East Sider what it was. Not for the first time, and not for the last, Barneys lured an uptown girl downtown.

· · ·

It wasn't just women's. In the late '70s, the whole store was changing and expanding, growing, sometimes gracefully, sometimes with slight difficulty, into its modern form. In the post-Barney era, we were busily working to improve, update, refine. Barney's name would forever be on the door, and on his visits to New York, he'd walk the floors and introduce himself to the customers. When something really got under his collar, he'd grab whatever salesman happened to be nearest to him, croaking, "Look at this overcoat Gene brought in, it goes for 1,700 bucks. My first car wasn't 1,700 bucks!" One time, incensed by some minor fault, he fired a floor manager on the spot. The guy, duly chastened, went across the street to the office, where HR was set up, to say his goodbyes. But Barney was no longer in charge, and HR just laughed. "He does this every once in a while," they told him. "Go home, come back tomorrow."

For some time, the old and new Barneys would coexist. Boystown, the unofficial atelier for husky middle-schoolers since before I was a bar mitzvah boy, was still Boystown, butting up against what we called the Underground and soon, in an effort to simplify, would call simply N.Y.C. N.Y.C. was a young man's shop—in the store's ledgers, it was still called Students—which carried both less expensive and smaller clothes, suits all the way down to a 34 short. There was a tailored clothing room, a furnishings room, and a sportswear room, and, if you can believe it, a Western-clothing room, which we used to advertise as the "Chelsea Corral." Custom cowboy boots in wild colors, bolo ties, ten-gallon hats, the whole bit. Randy Jones, the cowboy from the Village People, was a frequent customer.

For many years, the Underground had been the place to find the coolest clothes at Barneys. It's where, for example, we first started carrying Paul Smith. It was where we started Willi Smith, the young Black designer whose unstructured, pop-colored jackets and track pants were a sensation before he died, too young, of AIDS. Calvin was down there, too, and his nylon bomber jackets—with fashion-y touches like extended shoulders and deep pleats down the back—flew out the door. A bargain at a hundred bucks.

But with the designer men's market exploding, the action began to move upstairs. In 1979, Fred hired Massimo and Lella Vignelli, the husband-and-wife design duo famous for redrawing New York's subway map, to redesign the International House, floor by floor—if women's was going to be getting a new look, Fred saw no reason why men's should lag behind. Lella led the charge. It took years, but the store quickly shook off much of the shopworn look it had acquired over decades. "What happened to the plain pipe racks?" a guy who had been a customer since the early days asked Barney. "I sold 'em to Syms," Barney cackled.

In their place, we now had spaces like the Grey Room, as Fred called it, the beautiful, gray-flannel-walled section on the second floor where Armani had pride of place, alongside other international lines like Versace, Ferré, and Basile. The suits were hung facing out and customers could now see the silhouette—not the typical row of sleeves. As she had with other retail projects, Lella hit on the idea to make the space modular; she once described it as following the "theory of the guy with a hot dog cart: if goods do not sell on one corner, he will try another one."

The Grey Room had sliding panels of walls and mirrors, which could change the layout of the room in an instant—and that was important, since nothing looks worse than empty racks. The genius of the design was that the sliding panels could cover empty sections in a flash, so when the Armani merchandise sold out nearly on arrival, customers never realized that anything was missing. Tom Kalenderian, who joined Fred's team in 1979, recalled having to replenish the ties in the dress furnishings corner on the main floor many times a day.

On the third floor, which in the old days had been defined (or defamed, depending on your point of view) by the cheapie New Yorker Room, the growing women's sportswear section was joined by an international sportswear section. Though the full designer and international collection shops were up on four and five—Fred finds like Zegna and Brioni—the newer brands Michael and I were ferreting out in Europe first joined the assortment on three, which quickly became the most avant-garde, new-Barneys area. If you wanted basics, there was plenty at Barneys to content you. But if you wanted bigger, brighter, darker, extreme skinny to extremely oversized, you went to three.

Three was where we began selling the Parisian maximalists, some of the greatest showmen fashion has ever known, the generation raised at Le Palace. They inaugurated a new look in fashion, both for men and for women, one that was hyper-structured and exaggerated the body. Claude Montana, with his linebacker-shouldered leather jackets. Thierry Mugler, who staged fashion shows like rock-concerts-cum-circuses. Jean Paul Gaultier, the so-called enfant terrible, the first of the first to put men in skirts. (We didn't buy the skirts.) Gaultier, in fact, had left school before graduation to work for Cardin on his American licensee collections—there's a good chance he'd been in Barneys long before we even knew it.

. . .

The store was changing because men were changing. If the '70s had taught us anything, it was that men, even salarymen, were open to looking more stylish—they just needed someone to show them the way. They'd traded their sack suits for form-fitting ones by Cardin and Saint Laurent. They'd made (thanks to Fred) Armani into a sensation, the suit as sexy, as something you might want to wear even if you didn't have a boss breathing down your neck saying you had to. "The Business Suit, like jeans and bedsheets, has succumbed to The Age of the Designer," the papers loved to announce. Stores like Barneys were an integral part of that education process. But we weren't the only part. Magazines were another part of the revolution, and none more than *GQ*.

Not too long before, a man with too much interest in fashion was greeted with suspicion: most people would assume he was gay. But while gay stigma would take much longer to dissipate, fashion stigma started to melt away. *GQ* treated men the way the women's magazines treated women: They made them, and let them be, unabashedly handsome. The message was clear: You didn't have to be gay to want to be well dressed and well groomed.

Especially after Condé Nast, which published women's magazines like *Vogue* and *Mademoiselle*, bought it in 1979, *GQ* committed to fashion like never before, far more than its closest competitor, *Esquire*. Issue after issue, there would be fifty or sixty pages of fashion. The other magazines might do eight or ten. But if it ran in the pages of *GQ*, it had to be available for readers to buy somewhere. And thanks to Bob Beauchamp, *GQ*'s fashion editor, that place more often than not was Barneys.

I'd met Beauchamp on the fashion circuit and we'd hit it off. So when he or his editors would photograph some piece of clothing that they loved, and discover after the fact that none of the stores actually planned to carry it, he'd call me. There might have been a reason we hadn't picked a piece—not everything the magazine shot was "Barneys"—but in the spirit of collaboration, we'd arrange to get in whatever they were going to feature, and backed into a de facto exclusive on exactly what they'd be touting as the most stylish of the season.

The rewards were obvious. The store was packed, day in and day out, minting cash. Celebrities flocked in—walk into the store, and you might stumble over Diane Keaton sitting on the floor by the door, waiting for Warren to finish up (it happened), or Rod Stewart in third-floor sportswear, or Mike Nichols, or Baryshnikov. So did CEOs, whose town cars idled outside. George Steinbrenner. Harry Helmsley. Even Trump. "When Donald is in a very good mood," Ivana Trump told a reporter, they head to Barneys, where he was in the habit of buying ten or fifteen suits at a time.

We opened at nine, and the lull before customers began arriving was typically brief. On Saturday mornings, Fred would arrive by ten, and demand to know if everyone had taken lunch already—if not, they were too late. There were only two reasons you got a Saturday off, and that was you were getting married or you were dead. On a Saturday, a good salesman might write $5,000 or $10,000 worth of business; we had salesmen from the industry who worked part time, two nights a week and Saturdays, and made more than they did at their full-time job.

It wasn't only the salespeople. Fred used to insist that buyers come in on Saturdays, too, at least twice a month, and sometimes more. That was part of the Barneys difference. At other stores, the buying office and the store might as well be in different states. At Barneys, they were one. Fred, a merchant in the most traditional sense, would have it no other way. "I learned so much from him," Paul Smith told me. "Lovely, old-school shopkeeping. Fred, you walk through the store with him, he'd know the name of the staff, he'd talk about how a certain brand was doing, how a certain shoe was doing. Amazing. Hardly anybody knows how to run a store anymore."

Because of that perma-presence on the floor, we got very good at understanding the customer, what he wanted, what he needed, what he didn't. As Tony Kairouz, our head tailor, once told a magazine, "When you have customers like George Steinbrenner, it's more important to understand psychology than to make small stitches." The golden rule: "Whatever the problems are, you must blame them on the garment, not on the customer."

. . .

While we were flying high, the disco scene was about to come crashing to the ground. Studio's rise had been so meteoric—in two years, it had become unquestionably *the* place—and its owners so addled in the glow of its success (and the nitro boost of an endless supply of cocaine), that it was inevitable the cops would start asking questions. In this case, they skipped the questions, and proceeded directly to the raids. In December of 1978, at two o'clock in the morning, agents from the DEA and the IRS raided the club, leaving with boxes and boxes of documents and a trove of cocaine and ludes. That didn't dim the lights, at least not immediately—Halston showed up the next night as a show of support and Bianca flew in from London to be seen there, too, to buck up her old friend Steve—but the following June, Little Stevie and Ian were indicted by the feds on charges of tax evasion, conspiracy, and obstruction of justice. The party that never ended, ended.

It was sad to see it all happen. I liked Steve, and had since our Syracuse days. But he had his demons. Though Ian would go around swearing he didn't know Steve was gay until shortly before his death from AIDS complications years later, I don't know how anyone would've missed it; and there was certainly no missing his prodigious appetite for drugs. It made him reckless, and Studio's spot on top of the world made him feel invincible. Steve and Ian became an object lesson in the old truism that loose lips sink ships. All the attention had gone to his head, and he bragged to *New York* magazine that Studio 54 was making more money than the Mafia. That's probably what sent the feds in. I had heard rumors of garbage bags of cash being carted around, but no one seemed to mind when their noses weren't getting rubbed in it. But Steve couldn't help himself. His lawyer, the notorious McCarthyite Roy Cohn—himself a Studio regular; you'd always see him on those hanger-on couches for celebrity entourages—probably didn't help matters much, either. I don't think he was any more beloved by the feds than Steve and Ian were.

Steve and Ian were both convicted and sentenced to three and a half years in prison. In 1980, they started their sentences and sold Studio from behind bars. The "new" Studio was never the same, and disco itself was starting to fade. On the rise was a related, but even stranger, trend: roller skating.

Roller rinks had begun bubbling up in the late '70s, generally to skepticism—skating felt at first like kid stuff. But by the beginning of 1980, when the city's largest rink, the Roxy, opened due west of Barneys in a former trucking warehouse at 515 West Eighteenth Street, the trend seemed to be all but confirmed. "People who said they'd never do it, they're doing it," one proprietor told *The New York Times* that year. The Roxy was popularly known as "the Studio 54 of skating," even if, as its owner told *Women's Wear Daily*, "disco is dead." We ended up throwing a big party for David Hockney there, "David's Evening on Wheels"—one he only showed up to well after midnight. We even put on a fashion show on skates, which was a riot—less the show itself, and more beforehand, when we auditioned models and had people rolling through the store. (Not all models can stay upright on skates, it turns out.) If it was happening in downtown New York, Barneys wanted a piece of it, and roller skating was.

Skating was camp. It was a goof. But it was also fun. I never took it seriously, the way the gay guys did—those guys were good skaters, though part of the appeal was the short shorts—I'd do a few loops around the rink then get bored and smoke a joint. But it was enough of a sign of the times that even before the Roxy officially opened, I rented it for my twenty-ninth birthday in November of 1979. In the photos I still have from that party, you can see me as I was then, on the precipice of thirty but not yet ready to grow up. I'd invited three or four dates to the bash, and someone had made a cake that was decorated with a spurting cock, a vagina, and a syringe, to make the sex, drugs, and rock 'n' roll of it all unmissable—although, to really drive the point home, when it came time to blow out the candles, I made a show of licking the cake instead. My mother is standing right next to me in that picture, looking pretty unbothered, all things considered.

Looking back now, it seems like one of the last stands of my misspent, well-spent youth. I was growing up, however slowly. Seven years into my tenure at Barneys, I was a long way from the warehouse where I'd started—and, more important, what I was doing was working. And I was starting to think—just a little, without even acknowledging it to myself—about settling down. The arrest of Steve and Ian was a cold shower, the brusque intrusion of reality: All parties end, and it's better to leave early than stay too long, when the cops break down the door. The year before, Bob had married Holly Pearl, an investment banker, in a lavish wedding at the Plaza; I'd been his best man. I wasn't eager to follow in his footsteps, until I met someone who struck me unquestionably as the marrying kind. Whether or not I realized it at that moment, two months before, I had.

# 11

# WORK IS PLAY,
# PLAY IS WORK

## 1979–1981

It was love at first fashion show.

Bonnie Lysohir was a button-nosed, all-American beauty, the kind of girl that teenagers pinned up in their bedrooms. Despite her corn-fed looks and blond bowl cut, Bonnie had grown up in Forest Hills, Queens, not the plains of Kansas. But regardless of where she came from, in the '70s she was a regular on the covers of *Seventeen* and *Mademoiselle*, young girls' magazines more interested in wholesomeness and fun than high fashion or international allure. She showed up on *Good Housekeeping* and in ads for CornSilk face powder. Photographers loved her. Arthur Elgort shot her often. She didn't look like anybody I'd spent the last few years dating. I'd worked my way through the *Sports Illustrated* girls of northern Europe, but I always knew somehow that those weren't for keeps.

We first met at the Barneys office in September of 1979. We were staging a big fashion show and benefit spotlighting

"The Best of Barneys," and Bonnie was going to be one of the show's models. That, in itself, was unusual—she was more of a print model than a runway girl. (She still moans about a disastrous show she did for Geoffrey Beene where she lost a shoe on the runway.) But Paul Cavaco and Kezia Keble, a young couple who were becoming known in New York as stylists, had booked her, and she had come to the office for her fitting.

Our first conversation was a disagreement. The night before, by total coincidence, we had both been at one of the No Nukes concerts at Madison Square Garden, organized by Jackson Browne, Bonnie Raitt, and Graham Nash. Over four nights of sold-out shows, many of the greats in rock played, all to advocate for disarmament: Bruce Springsteen and the E Street Band; Tom Petty; Crosby, Stills and Nash; James Taylor; Chaka Khan. I loved it, obviously. "Wasn't it great?" I asked her. "No," she said flatly. Bonnie always hated big crowds, big gatherings, and she didn't hesitate to tell me so. I thought, *Who is this chick?* I loved that she wasn't intimidated or shy. I later found out she barely knew who I was.

"The Best of Barneys" benefit was for The Actors Fund—and also, in a way, for the benefit of Barneys itself. Women's was so new to the store that plenty of people didn't know we even carried it. "I don't wear men's clothes!" Ethel Merman, a guest that evening, barked when a reporter asked her if she'd been to Barneys before. (She wasn't exactly my target customer.) So we had cocktails to start the evening in the Penthouse, to clue everybody in that Barneys was getting into the women's game. Then it was across the street to Barneys' parking lot, where we erected an enormous white tent, for dinner, dancing, and the fashion show.

It was a huge show. We created an X-shaped runway that the models would crisscross—dozens of them, men and women both. I pushed so many clothes on Kezia and Paul in my exuberance that they ended up having to divide into groupings by shoulder styles to keep it all straight.

This was the kind of event we'd soon be doing more of—this was not your grandfather's Barneys. This wasn't even *my* grandfather's Barneys. At the party were Gregory Peck, Glenn Close, and Angela Lansbury; Bill Blass and the designer Pauline Trigère; and a former New York City mayor, Robert Wagner. For entertainment, Barbara Cook, the Broadway star, sang; Gregory Hines danced. It all came off without a hitch, and afterward, I asked Paul to introduce me to the girl who'd hated the No Nukes show.

She gave me her number and agreed to have dinner. Her friends, I later found out, took a bet on whether I'd have my hair down or pulled back in a ponytail, whether I'd be wearing jeans or khakis. And? "You're everything they thought you wouldn't be," Bonnie said.

We didn't get serious right away. She was in the midst of a divorce from her first husband, and I didn't think I was quite ready to hang it all up yet. I was still young, still fun, reliably energized, both by youth and drugs, and taking on more ownership of the best store in the world. Add the fact that I could basically count on being the only straight guy in most of the rooms that I walked into, and it was a heady mix.

But there was something about Bonnie. For all her quiet sweetness, she had a touch of grit that I loved. She was unpretentious, a straight talker who took no shit. And she had great taste: She dressed simply but elegantly, never like a fashion victim.

We began seeing more of each other, arranging to meet where we could. Not long after we started dating, she was shooting in Senegal, I was in Florence for Pitti, and she found a way to fly to Italy to see me. She had seen the world of women's wear as a model, jetting around from Africa to Japan to everywhere in between, but this was her first experience of menswear: She toured the Pitti show, met the buyers, met Fred. And like Fred, she was seized, nearly instantly, by a profound appreciation for the clothes, the precise ways they were tailored, the beautiful fabrics from which they were made. "I just fell in love," Bonnie said. With me, but not only with me. Bonnie fell in love, as I had, with merchandise.

. . .

Once we got women's firmly established in the Penthouse, it continued to grow, and that growth required new blood. The timing, once again, was right. Louise Ohm retired in 1980. She had been a major force in getting Barneys' women's department off the ground, and I was grateful, but we had grown from a small corner to two floors, with plans for a full store—even if she'd stayed, we would've needed a bigger team. But by 1980, then in her sixties, Louise had had enough. She and her mink moved back to Minneapolis, where she lived out the rest of her life; she died in 2016, two years shy of her hundredth birthday.

The year Louise retired, I hired a brisk, chic woman named Barbara Warner to replace her. Barbara had strong, patrician features and short, curling blond hair. (*Vogue* called it a "non" haircut, perhaps not entirely flatteringly.) What's more, she had industry chops. She'd worked at Lord & Taylor and Bonwit Teller, building up an impressive designer sportswear business. Her style wasn't funky or esoteric, exactly—she loved classics—but long before it was common practice, she was mixing high and low, designer pieces with Hanes T-shirts and running sneakers. She called it "breaking" a look to throw a plain white tee on with a Versace suit or a Norma Kamali skirt. "I love expensive designer clothes," she once said, "but I don't let them wear me." She used to tootle to work in a white VW convertible.

The whole team could basically fit into that convertible. While the big guys uptown traveled with their armies, we were a handful—me, Barbara, and a few young ladies handling contemporary clothes or shoes. In the early '80s, Bergdorf's sent twenty-three people to the European shows. Barneys sent three. And we *still* managed to negotiate exclusives out from under their noses.

Fred was warming up to the idea of women's. He came by my office one day to have a chat. "Looks like we're starting to get serious about this," he said. The needle was starting to move: Women were coming in and clothes were flying out. That was enough to get Fred on board. "Listen," he said, "Should we really go into women's in a big way? Or . . ." You could see the gears turning behind his eyes. "Should we go and buy someone else who already is?"

"What do you have in mind?" I asked.

Fred had always had a real appreciation for Henri Bendel. It was a competitor, but it was also the best store of its kind, a historic merchant (it was originally founded in 1895) that had been brought up to date in the best way by Gerry Stutz, its president. She had come on board in 1957 and totally reversed its fortunes, taking a store that had been losing $1 million a year and ushering it into the black. She and her team had a great eye for designers—people like Sonia Rykiel, Jean Muir, and the up-and-coming American designer Stephen Burrows—but also a real understanding of how to merchandise and design a sales floor.

Bendel's was owned, though, by Genesco, a Nashville-based footwear and apparel manufacturer we knew from the men's shoe business. Genesco had owned a number of great stores and brands, like Bonwit Teller and the French footwear label Charles Jourdan, but was finding its diverse portfolio hard to manage, and in the late '70s, had been selling them off to focus on its core business. It sold Bonwit Teller in

1979 (including the Fifth Avenue building, land lease, fixtures, and air rights to Trump) and word was, it was open to a deal for Bendel's. Others had been kicking the tires—including, apparently, Fortnum & Mason, the classic English department store, which would have appealed to Fred—and I think it gave him the idea. Why not buy it?

I loved it. Bendel's was part of what got me into women's in the first place—remember, it was Marion Greenberg, Bendel's "Fancy" buyer, who gave me advice early on—and the store was a great complement to Barneys. Like Barneys, Bendel's wasn't a chain of department stores: It was one perfect store. Henri Bendel had been a Barney-ish figure in his own right, albeit a generation older: Like Barney, he was the son of Jewish immigrants, and he, too, had started downtown—his first shop was on Ninth Street. Joining the two companies would be like a marriage of two great families. "Barneys Bendel's," Fred mused. "It has a ring to it, doesn't it?"

In May 1980, we organized a bid. Eight million for the business, including an option to purchase its priceless real estate—Bendel had bought 10 and 12 West Fifty-Seventh Street fifty years earlier, in 1929. Owning Bendel's would have supercharged our women's business immediately *and* taken us right into the heart of our competitors' neighborhood, across the street and down the block from the big guns of women's. To our great joy, Genesco accepted our bid.

There was a catch; there's always a catch. Gerry Stutz had, in her contract, the right to match any offer on the store. She *was* the store: She had dragged it to success, despite all her doubters. (The "Street of Shops" took a few years to catch on, and the old-timers used to call it the "Street of Flops" or "Gerry's Folly.") I'm sure she wasn't relishing all of that getting turned over to some suit sellers from downtown. As the *Times* put it, "Henri Bendel is a reflection of her taste, her wants, her needs and even her dreams." So she pounded the pavement. Within thirty days, the timeline specified, she drummed up a matching offer.

With the help of a mysterious European investment banker living in New York—a woman so unusual the *Times* wrote a swashbuckling story about her brokering grain deals with Idi Amin and camouflaging herself as an Arab to sneak into and out of Beirut during the Lebanese civil war—she put together a consortium of overseas investors that would leave her in charge of the store, as well as part owner. In the press, Stutz called them a group of interested Swiss backers, though in reality, they were a hodgepodge of shell companies that stretched from Europe to Panama to the Dutch Antilles; even Stutz, it came out years later, didn't know them all. But it didn't matter. Genesco had no choice but to accept.

I had my heart set on this, and it was gone. But it just motivated me more. And not only me. The Bendel's bid got my father hooked on women's. Once he set his mind to something, there was no turning back. If we couldn't get Bendel's, we'd do it better as Barneys. The Gordon Chadwick-designed Penthouse was too small for our growing ambitions. I went on a rampage, going hard after the designers that Bendel's had and convincing them, one by one, to sell us, reasoning that we were downtown and obviously not competing with them. Chanel. Sonia Rykiel. Jean Muir. At long last, Chloé. Fred blessed the creation of a larger space at the top of the store, with grand, beautiful windows and skylights. And we found the perfect person to build it: a young architect named Peter Marino.

· · ·

Those who know Peter now know a palace architect in the uniform of a leather daddy. Peter has spent the last thirty years designing for the richest people and richest brands in the world: the Wertheimers of Chanel, half the brands of LVMH, the Agnellis, Valentino, Yves Saint Laurent. He dresses in black leather (lighter lambskin for the summer, heavier horsehide for winter), mostly of the sleeveless variety, and wears nothing but motorcycle boots, though in his case, the shoe fits, because he does ride motorcycles. He has a waiting list a mile long, and that's *if* you can afford him.

But Peter then was a different person, probably unrecognizable to anyone who air-kisses him today. The young Peter wore loden jackets, English shirts, and little spectacles; no animals died in the making of his wardrobe. He spoke with an accent that traveled the world—"My parents spent a lot of money so I wouldn't sound like I came from Queens," he once said—though it usually hovered somewhere around England. But he was always a chameleon. Andy Warhol, who gave him his first big break in the 1970s, remodeling Warhol's East Side townhouse, had already noticed as much before Peter turned thirty. "I told him how he owed his whole life and architecture career to us—how we gave him his first job—took him out of his business knickers and gave him his long pants," Warhol wrote in his diary in 1977. "And he said that well now he was in Armani suits and that we sure didn't put him in those."

If he was in Armani suits in 1977, they most likely came from Barneys. And if Warhol gave Marino his first big break, Barneys would be the one to give him his second. Phyllis had discovered Peter as a young associate, and had him design a candy counter for the store, where she sold Li-Lac chocolates. (Li-Lac, like Barneys, was a New York institution: They were founded the same year, 1923.) Phyllis never lost touch with Marino after that candy counter, and when we decided the women's Penthouse needed a more modern look, Marino got the job. He was newly out on his own—he'd founded his own practice in 1978—but Peter turned out to be a rare thing: an architect who was actually good at interiors. Most architects doing interiors skew cold and spare, but not him. On his way up, he'd worked for George Nelson and I. M. Pei.

Peter worked on redesigning the Penthouse into what we'd call the Duplex through the first two years of the '80s. When it opened in September of 1981, the Duplex laid the groundwork for a whole new feeling at Barneys. Literally, the light was let in. Marino opened up a skylight in the roof, and bragged to the *Times* that "The woman who shops here never has to walk more than 20 feet to see herself in natural light." Key designers each had their own individual boutiques, connected by cobblestone floors and park benches, like an outdoor galleria. The spaces reflected their residents: Armani got shoji screens in Japanese silk. Versace, leather and suede. Ralph Lauren, American oak. And so on. Marino always gave Fred credit for teaching him everything he knew about retail, and for many years, the affection between him and Barneys was mutual. We would be loyal to Marino long after: He was one of the key architects and designers of Barneys' women's store a few years later, and of Madison Avenue after that.

Because, of course, a women's store was already percolating in my head. Basically from the moment we opened the Duplex, I began fantasizing about it. But the grand, gorgeous one that we eventually built next to the men's, the one that would supersize Barneys' ambitions in women's wear, that would compete with the biggest stores in the world and—if I can say so—best them, was still several years off.

. . .

Once it got into my bloodstream, fashion was just another drug I couldn't get enough of. From Europe, we pushed farther into Japan, then beginning its rise in global fashion. On a tip from a designer friend of Schreier's, we flew there to check it out.

The only Japanese designers I knew (and that we carried) were Kenzo, who set up his studio in Paris, and Issey, who showed during the Paris collections. But going to Japan in the late '70s opened my eyes. The most fascinating designers were working away in little pin-neat studios in Tokyo, totally unknown in the United States. All the big stores, the ones with staffs ten times the size of ours, the ones with regional

At the Duplex, our dedicated women's area,
in front of the Chloé boutique, Fred's favorite (at last).

offices in Europe and Asia, the ones who were making their own private label there, had no idea. Japan was like nothing else I'd ever seen. On one of my early trips, I remember going to a park, where some kind of convention was going on—a gathering of Elvis impersonators, of all things. But it wasn't one Elvis impersonator, or a handful of Elvis impersonators. It was *hundreds* of Elvis impersonators, schmoozing and gyrating their hips and "Hey, baby"ing each other.

Straight off the plane, we headed for the clubs. If you want to get the feel of a city, you have to go where the people go, and the people we wanted were going to Roppongi, the ritzy nightlife district. Tokyo isn't a big city; what it lacks in acreage, it makes up for in height. People partied vertically, packing into nightclubs stacked in towers—you'd travel between them by elevator.

The people I saw there were some of the trendiest kids I'd ever seen in my life, totally different from anything in New York. For one thing, they all wore sneakers, which would be enough to get the door slammed in your face at Studio. And their clothes—they all wore black. "Basic black" would become the uniform of New York, but later; it would become associated with Barneys, too, but that would come later as well. Maybe it was the black shopping bag we introduced in the '80s that lingered in everyone's memories, but in the '70s and early '80s, Barneys was about color; black, at the time, was hard to sell. The Japanese loved it, and wore it monochromatically, black on black, and a rich variety *of* blacks. It wasn't only America that was slow to come around. When the new guard of Japanese fashion—Yohji Yamamoto, Rei Kawakubo of Comme des Garçons, and others—came to France to present their collections there, the French sniffed at the black-clad early adopters who swarmed their shows and called them "the crows."

The fit was totally different from European fashion. They didn't care about showing off the body, about following its natural lines. Saint Laurent was tapered, tailored. Armani, tailored. The Japanese thought about shape differently. Their clothes were boxy, freeform, almost cubist; they hung off their bodies. They were precious about perfection, but un-preciously so: They loved uneven hems, rips, and tears. I remember the first pair of distressed jeans I ever saw was in a shop in Tokyo. They were charging a fortune for these jeans and I looked down and saw they had holes in them. I freaked out—did this place have a moth problem, or what?—until I realized it was intentional. Then I was obsessed.

We gawked like tourists, then dove in to see what we could find. The discoveries were constant. Yohji Yamamoto was a thirty-seven-year-old hipster with long hair who played guitar. Perfect: I was a thirty-year-old rocker with long hair who played guitar. He didn't say much, but he said it in clothes. His women's collection—long, layered pieces, beautiful voluminous coats with big buttons—was exquisite, and we snapped it up basically on the spot. His menswear was less appealing at first. It was simple to a fault—it looked like Brooks Brothers at ten times the price, not what I came to Japan to see. So we passed on that, a decision I'd come to regret, and it was several years before he gave us another crack at it.

With his girlfriend at the time, Rei Kawakubo, the situation was reversed. Kawakubo, without formal fashion training, had been making her line Comme des Garçons ("Like the boys") for years. Rei made Yohji look chatty by comparison. She was a sphinx—"We do get a few smiles out of her once in a while," one of her assistants said around this time, "but she doesn't say anything unless absolute necessary"—and favored a blunt pageboy haircut from which she has never deviated. Her women's wear didn't do much for me at the time, too Rykiel-ish, with its little knit-tie blouses. In her case, we bought it anyway. But her men's was strange and wonderful, all black and blue, in simple, workmanlike shapes, uniforms for foot soldiers of the fashionable apocalypse. We became her first customer in New York.

There were many others. Kansai Yamamoto, more psychedelic than the rest of his cohort, whose huge-legged jumpsuits David Bowie wore in his Ziggy Stardust and Aladdin Sane phases, when he looked like a glamorous alien. Matsuda, a knitwear genius. We even went to see Miyake in Japan, and found he had lines that he didn't bother bringing to Paris, and pieces that the international market didn't get to see. We started buying the collection direct from Japan, and got colors no one in the rest of the world had, ones that were more muted, and more beautiful, than the ones at the Paris trade show.

I brought all this back and decided to make a statement. Japanese fashion was going to be a big part of the future, and I wanted to plant the flag at Barneys. We negotiated for exclusives and designed space for it: a corner of the men's sportswear section for guys, a cordoned-off section of the lower floor of the Duplex for women, under a neon sign that read Tokyo. No one had ever seen anything like this stuff before. It took off like wildfire. It didn't matter that the sizing was impossible—Americans being a lot bigger than the Japanese, we were buying every large and extra large we could get our hands on—and that half of it was one-size-fits-all anyhow. When we toured the showrooms, I used to get my kicks making Michael try everything on. It was hysterical to watch him wriggle around trying to get the pants buttoned and the shirts to close.

· · ·

The city was changing all around us. The '80s were underway. The disco scene had skidded to a halt, and in its place artier, more avant-garde clubs were bubbling up downtown, light-years away from Bloomingdale's Country. Downtown—way downtown, long taxi rides to nowhere, Tribeca before it was even widely known as Tribeca—was an industrial no-man's-land, colonized by artists and scuzzy types in old warehouse and factory buildings, on dark, still cobblestoned

With a very young Rei Kawakubo of Comme des Garçons. Rei was one
of the great designers we picked up first, and as her star rose through
the '80s, people would flock to Barneys to buy Comme des Garçons.

streets. Streetlights were sporadic. The glossy, ritzy Tribeca of today was unimaginable then. Down here, the hot club was the Mudd Club on White Street—the closest cultural landmark was the entrance to the Holland Tunnel a couple of blocks away—with its Weimar-decadent vibe and the buy-in of the neighborhood's artists, noise musicians, and fashion weirdos. The drug of choice wasn't coke, as it was uptown, but a new scourge that was quickly becoming adopted by the hipster set: heroin.

If the Mudd Club was the first place with a downtown sensibility—one that appealed to plenty of people uptown, too—that vibe was perfected by AREA, which would be opened in 1983 by four Mudd Club regulars, California transplants Eric and Christopher Goode (brothers), Darius Azari, and Shawn Hausman. AREA was part club, part art project: The foursome would decide on a theme, the more abstract the better, and construct the entire club, including natural-history-museum style dioramas, to reflect it. Some were clear enough (Suburbia, Disco, Carnival) and some were memorably abstract: Obelisk. Gnarly. Faith. (The guys invited Archbishop O'Connor to that one; his secretary sent back a gracious note of thanks but no thanks.)

The themes changed every six weeks, at which point the four guys, and whatever help they could enlist, had about seventy-two hours to demolish the previous theme and erect the new one. They turned a swimming pool into alphabet soup with noodles for the Food theme, and built a ranch house for Suburbia, plus man-sized boxes of Trix and Tide for the dance floor. Thousands of people would come to see each one. Plus, of course, the regulars: Steven Meisel and Teri Toye, Andy Warhol, Calvin Klein. Artists would regularly design for the dioramas, or perform in them: a young Robert Downey Jr. was paid minimum wage for his labors, and the club's semi-resident mascot was a performance artist called Joe Bernard, who, under the nom de drag Zette, would appear as various historical women, from Joan of Arc to Mary Richards from *The Mary Tyler Moore Show*.

Whether I realized it at the time or not, AREA's showmanship and performance-art dioramas helped me reimagine what Barneys' own windows could do. The appreciation went both ways. For the first party of every new theme, the four AREA founders would go out and buy an outfit for opening night. Their tradition, Shawn Hausman told me years later, was to head to Barneys for it. "That was our go-to place," he said.

# 12

# THE BASCO BOYS

## 1981–1982

In June of 1981, I was holding court at the Cutty Sark Men's Fashion Awards at the Playboy Country Club and Golf Resort in McAfee, New Jersey, rubbing elbows with the so-called power players of men's fashion. Established by the whiskey the year before, the Cutty Sark Award was a sterling-silver replica of the namesake clipper ship, but more important, it offered bragging rights, and the labels that had helped to make Barneys Barneys were competing for top honors. Giorgio Armani, Daniel Hechter, and Gianni Versace were all in the running for Outstanding International Designer—we sold all three. (Armani won.) Pierre Cardin was up for a Special Designer Award; we sold him, too. Calvin Klein was nominated for Outstanding US Designer. And for Most Promising US Designer, the ingenue prize, the Cutty Sark went to a duo: Lance Karesh, and a newbie designer named Gene Pressman, for their label Basco.

Lance was Schreier's Japan-obsessed designer friend. He was New York to the bone, a street-smart tough guy from

Brooklyn a few years my senior whose father had manufactured children's coats. He was bald and rangy, but he always had a hot chick; he had the kind of cocky confidence that belied his looks. He'd been a schoolteacher once upon a time (with his volcanic temper, that was pretty hard to imagine), and then had actually worked for a while as a sales guy in Barneys' Underground. He found his footing as a Seventh Avenue designer specializing in the Juniors market. His style was American classics with just the right little tweaks, but he had a relentless appetite for what was new and cool.

Basco—formerly Barneys All-American Sportswear Company—had been born a few years before, in 1978. It seemed like a no-duh proposition to me: Barneys had the world's best labels, so why shouldn't it have one of its own? As much as I loved the sophistication of Europe, the total dominance of European design over its American counterpart was irritating. If they could do it, why couldn't we?

It was probably a bit of brass-balled hubris to imagine that on top of everything else—men's sportswear, women's wear, international travel—I could toss off an entirely new label. But the spirit of Barneys in those days, and one of the keys to its success, was a willful disregard of anything that might stand in our way. Fred was methodical, logical, but I was 100 percent diesel fuel: all gas, no brakes. I spent all day in and out of designer showrooms and specialty stores, and I knew what it took. I could do it as well as they could. Couldn't I?

Not at first, no. The first year of Basco, while not an unmitigated disaster, was far from a success.

I worked on the first collections with a moonlighting designer named Howard Dickinson, an Englishman who lived in Paris and worked for Cerruti, where I must have found him. He was a charming guy, with art school instincts and European finesse.

The problem was that Howard's sensibility was a little too refined for what was meant to be American sportswear—All-American it wasn't. "It's not a look for everyone, but it's a look nonetheless," *Daily News Record* wrote. We bought the most beautiful Japanese fabrics, found factories in Allentown, Pennsylvania, to make the collections, but Howard's designs were Euro-chic: big, billowing trousers, shirts with asymmetrical plackets or shoelace neckties. The factories would go nuts—they couldn't make sense of any of it. And though buyers from all over the country came to check out the collection, and many bought it, wanting a little bit of Barneys magic, the store's own buyers whispered what the others wouldn't: *This will never sell.* Schreier, who bought it for Barneys—whether he wanted to or not—probably whispered it the loudest.

He was right. Drunk on fashion, I had tried—with Howard's help—to make fashion, but I started to realize I didn't actually like what I was making. It looked like David Bowie in his most weirdo days. That's not me. I was still showing up in Bass Weejuns. And Howard was just gigging with us, anyway—he'd come over once a month or so and work twelve-hour days, but he couldn't get away from Cerruti long enough to really manage things. It was time to try something else. We parted on good terms, and I set out to find someone new.

Lance fit the bill. He brought a more classic, American-guy vibe to Barneys All-American Sportswear, and finally it did look all-American. Great little ski sweaters from the '50s, cool shirts, leathers, outerwear. We shortened the name to Basco.

We were a good team. The press took to calling us "the Basco Boys": Lance knew how to design, and I knew how to merchandise. It didn't hurt that we always had a good time together. Lance didn't suffer fools or doubt. He had an attitude, and he was sure—even before he had any real right to be—that his way was the right way, and he didn't think much of many of his competitors (real or imagined). Ralph Lauren's name was abused often in the Basco offices. Tommy Hilfiger was a "no talent," as Lance used to bark. (Both of those guys built billion-dollar businesses, so he may have been a little hard on them, as it turned out.)

He may have been superior, but he wasn't a snob. He was genuinely excited to design uniforms for the New York City Parks Department, as we did in 1982. Lance dove into the ranks of the rangers to understand what they actually wanted and needed, coming up with flannel-lined jean jackets, chinos, tees, and nylon vests—things you could sell (and wear) today—all of them affordable on a municipal budget. "After all," he said, "you can make a beautiful uniform for the same amount of money as you can an ugly one."

Lance made two important changes to Basco. The first was that he made it truly American. Lance lived and breathed Americana—he used to say that if he could pick anyone to dress it would be Archie and Jughead. Later on, when we were doing fashion shows, he staged one at Howard Johnson's, treating editors and buyers to fried clams and ice cream. He wore vintage back when vintage was still called, derisively, "secondhand." (It only became "vintage" once the whole idea got chic.) He made it look funky, not preppy—Ralph Lauren, Perry Ellis, those guys were doing preppy. Lance was doing history, but in such a way that it didn't look dated or costume-y. He'd haunt thrift shops and flea markets, not only in New York, but also the puces in Paris and the shops of Harajuku in Japan. He wore what he'd rummage. He'd turn up anywhere laden from his explorations—I used to call him a bag lady, and I later learned from his wife, Barbro, that he had a whole garage full of his archived finds. His preferred colors were those that had lived hard lives and aged in attics and basements: dusty, beautiful greens, wines, and blues that had earned their exhaustion.

The other big change was price. Howard and I spared no expense, buying up the finest fabrics, making everything in the United States. Lance, who had experience manufacturing in Hong Kong because of his time in the Juniors' market, saw a better way. It hurt a little to take the production of an all-American sportswear collection out of America, but what Americans want even more than local craftsmanship is good prices. At the time, fashion manufacturing was nowhere near as prevalent in China and Hong Kong as it is today. But with Lance's know-how, and the help of a few on-the-ground agents—guys like Bobbie To, a flamboyant local celebrity (he kept a staff of pretty Chinese women he referred to as his "dragon ladies") who knew what seemed like everyone in the sweltering city—we found factories willing to accommodate us. For Lance, there was an additional advantage: Very few direct flights to Hong Kong. In those days, you would fly fourteen hours to Tokyo, then on from there to Hong Kong. And if he had to stay in Japan a few days to shop and party in his favorite city on earth, twist his arm, he'd do it. "They're so *funky*," he used to moon.

The response was immediate, even more when we added women's to the men's line. Stores began placing orders, then larger orders—even those who would've preferred to spurn anything having to do with the Pressmans or Barneys. One of the *Times'* fashion critics came to see it, and told his readers this was "exceptional stuff." We took the collection to Pitti in Florence—American stores bought it there, liking to feel like they were getting in on a European secret (direct from Seventeenth Street).

In 1980, we were doing $300,000 in sales a year. A few years after that, $20 million. We moved, first to a showroom on Seventeenth Street, then up to Forty-First Street, right off Bryant Park. We started doing shows, first little ones in the showroom, and then bigger and bigger. Despite his fiery temper, Lance could sweet-talk with the best of them, and had a nose for models. A young Andie MacDowell was one of our campaign girls, and walked in a Basco show. So did Christy Turlington. And so did Naomi Campbell. Even if, as Lance stage-whispered, "She can't fucking walk!" (That goes to show how early in her career she was. Needless to say, she learned and learned well.)

By the late '80s, Basco was sold at five hundred stores. And prouder still, Barneys was one of its smallest customers.

. . .

Basco came along at the right time. After years of European dominance, American design—formerly mostly restricted to Seventh Avenue knockoffs—was beginning to flourish in its own right. A new guard of proudly American designers were going back through their own history, playing on their own traditions, not as firmly in thrall to Saint Laurent as their predecessors.

The American era had been a long time dawning. Ralph Lauren had left the sales floor at Brooks Brothers in the late '60s, founding his namesake company (well, his *new* namesake—he was Ralph Lifshitz from the Bronx) in 1967. Calvin Klein started his coat line the next year, in 1968, the same year as Stephen Burrows, a recent FIT grad whose vibrant women's wear would become catnip to celebrities like the Supremes. Halston and Bill Blass—who dressed Studio dollies and Upper East Side matrons, respectively—in 1968 and 1970. When the famous Battle of Versailles, a runway show held for fundraising but really for bragging rights, was staged in 1973, pitting five French designers (Saint Laurent, Cardin, Emanuel Ungaro, Marc Bohan of Dior, and Hubert de Givenchy) against five American ones (Halston, Blass, Burrows, Oscar de la Renta, and Anne Klein), the shock heard 'round the world was that the Americans actually *won*.

Our own Rat Pack: Me with my partner in crime, Michael Schreier,
far right, and Michael's friend Lance Karesh, who would become
the designer of my collection, Basco. Far left is Murray Korn,
who owned the Philadelphia men's store Dimensions.

Fred's eye was more on Europe than America. Europe was his ideal and his dream; Fred respected the American manufacturers, like Oxxford and Hickey Freeman, but fell in love with European quality and design. And because Barneys didn't start experimenting with women's wear until the mid-1970s, many of the upstarts were finding their way to other stores, whose early patronage helped secure their futures. It was Mildred Custin of Bonwit Teller who took a chance on Calvin, when he wheeled in a rack of coats and dresses off the street himself, and was mistaken for the delivery boy. Gerry Stutz of Bendel's gambled on Burrows. Lauren was the one who got away—Bloomingdale's men's shop locked him down for an exclusive in 1969, one that took years to break. It was a particular point of pride for Fred when he finally did—and Ralph was a finicky pain in the ass ever after.

But by the late '70s, America was heating up, and Barneys was making up for lost time. My style is and has always been based on American pieces; one of the contradictions of my life has been that I may have fallen in love with Italian-made blazers, hole-ridden Japanese avant-garde sweaters, and everything and anything Azzedine turned out of his little atelier in the Marais, but I was also the staunch American classicist in blue jeans and penny loafers. There's no contradiction between Comme des Garçons and Brooks Brothers—and it's only the victims who insist on wearing 100 percent one or the other. If you have taste and an eye, you can have it all.

I did, and so did Barneys. By 1980, we were running major ads in magazines like *GQ*—then in the thick of its all-American era—proposing fall wardrobes for US guys inching into fashion. These spreads included pieces like Versace suede pants ("buttery," we called them) and Missoni sweaters. But it also included the staple pieces I'd been wearing my whole life.

Read those ads now, and the pieces we were promoting—things you'd never have found at the old, sea-of-suits Barneys—are things you could still sell today. Levi's 501s ("The button-fly, red-tab Levi's that started the whole thing"). Varsity jackets, in reprocessed wool with real leather sleeves ("the real thing"). Sperry Top-Siders, suede bucks, and Bass Weejuns.

The '80s seemed to promise rosier, prouder days ahead for America. If the '70s had been the decade that brought America out into the wider world, from the boom in jet travel to the morass of the Vietnam War, the 1980s brought an instinct to retrench, to celebrate Americanness. I'd spent so much of the previous decade scouring Europe for the kind of sophistication that barely seemed possible in the States, that I'd nearly missed the mood of the rest of the country.

Preppy—the look of classic Americana, taken well past its logical conclusion—was ascendant. The joke-but-not-a-joke *Official Preppy Handbook* was published in 1980 and quickly went on to top the bestseller list, selling more than a million copies. It was soon being considered for TV specials, films, even a Broadway musical. Everyone wanted a piece of preppy. The Lacoste polo—French provenance notwithstanding, it was now licensed for America by Izod, owned by the same all-American corporation that gave the world Wheaties and Cheerios—hit record sales in 1982. The preppy look connoted not just national pride, but money and power. It didn't escape notice that Ronald Reagan, who was elected president in 1980—a former Hollywood actor who looked like the movies' idea of a president—had a habit of selecting preppies to be the new face of American diplomacy. "What else will distinguish the new administrators?" the politics writers wondered. "There will be more members of country clubs and more lunch-time squash players. There'll be less denim, and more khaki, along with Lacoste shirts and tassel loafers. . . . the typical Reaganaut fits at least partly into the mold of a middle-aged 'preppy.'"

American designers were coming into their own. It wasn't just that they were talented—though they were. It was that, in a way that had hardly been seen before, they began proposing not only fashion, but a full American lifestyle. When Ralph launched Polo—his little pony-embroidered polo shirts fighting with their croc-stitched Lacoste competitors for dominance—he was crystallizing an American dream that went beyond any single item of clothing. It was the *idea* of a polo shirt or a cable-knit sweater, distilled in the golden ad campaigns he hired a former model-turned-photographer named Bruce Weber to shoot for him. When Perry Ellis staged his runway shows, the crowds went crazy for his genteel vision of an unruffled American aristocracy—and Perry was his own best model of that. It was like pandemonium. The Barneys buyers compared those shows to Kenzo's shows in Paris: people standing on top of the bleachers that pulled out from the walls of Ellis's showroom, screaming their heads off for the looks they liked. It looked so new, and so fresh, I remember them enthusing to me. And so *American*. There, right into the middle of the mix, went Basco.

Nor was this American spirit restricted to men's. We were buying up new women's designers, too, especially in the nascent contemporary market, of lower-priced, easy-to-wear sportswear. The lower-level of the Duplex featured younger-leaning lines like Betsey Johnson, formerly of Betsey Bunky Nini, a kook who would cartwheel down her runways. Or WilliWear by Willi Smith, a native New Yorker with an intuitive feel for what people wanted: unconstructed casual wear in bright colors. To complement it all, one of our young women's wear buyers went to the Army Surplus store and scooped up armfuls of old standard-issue military pants, and took them across the street from the store to the tailor shop, where she instructed the befuddled seamstress on duty to turn them into miniskirts. In Barneys' fifty-plus-year history, it seems safe to assume, no one had ever asked one of its tailors to do that.

. . .

By 1981, Bonnie and I had gotten pretty serious. If I had been dating around wildly through much of the '70s, unwilling to be pinned down, part of that was never meeting anyone who demanded much more of me. But Bonnie, despite her cutesy looks, could be tough. She had already extricated herself from one husband who wasn't doing it for her. We were on and off for a while, but before long, I knew I had to make a choice (and if I didn't, she told me). She let me know, in her quiet way, that she wasn't going to put up with screwing around. She was someone worth making a change for. Phyllis had never thought any woman was good enough for me, but when I introduced her to Bonnie for the first time, she liked her. Something clicked. Bonnie was the marrying kind.

So in October of 1982, a few weeks before my thirty-second birthday, Bonnie and I were married. We'd been together for close to three years. Bonnie was growing up, maybe faster than I was. She saw the writing on the wall, that modeling is a young girl's game. She'd decided to segue to acting, hoping to make it to the screen. Her best friend from her modeling days was a girl named Randi Oakes, who'd gone out west and ended up as a lady patrolman on *CHiPs*—one named Bonnie, incidentally—and the two of them had stayed close, running up long-distance phone bills in the days when there still *were* long-distance phone bills. I think Bonnie figured if Randi could do it, so could she, and she threw herself into acting classes with the kind of faux gurus who always seem to end up instructing pretty girls in acting without having much in the way of credits themselves.

She made a little headway, getting cast as the girlfriend in a few episodes of a long-forgotten sitcom that premiered that spring called *One of the Boys*, which had some heavyweight talent—Dana Carvey, Nathan Lane, a young Meg Ryan—all of whom did better later. In an odd twist of fate, the plot of *One of the Boys* was like a mirror image of my own earlier life: A grandfather moves in with his college-aged grandson. Switch the move-in direction, add some deli, and you've got me and Barney on Park Avenue.

But Bonnie's patience was waning, with the uphill climb of acting work (*One of the Boys* was not destined for great success, and only lasted a few months), and with me. I was in the throes of a wild, protracted youth. I still had some rough corners to sand down. Bob Beauchamp, who came to Japan with Michael and me, recalled us getting into a fight so physical, in the rain and the mud, that Michael ended up walking around for the rest of the day with my muddy footprint stamped on the front of his shirt. He just told everyone it was fashion. Traveling to Hong Kong for Basco around that time, I had gotten cold-cocked in first class by a Dutch psychopath who objected to my taking the "girlie" fashion magazines, an altercation that began with him slugging me and ended with Bonnie screaming and jumping on his goon hanger-on, six flight attendants restraining him, and a long, tedious afternoon in the Hong Kong police station once we landed. Best of all, when we finally got to the factory, I had an interview scheduled with the *South China Morning Post*, who couldn't resist mentioning my livid black eye.

As crazy as it seems now, in those days, it just felt like part of the whirlwind. (A few months later, paging through a magazine in the dentist's office, I came across an article about a Dutch fugitive wanted by Interpol who sounded suspiciously like my assailant.) Part of that rambunctiousness was amped up artificially, thanks to a fair amount of cocaine. Bonnie had let me know, in her subtle way, that it was time to put up or shut up. Being with her symbolized a new chapter of my life, and it felt good to be settling down.

The person who was most excited about the wedding wasn't me *or* Bonnie—it was Phyllis, who decided she would host it. It was practically more Phyllis's wedding than ours. She was rightly house proud; their home on Osborn Road had been built by Rosario Candela for his own family in the 1930s. The Italian American architect was better known for having designed many of New York City's most beautiful apartment buildings, including 740 Park, where Chryslers, Rockefellers, and Lauders lived.

The wedding would be a coming-out party for Mom's stock as much as for Phyllis herself. After a few years, she had grown bored of windows, and wanted to find something that would engage her more. Having kept a beautiful home, she realized that her natural entry point into this sea of suits was in what she started calling "gifts." There's no single good word for what Phyllis's bailiwick at Barneys grew to be. But what began as a few little knickknacks, antiques, and treasures she would pick up on vacations with Fred when they'd scour the flea markets, eventually grew to include antique silver, artisan ceramics, the most beautiful table linens, Murano glass, and estate jewelry. It was in Europe that she found and sourced things that many American customers had never seen, and, short of a plane ticket to Paris, wouldn't have had access to: Bonpoint, Diptyque, and D. Porthault.

In a few short years, her little gift counter had grown into "Chelsea Passage"—officially opened in 1980, it was so named because it was stuck in the passage between the adjacent America and International Houses—which she stocked with vintage china and ceramics, antique silver, vases, and decor, all the things you'd need for an elegant wedding. She selected the best of everything, had it sent to the house, and erected a huge tent in the backyard for cocktails and dancing. When Bob had gotten married four years before, he and Holly made it into *The New York Times* Weddings section, but for us, the stage was even bigger: Mom negotiated for full coverage of her table settings and decor in the *Times*' design magazine, on the WASP-y condition that they not use any of our names.

On the third of October—a Sunday night, 7:00 p.m.—guests began streaming into the house, a cast of thousands (or so it felt), most of whom I barely knew. It was allegedly friends and family, but that category included plenty of people I'd never met in my life, coming up to me with congratulations.

The Pressman boys were in their best black tie. Fred, Bob, and I, at least. Even Flippy, our schnauzer, got a bowtie. But not Barney. He wore a gray suit and a clubby striped tie; maybe Florida had permanently shut the door on formality for him. Bonnie, who had a refreshing apathy about tradition, had bought herself a vintage 1920s gown trimmed in antique lace, sleeveless, tea-length, without veil or gloves or any of the usual bridal accoutrements. She wore a simple strand of pearls and a sprig of baby's breath in her hair. She looked like the fresh-faced, sunny American girl she was, the one all the readers of *Mademoiselle* and *Seventeen* knew her as—and Arthur Elgort, her favorite photographer, who had put her on all those covers, was there to see her wed. His camera didn't leave his neck the entire night, not even when he did the twist with Bonnie on the dance floor.

A rabbi led us through our vows in the living room, standing before a trio of churchlike gothic windows in a thicket of potted firs. Bob was my best man, as I'd been his. Fred and Phyllis, Barney and his wife Isabel, Nancy and Liz and Bob's wife Holly watched from one side. Friends of my parents perched on the sofas, as if waiting for the cocktail party to start.

The night was a blur. Looking back at the pictures now, I see constant movement. I'm up there jamming with the band. I'm dancing with Bonnie. I'm dancing with Bob, as a joke, at least for the sake of a picture. I'm dancing with Mom, whose hair at fifty-three was starting to go gray but who has a huge smile on her face in her spaghetti-strapped, long-skirted black dress with its bands of sequined stripes. I don't know if I ever saw her happier. Maybe it was seeing her eldest married, or maybe it was the dance she'd never got to have at Euey's wedding. Or maybe it was just that, in deference to the occasion, I'd cut my hair.

My wedding to Bonnie at my parents' home in Harrison, 1982.
Me dancing with my mom, Bonnie, in her vintage wedding dress,
dancing with my dad. Phyllis was beaming ear-to-ear, relieved.

Me and Bob, left; me and Fred, a mutual appreciation society, right.

# 13

# CALLING ALL MEN

And now, for a commercial break.

Advertising is as critical a part of Barneys' success story as the clothes we stocked, the way we displayed them, or the people we hired. It's come up here and there throughout this history, but it's such a crucial part of the overall package that it deserves its own moment of reflection. So here we are.

From the very beginnings of Barneys—well before the advent of television, even before most newspapers were printed in color—advertising made the difference in Barneys' business. Its ads dominated the radio waves. To New Yorkers, Barneys had the name recognition of Santa Claus. Even well into the television age in the 1960s, Barneys remained one of the largest buyers of ad space in the New York radio market.

Barney himself saw the appeal of a strong message delivered and delivered and delivered. But he had help, too. One of the store's earliest ad wizards was a guy with the imposing-sounding name of Emil Mogul. Mogul had been a part-time sales guy at Barneys in the 1930s before going on to work at a succession of local ad agencies. At one of them, Mogul wrote and produced the famous "Calling all men" ad that helped make the store a household name in New York.

Barneys' first radio ads date back to 1933, when it sponsored a daily program of Irish music, and the "Calling all men" line to 1935. Not everyone was a fan. "'Irritate 'Em, Then Sell 'Em' Basis of Barneys Sales Gain," ran a headline in *The Billboard* in 1937. "Many of those familiar with the slogan, and the intonations used in its delivery, consider it to be a direct irritant," the report read, citing a few other brave companies who tried a similar strategy. (One Cleveland coal company assaulted listeners with sounds like heavy artillery, before announcing, "another ton of coal has just been delivered.") "Barneys," the paper concluded, "tops all in this field," which seems like a harsh verdict until the writer has to admit that Barneys had also doubled its business. So, "corn pays." Barney knew that already, and rewarded his irritator-in-chief. In January of 1940, Mogul announced the creation of his own firm, Emil Mogul Co., telephone ELdorado 5-1756, with Barneys as his marquee client.

Mogul quickly began ramping up the frequency. "Only a Hole in the Wall, but That Was Before Barneys Found That Radio Could Do a Job for It," blared *Broadcasting*, an industry broadsheet, in 1943. That's probably putting it a bit strongly, but the numbers make a strong case for the difference a catchy ad can make. "It would be hard to find a listener in the New York area unable to repeat the commercial in part, or word for word," the article read. "It is hammered out up to 70 times weekly on some stations." It ran for almost five hundred consecutive weeks, and helped goose Barneys' business to $1.5 million a year, equivalent to about $27.5 million today. Even the encroachment of war didn't slow Barney's gusto. "Threatened with curtailment of merchandise by current wartime restrictions on men's clothing, Barneys met the challenge by throwing the spotlight on its boy's department," the paper noted, with a new ad to match. The kid who played Robin on the radio serial *The Adventures of Superman* recorded a "Calling all boys" version to bring in the kiddie crowd.

For decades, radio listeners heard about the merits of Barneys—its location, its long hours, its free parking. Barney was fiercely loyal to the medium. In the mid-1960s, one New York station, WNEW, held a luncheon to present him with a gold record commemorating thirty consecutive years of advertising with them. Barneys' ads had only ever been paused for Christmas and days of mourning, when station policy dictated.

Though Fred smiled gamely through the photo op, his interests were elsewhere. It was time to move in a more modern direction. Radio spots and Barney's other preferred marketing tactics—like sending girls up and down Seventh Avenue wearing barrels advertising the store—were coming to seem like relics of a vaudevillian past. Fred wanted to put his own stamp on the message. The timing, once again, was right. In 1966, Mogul retired, and the company merged with an up-and-coming firm co-run by a young gun named Jack Byrne.

Byrne was looking to make a splash, and Fred was looking to tune up Barneys' image, in line with the fine European product he was beginning to import and the expanding store in which he was displaying it. Under Barney, the store's ads tended to emphasize breadth: There was no customer they couldn't fit (one print ad featured the Jolly Green Giant with the promise, "We can fit him, too") and they kept sixty thousand suits on site to offer him any kind he might ever want.

Barneys had dabbled in television already. In 1968, we won an award for an ad emphasizing Barneys' famous breadth—a sixty-second spot that made the point by showing a cleaning lady counting every suit in the store, losing her place around 59,999 and having to start over again. But in the 1970s, we took it to an entirely new level. The first Pressman/Byrne ad set the tone for the new Barneys. No longer merely a sea of sleeves, an emporium with something for absolutely everyone and two pairs of pants for every jacket, it was now a place of connoisseurship. "Select," the ad told men, "don't settle."

The famous 1970 "You'll All Need Clothes" ad came out of this partnership, one of its earliest and most durable successes. Everyone in advertising remembers it—a kid Barney on a Brooklyn stoop with young Bogey, Louis Armstrong, and Fiorello LaGuardia, spitballing about their destinies. Script duties were handled by Steve Gordon, a few years before he went to Hollywood and was nominated for an Oscar for writing *Arthur*.

Though it won a Clio, the ad industry's Oscar, and entered the TV hall of fame, it was a bigger headache on set. It took "Little Barney" fifty takes to nail his now-immortal line, "You'll all need clothes." All the other kids were egging him on, but he flubbed it over and over and over again. I asked Steve Horn, the director of the spot, if they ever thought of firing him. "When a kid looked like that?" Steve said. The child actor was a roly-poly Barney doppelgänger, who managed to look both ten and seventy-five years old at once. "There was no way you were gonna get another kid. I mean, the timing is perfect on the final take. And it's lasted fifty years."

Byrne was one in a long line of Barneys ad men. The '60s and '70s were the glory days of American advertising—the *Mad Men* era—and the guys who ran the boutique-sized agencies popping up were cocky, competitive, and cutthroat. (One young worker joked that at Ally & Gargano, Barneys' agency in the late '70s, receptionists would answer the phone, "Ally & Gargano, fuck you.") Fred had his pick of the best. The Barneys account was a major plum for ad guys, as well as a major undertaking.

An award-winning ad from the agency days: A Barneys
cleaning lady hand-counting all of Barneys' zillion suits.

"Little Barney" from the famous (and also award-winning)
"Men of Destiny" ad from 1970. Little Humphrey Bogart, Little Louis
Armstrong, Little Casey Stengel, and Little Fiorello LaGuardia had
dreams of the movies, the jazz club, the baseball field, and city hall,
but Little Barney knew his path, too: "You'll all need clothes."

It's hard to conceive now of the scale of Barneys' advertising operation. It was a multifront war. There were TV ads, complemented by weekly newspaper ads, full pages in *The New York Times*—which Fred had finally broken his way into, despite pushback from the paper and its bigger-ticket advertisers, the same ones that historically hated Barneys for discounting their labels in the Barney days. Then radio ads. Agencies burned out on the volume. And Fred kept a close eye on each and every ad. Still, the ad guys all fought for the privilege. They knew that when you worked on the Barneys account, awards would follow.

Straight through the '70s, Barneys was a mainstay of the Clios, winning in the retail category just about every year. It hardly mattered which agency it was. In the early '70s, with Scali, McCabe, Sloves. Then Ally & Gargano, the combustible partnership between Carl Ally and Amil Gargano, which brought a little more humor and cosmopolitanism to Barneys' message. One award-winning ad, "The Out of Towners"—another Steve Horn production—showed people from all over the world coming to Barneys and bringing their treasures home. "A rancher from Nevada brought back seven Lanvin suits," an announcer's voice intoned. "A Turkish pasha brought back two suits by Oxxford. A Japanese diplomat brought home English tweeds by Burberry. And for a basketball player from Bulgaria, it was one dozen Yves Saint Laurent shirts." Some of the ads weren't even about Barneys at all; we ran campaigns reminding people to vote, and spotlighting Fred's work with the Fresh Air Fund, the nonprofit that gave poor children from New York City a taste of country life. "Show a Cow a City Kid," one of my favorite taglines ran.

Around this time, I started getting more involved in the ad business. 1976 was also, you'll remember, the year Barneys introduced women's wear, and I got Fred to let me run point on a women's TV ad. Finally, my old Syracuse film education was coming in handy. Together with Ally & Gargano, I envisioned a mock-French art film—the best fashions were French, after all—and they trundled to Paris to shoot at the

Palais Royal. The location was French, the director was French (the great art photographer Sarah Moon), and wildest of all, this American commercial was in French, with subtitles. Two lovers have an intimate conversation on celluloid, worthy of Godard. "Juliette, où as-tu trouvé ta chemise?" asks the man. (Subtitle: Juliette, where'd you get your shirt?) "Bahr-neyz," Juliette replies. "Bahr-neyz? Où est-ce, cela?" Barneys? Where's that? But that question, of course, any New York viewer could answer already. Fin.

What became clear to me early on was that having the best stuff wasn't enough. A store might have the greatest buy of all time, the best selection of brands, but if no one goes to it, a lot of good that does. Advertising, and all the ways it's disseminated, is an essential component. For a lot of companies, the advertising reinforces the product, but in Barneys' case, it led the way, to introduce and educate the customer; the message was as important as the product itself. Even the name—in 1981 we changed that, subtly but decisively, by dropping the apostrophe. "Barney's," with its permanent aura of Barney Pressman, wasn't big enough for what we had in mind.

Barney was a legend, and there was no thought of cutting him out; we hadn't spent fifty years drilling his name into customers' heads for that. But Barney's-with-the-apostrophe felt like a local hangout, mom-and-pop, a Barney's Beanery type of place. That was too small for what we were dreaming of. Working with Ivan Chermayeff, the graphic designer who created indelible logos for Chase Bank, Mobil, and the purple torch of NYU, we rechristened ourselves Barneys New York, with a new logo to make our case. In elegant serif font, with "Barneys" exactly the same width as "New York" under it, it was regal, like a new cornerstone to build on. It looked beautiful on the new shopping bags we designed which were—dangerously—jet black. "Would men go for black?" Fred worried. In those days, men were wary of any shopping bag that looked too fashionable—which must account for the brown-paper Barneys bags Massimo and Lella Vignelli had designed for the store a few years earlier. But as talented as the Vignellis were (and good friends of Fred and Phyllis besides), their bags and tags just weren't stylish enough. The bags, like the ads, had to lead the way. These new ones did—before long, they became status symbols as much as any handbag, shoe, or suit carried inside them.

As I got involved in all these decisions, I realized I needed to get my own people in to help.

Marc Balet was the first. A trained architect—he'd won the Prix de Rome right out of the Rhode Island School of Design, and had a solo show at the Whitney before he was twenty-five—he washed up in New York after a few years bumming around Europe and had established himself as an art director, both at Warhol's *Interview* magazine, and freelance for clients like Armani and Saint Laurent. Marc seemed to have a charmed life—the first photographer he ever worked with was Helmut Newton. But he was good. I knew him slightly from out and about; as an art director, he used to book Lena, my old Swedish girlfriend, for jobs in the late '70s and early '80s. I met him again through Andy, who attended anything and everything. (In his published diaries, Andy recalls coming to the opening party for the Duplex. "It's nice up there," was his official review.)

*Interview* was a great gig—it opened doors for you everywhere—but Andy barely paid, so everyone who worked there had little hustles on the side. Marc was no exception. When I gave him a tryout to design print ads for Barneys, ones that were more fashionable and contemporary than the ones we'd been doing, he jumped at the chance. By that point, Ally & Gargano had given way to another agency, Epstein Raboy, but I made very clear to them that Balet was in charge. Albert Watson shot that first ad at an apartment overlooking Central Park West, with the society girl Linda Hutton as the model. The result was gorgeous. Balet got the job, and for the next few years, worked on the print ads. As was the Barneys way, we found people early and took chances on them before others would—the question was always "why not?" For one subsequent campaign, Marc booked a young photographer named Steven Meisel, who had a studio on Park Avenue South. Today, Meisel is probably the most important fashion photographer alive—he shot every single cover of Italian *Vogue* for almost thirty years—but at the time, he was so green that Marc had to rent him equipment to use.

My philosophy was, you pick the best people and then you let them do their thing. No micromanaging. I wanted to be kept in the loop, but I didn't breathe down anyone's neck. Especially in those early days, we operated like a pirate band. Money could be found when money was needed, but these weren't cast-of-thousands productions. For those early print ads, the ones that would run full-page in *The New York Times*, I gave Marc a long leash. He delivered. That early Meisel ad featured a young model who would become enduringly associated with Barneys: Linda Evangelista. We booked many models over the years, and a fair number of "real people," too (always and only if they were actual customers, though). But no one represented Barneys' combination of elegance and restraint, mystery and allure, eclecticism and ease, like Linda. Meisel shot her—the first of a million times he would—jumping rope, reading the paper, hollering through a megaphone. It had a kicky, tossed-off charm that suited the new vision of Barneys perfectly. And it did because it *was* tossed off. Balet was heading out of his apartment to the studio when he realized he had no idea what he was going to shoot. He grabbed whatever he saw around his place and threw it in a garbage bag to take with him. You can't fake ease.

When you find the best people, and let them follow their own lead, magic happens. The real job is finding them—the work takes care of itself. That was the case with a young art director I brought in named

Paula Greif. I'd known Paula since I was a kid; her family lived in Harrison. But she'd caught the New York City bug early (she once told me she painted her childhood bedroom silver, in imitation of Warhol's Factory) and dove into a bohemian life. After three different art schools, she finally graduated from the School of Visual Arts in the mid-1970s, then ran off to Milan to work for Franca Sozzani at *Lei* before Franca took over Italian *Vogue*. When she got back, she worked for *Mademoiselle* by day and haunted the Mudd Club by night (she was at its opening), living as a kind of high-end rock 'n' roll groupie. (Though her boyfriend at the time was Richard Prince, the artist.) She'd throw her artist friends bones when she could—*Mademoiselle* briefly hired Prince to select its cover images—and freelanced on the side, designing record covers. When I met her again, she had just directed her first video: the defiantly lo-fi music video for "How Soon Is Now?," a moody '80s anthem by the English band The Smiths.

Around 1984, 1985, Paula joined Barneys. It was still a pretty ragtag crew, though we'd poached Neil Kraft, who'd been our account guy at Epstein Raboy, to run a little advertising department. Paula's first big assignment was to do a TV commercial for the women's store, which at that point, was meant to be opening imminently. Like we did with the Ally & Gargano team a few years before, we sent her to Paris. The commercial she turned in was the opposite of anything polished, slick, try-hard—it was one only she could make. Like the Moon spot, it had the feel of an art-house movie, a pastiche of quick shots and cutaways of a young Paulina Porizkova, all of about twenty at the time, walking, working out, gliding down a staircase. Paula and her director of photography shot it on a fifty-dollar Super 8 camera found at Olden Camera in Manhattan, a little shop not too much younger than Barneys itself. Paula's friend and fellow Mudd Clubber Arto Lindsay wrote a jazzy score. It didn't shove anything down your throat. It was, as we would say now, a vibe—and ages before anyone thought to do ads that way. We were a long way from advertising by irritation, from earworms like "Calling all men." But we had a major impact all the same. Everyone talked about the Barneys ad, the new, cool, mysterious style of whatever was to come. And nobody talked more than other marketers. Nike later booked Paula and her team on the strength of that ad, and Coca-Cola tried, too. "They wanted a commercial that looked just like that," she told me. "But with a gulp shot."

# 14

# AZZIE

## 1982-1985

In the ranks of fashion designers, there is Azzedine Alaïa, and then there is everybody else. There are a million talents out there, but there was only one Azzedine; there are a million craftsmen, but he was one of the rare artists. Rib-height, curly-haired, forever dressed in his uniform of Chinese silk pajamas, Azzedine might not have been the likeliest candidate to be the brightest light of French fashion. He wasn't even French—he was North African, and the French were forever referring to him as "the little Tunisian."

But from the first time I met him, at his tiny apartment and studio on rue de Bellechasse in the 7th arrondissement, I had a feeling about him. That first meeting he didn't even have a proper collection; he worked as a private tailor for some of the richest women in Paris. (His antagonists sniped that he was knocking off Chanel couture at their request.) He had never had a fashion show, and he had no patience for buyers or most of the fashion press. He wouldn't even condescend to speak English—he claimed he couldn't—even as his international profile grew and grew. He didn't, to put it politely, give a fuck. Naturally, I loved him. And he loved me. As different as we were—tall and short, straight and gay, American and French-Tunisian, obnoxious and even more obnoxious—we were kindred spirits all the same. In the many years of our friendship that followed, he'd always ask me, with a totally straight face: "Did you bring it?" I'd say, bring what? He'd go, "My passport, my American passport. It should say 'Azzedine Pressman.'" And I'd always respond, I'm working on it.

I met Azzedine through Andrée Putman, an imposing interior designer with impeccable taste. By the time I met Andrée, she was already well known in Paris, both from her work and from the social pages of *Paris Vogue*. She designed a chateau in Brittany for Karl Lagerfeld, and showrooms for Yves Saint Laurent in Philadelphia and San Francisco. Not bad for a former magazine journalist in Paris with no background in design. But Andrée had something no training could offer: taste. She was a style elitist—she used to crack my mother up by stage-whispering "how vulgaire" when brought to the home of someone whose style she didn't appreciate—with sensitive antennae for beautiful pieces, and the drive to haunt the flea markets and antique shops to find them before anyone else knew to look. She was, by her own description, an "amateur archaeologist," and in 1978, had founded her own company, Ecart International, to re-edition pieces by early-twentieth-century greats like Eileen Gray and Robert Mallet-Stevens. Clients like Lagerfeld began to ask her to design rooms around her pieces and by the early '80s, she had become the most sought-after interiors guru in Paris.

The fashion community loved her. Nearly six feet tall, with a deep, gravelly voice and large features, she was more striking than beautiful—"A classic belle laide," *Vogue* called her, a little insultingly, "part Cubist Picasso, part Expressionist Grosz, and part Primitivist Modigliani"—but she had the kind of taste that passes for a moral authority. ("How vulgaire!") She wore Mugler's hourglass skirt-suits, and leather accessories by Alaïa. Taken with her look, I asked her to introduce me to whoever made these pieces, which is how, in 1979 or 1980, I found myself in his little studio. There was no ready-to-wear at that time, but Azzedine pulled open a drawer, and there inside was an elbow-length black leather glove studded all over with metal grommets. With those metal eyes, it seemed to reference the opera and S-M at once. I bought up every pair he had, and asked for more. In the years that followed, there would be a million fibs told about who discovered Azzedine and who carried his collection first. And the truth is: With those gloves, we had it first, and no amount of revisionist history is ever going to change that. It's one of the reasons why Azzedine stayed so loyal to us for so many years, even as he got into spats with, and walked away from, many of his other "champions."

In 1981, we began selling those long, black, grommeted gloves, the same season Bill Cunningham (later *The New York Times*' blue-jacketed street-style photographer) was writing in *Women's Wear Daily* about "an unknown designer who might well be responsible for re-establishing the authority of understated Paris elegance." By the next year, Azzedine was launching ready-to-wear, for the fall season of 1982. Barneys was there. We bought those first collections straight out of his apartment, with his dogs running around—total chaos.

Soon we had company in the Alaïa showroom. Bloomingdale's bought it. Bergdorf's, now under the sway of its hard-charging fashion director, Dawn Mello, bought it. Andrée even designed a store in Los Angeles for Azzedine, which opened in 1983. Alaïa was a sensation. He was ushering in a new era of body-conscious dressing, of sex appeal, of sophisticated, cosmopolitan, un-basic black. "Black was the non-color of the year," the *Times* announced at the end of 1982—so Fred didn't have to worry about our black shopping bags. Other designers had made skintight clothes, and fitted jackets and skirts, but none of them, the *Times* critic judged, "quite like Azzedine Alaïa, the Paris-based Tunisian who gave fashion a good kick in the bottom merely by dressing that bottom differently." It was like fashion, the *Times* put it, as surgery. His clothes made women unbelievably sexy—which made a lot of sense when you realized that he'd tailored costumes, in his early years, for the dancers of the Crazy Horse burlesque.

Azzedine worked like no one else in fashion. He touched everything that passed through his atelier, which he treated like a family home, with a small team he treated like a family. Every day, they would all sit down to lunch together, prepared by the atelier's chef: Azzedine and his partner, Christophe, the loyal handful of designers and assistants, even the cleaners. That chef was always in a bad mood, because Azzedine would forever be inviting people to come for lunch and forget to tell anyone about it. "We sit down and there is Tina Turner having lunch with les petits mains of the atelier," Farida, one of his muses, later remembered.

There were no working hours at chez Alaïa; he worked day and night. "Come to work at nine o'clock in the morning, at midnight, you're still there, and at four o'clock in the morning you're still there," Sophie Théallet, who worked for Azzedine when she was starting out in the late '80s and is now a wonderful designer in her own right, told me. Azzie expected everyone to follow his schedule, whatever that might mean, and everyone did; if he wanted to drape on his favorite model, Naomi Campbell (she called him "Papa" until the end of his days), in the middle of the night, then it would be "Naomi, wake up!" At night, Azzedine himself would cook for whoever was there, and everyone would stay to dinner; Sophie at the time was friends with all the young, party-hopping actresses in Paris, like Béatrice Dalle, and Azzie would insist that they come, too.

There wasn't much hierarchy at Alaïa's. Other designers might function like top-tier executives of their own studios, giving directions to young designers for them to execute, but not Alaïa. Someone like Jean Paul Gaultier, for whom Sophie had worked before (one of her coworkers there was a young Belgian designer, Martin Margiela, who'd soon go on to international fame), would give ideas and inspirations and his designers would develop them. At Alaïa, that would have been unthinkable. Touching a garment was a privilege only granted after years and years of watching the master work.

If that sounds slow, it was. Azzedine worked on his own schedule. The kind of tailoring he was doing was exact and precise, and he refused to cut any corners, even on the interior of a garment. "We could work on a jacket for two or three years," Sophie recalled. "Sometimes you'd go, 'Come on, Azzedine, you're crazy. Nobody's gonna see this!' And he'd say, 'No, no, no, this jacket is not ready. There is no way that I'm gonna sell it.'"

Over the years, this anal retentiveness ended up hurting him. It drove the stores crazy. Since you never knew when Azzedine would show his collections—he never cared to follow the dictates of the fashion calendar and show during the official Paris fashion weeks, or any other fashion weeks for that matter—buyers had to be ready at a moment's notice to be summoned to his studios, on the rue de Moussy, or later, rue de la Verrerie, for a presentation, even if that meant jumping on an international flight to do so. As a retailer, you never knew when the collection would actually be delivered, which can create a huge headache, and many stores stopped working with him.

But never Barneys. Alaïa became a mainstay of Barneys and a favorite of both customers and staff. It felt like half the buyers wore it— there were times when I considered telling them to knock it off and leave some of it for the clientele.

. . .

It was around this time I made a huge change in life. I had been a New Yorker since the early '70s, but the city wasn't conducive to good behavior. I knew too many people and had too much history there—friends, women, dealers.

You can have a flourishing career, or a flourishing drug problem, but very, very few people manage both. And as our ambition for Barneys grew, and we built it bigger than it had ever been built before, it became clear I was going to have to make my choice between the two. I worried I was approaching a point of no return. Newlywed though I was, I was still going pretty hard. My bingeing had gotten so crazy that I woke up half naked one morning in Central Park, with very little idea how I'd ended up there. I was marauding. Everybody was doing it . . . but I was doing it more. After my morning in Central Park, I decided it was time to move on.

I knew I needed to get out of town. We started to look around for a place. Fred and Phyllis had Harrison; Bob was living in Greenwich; and after a long search, Bonnie and I landed on Larchmont, buying a beautiful rolling property that allegedly used to be Bugsy Siegel's. It had all the trappings a silver-spoon kid turned lucky adult could want: a swimming pool, a wine cellar, an underground garage for the Porsche Targa I couldn't drive when my license was suspended for six months for screaming down I-95.

I was lucky in another way: I was able to pull myself back from the brink with my own two hands. I decided to stop and I stopped—I didn't become a teetotaler, I had too good a cellar of Bordeaux for that—but the drugs fell away. It was one more step toward growing up. Everyone around me was. Most of my friends were married, some with kids. Some had left the city. The city, for its part, continued to be a hotbed of drugs, money, and parties—the '81 recession in the rearview mirror, money was about to *really* start flowing, and with it, more debauchery than even Studio had been witness to—but it wasn't really my scene anymore. I was getting a little bored of it all. Boredom probably saved my life.

Nancy had taken my place as the party Pressman, Nancy who by the mid-1980s was haunting the Limelight, palling around with the Brat Pack. I didn't blame her—she was twenty and a chip off the old block, the block being me. When she first started going out in New York, she was known as Gene Pressman's little sister. But when she took me to the opening of the Palladium a few years later, it was she who parted the crowds and got us in. The door gal sized me up: "Are you Nancy Pressman's brother?" I was amused—and proud.

The Palladium would become the big club of the 1980s, what Studio had been to the '70s. The two clubs had something in common: their owners, Steve and Ian. My old friends had been released early from prison in 1981 after their sentences were reduced in exchange for cooperating with the feds. Determined to return to the prominence they'd achieved with Studio, they got to work. They began planning the renovation and rebranding of a decrepit old hotel on an unappealing part of Madison Avenue, a no-man's-land in the East Thirties, and Ian rang me up one day to ask if I could recommend someone to design it. "Sure," I said without hesitation, "Andrée Putman."

Andrée had worked her magic, and the hotel opened as Morgans in 1984. Straight after that came the Palladium the following year, which reimagined the old Academy of Music movie theater on Fourteenth Street. Steve and Ian knew a thing or two about updating vintage spaces—Studio, remember, had been a TV studio—and this time they had an extra advantage, in the Japanese architect Arata Isozaki. Isozaki would go on to be recognized as one of the great architects of the twentieth century—in 2019, he won the Pritzker Prize—but it feels like a sign of the times that his first completed American project would be the interiors of a nightclub. Serious architecture critics descended from their perches to review it, incredulously.

It was *the* place, and so when *the* designer was looking for a show space, it made perfect sense to pair the two. Dawn Mello had continued courting Azzie through the '80s, and in 1985, she announced that Bergdorf's was throwing him an enormous fashion show. Keep in mind, Azzedine hated fashion shows, and had publicly vowed he would never do one. But this was an offer too good to refuse. It would be held at the Palladium, for an audience of more than a thousand, and the press reported that there had been more than ten thousand ticket requests. He was the designer of the decade, it was the club of the moment, designed in part by his consigliere, Andrée. . . . It was going to be an event. It was hard not to feel competitive, and I did. My ass was chapped beyond belief.

But Bergdorf's wasn't up to the challenge of dealing with an artist like Azzedine. This is a man who, when Barneys later did a series of windows dedicated to him, featuring adoring quotes solicited from celebrities all over, asked us why the Queen Mother hadn't bothered to sing his praises. He could throw a hissy fit with the best of them, and kept up feuds no one else would ever have dared, like his years-long spat with Anna Wintour, ensuring that his designs were effectively banished from the pages of American *Vogue*. And right in time for his big show, he got into a pissing contest with Mello, another woman no one in fashion would dare cross. But he didn't give a shit. Why should he?

He and Mello quickly came to blows over the cost of the production, which, probably just to piss them off, he insisted had to be huge: a set by Jean-Paul Goude, who had helped make Grace Jones a star, a commissioned soundtrack and more than an hour of looks reflecting the full breadth of his house's three-year history. Mello balked, and Bergdorf backed out. It was "a difference in philosophy regarding the scope of the presentation," she told the *Times*. Azzedine was more blunt when *The Washington Post*'s Nina Hyde asked why. "Bergdorf's should have spent less money on sending me flowers and be more willing to pay for the show," he said. He'd rather do it his way, on his own dime, than compromise.

The best of the best: Me with Azzedine Alaïa (Pressman),
my brother from another mother. What a find!

In the end, he didn't have to. The show, that early September of 1985, went on as planned, to a packed house of black-clad guests (as the invitation stipulated), everyone from Simon Le Bon to Joan Rivers to Francesco Scavullo, and most of the good designers in New York—Giorgio di Sant'Angelo, Koos van den Akker, Willi Smith, a young Marc Jacobs. Alaïa split the cost with Steve and Ian, and Barneys stepped in, like real friends do, to provide support dressing all the models. Azzedine, to the end of his life—he died in 2020—never forgot that. He'd fall in and out with other retailers (it took a while for Bergdorf's to win him back after that, with good reason), but never with us. How could he? He was Azzedine Pressman.

# 15

# YUPPIE CITY

## 1985–1986

The Palladium was just one more symbol of a new era in New York, one borne on a raft of new wealth and new interest in the trappings of it: design, art, fashion, excess. The markets were booming. Stocks were up, and corporate raiders were the new antiheroes. The leveraged buyout was invented; so was the junk bond. A new downtown art scene, centered in SoHo, was flush with interest and cash. We were entering the era memorialized in Oliver Stone's *Wall Street*, with Gordon Gekko and his decade-defining catchphrase: "Greed is good." Cash was readily available and it felt like the bubble would never burst. It was no accident that this was a time of major expansion for Barneys, for which we'd buy up the neighboring buildings on Seventh Avenue for an ambitious enlargement and the creation, for the first time, of a stand-alone women's store.

I had been dreaming about a separate women's store almost from the moment the Penthouse opened. With the Duplex as a proof of concept, we began working in earnest. Women wanted their own store, and I loved the idea of having my own playground. Fred was more cautious. He supported me, as always, but privately, he was much less sure—something I learned only when the store was about to open and he told a reporter that when I'd come to him to say let's open a women's store, he told me, "That's a great idea," and then said to himself, "That's not a great idea and I hope he forgets it."

Not likely. We'd conquered men's, that much was clear. The men's store was bringing in millions of dollars a year, and expanding its fashion offering seemingly by the day; some time in the late '70s, we made it into the Guinness Book of World Records for the largest privately owned menswear store in the world, something I only know because some high schooler ran up to my sister Nancy in the halls to show her. Now I wanted to make that kind of impact in women's.

The time, once again, was right. The hippies of the '70s may not have cared for clothes besides their bell-bottoms, but the '80s Man and '80s Woman were fashion obsessed. Clothes were a key part of the urban equation, the requisite uniform for a rising new guard: the Armani-suited boardroom guys, the Comme des Garçons–wearing artists. If the '70s had the hippies, the '80s had a whole new demographic: the yuppies.

The term—an acronym for Young Urban Professionals—was first coined in 1980, as a joke, almost a slur. But it quickly became omnipresent. In 1984, *Newsweek* declared it the Year of the Yuppie. The shoe fit. The Young Urban Professionals filling up cities were coming into their own—they even had their own presidential candidate, Gary Hart, an ambitious young senator who hoped to be the first yuppie in the White House. The yuppies had discretionary income and expensive taste, and were looking for somewhere to flex both.

After some hiccups in the early '80s, the economy was booming. Having tamed inflation and dispensed tax cuts like party favors at one of his black-tie White House bashes, Reagan was presiding over a historic bull market. Starting in 1982, the stock market climbed and climbed for five years straight. There was money everywhere, and people were ready to spend.

Go to the Armani floor in the mid-1980s and all along the benches and sofas lining the walls would be the suits that had been sold, tagged, and altered, and were ready to go to their new homes. On a good day, there might be fifty. Wall Streeters would come in, wanting to look like their bosses, and buy six suits at a time, with two or three shirts and a couple of ties for each. "I've never seen anything like that again," one of our buyers from those days told me recently.

It was a rising tide that lifted all boats. Barneys was "the place to be," remembers Gildo Zegna, the third generation (and namesake) of Ermenegildo Zegna, one of Milan's premier suit makers, who Fred and his team had brought to Barneys in the early 1980s. "There was a halo effect to selling a collection in Barneys. Since this predated social media, word of mouth was the best endorsement you could have for a business. To be known to have your collection available at Barneys added to the cachet of a brand." Men's was selling; women's was selling. Even boys' clothes were selling. In 1985, we did a big redesign of Boystown, the better to serve the kids of means—the kids were as spoiled as the adults. "We get the yuppies—the baby boomers who have the taste and the disposable income," Peter Rizzo told *DNR*. "They want quality and unique things for themselves . . . and for their sons." Several of the brands that we introduced first to New York were getting enough of a foothold to open stores of their own—Comme des Garçons opened in SoHo in 1983, and Alaïa in 1987.

The question of building a bigger, better mousetrap wasn't if, but when.

. . .

It took a cast of thousands to design and build the downtown women's store—we assembled so many that I probably should have had my head examined. There was Andrée, inevitably, who designed the grand deco spiral staircase that was the centerpiece of the store. Peter Marino, who carped at Andrée the whole time. Beyer Blinder Belle (Fred's preferred architects), plus Jean Paul Beaujard (Phyllis's favorite decorator and antique dealer, who worked on her section and on the restaurant), plus a Japanese architect I found, Setsu Kitaoka, who was tasked with making the contemporary store next door, and whose work was so austere and customer-unfriendly I eventually had it ripped out and redone. Why have one architect making you crazy when you could have a half dozen?

In anticipation of the women's store, we kept building out the team. Bonnie had come on board to manage footwear, something we wanted to make a priority—you just can't have a decent women's store without shoes. These days, that would get called nepotism, but for the Pressmans, it was simply the way things were.

Fred never forced anyone into Barneys. But Barneys was too big, too shiny, too successful for any of us to resist. It was Fred's delight to sit back and watch his beloved family get drawn in. First me, then Phyllis, then Bob, then Bonnie; later my sister Liz, who dabbled in children's clothes, and Holly, Bob's wife, who tried to make a go of a corporate gifting department. Nancy, the baby of the family, basically grew up in the store. Fred used to bring her along on Saturdays (the executive offices were open six days a week, unthinkable now) and send her toddling around to every cash register—we must have had forty throughout the store—getting what we called "readings," printouts of all the business done. She'd proudly deliver them to Fred, without ever having the slightest idea of what they were. I ended up taking her to Europe on a buying trip during one of her high school spring breaks. After that, the hook was in. She started working at Basco during high school, and basically never left. Nancy was like my little alter ego, a tiny partner in crime. I used to let her crash at my apartment in the city, and would take her with me to work out at the Atrium Club, one of the first boutique gyms.

Fred had his own menswear buying team—Peter Rizzo, Tommy Kalenderian, and Jody Kuss, his stalwarts—but it was up to me to build women's into a gang that could sustain the kind of mega new store we were envisioning. There wasn't a master plan, exactly. We hired on instinct, bringing together a diverse and totally dissimilar group of people. That was part of the secret of Barneys' success, and the key to its creativity. You couldn't, as Fred loved to say, stop giving direction for one second, but you also couldn't micromanage people or hire only in your own image. Barneys worked because everyone *was* so different. Some days, it felt like the inmates were running the asylum. But when it all worked, the machine hummed.

Barbara Warner had ably stepped into Louise's shoes as head women's merchant when she joined in the early '80s, though the two of them could hardly have been more different. Barbara was a classicist and an Anglophile, with a taste for luxury: cashmere, fine shirt-making, cuff links, the stuff of traditional clothing-with-a-capital-C. She'd hunt out the factories that made cashmere for Hermès and Chanel—little factories in Italy or just over the border in Switzerland—or traditional English craftspeople hand-knitting sweaters. She could be strident, even fearsome—the other buyers used to call her "Angry Feet," because you could always hear her coming, even in the little Chanel ballet flats she preferred.

We needed someone to build out the contemporary department, and Anna Wintour, who I had met when she was a young fashion editor at *New York* magazine, introduced me to Jayne Harkness, an English-rose type. She hadn't meant to work in New York, or in fashion, at all:

She'd wanted to be a costume designer, and had been within a hair's breadth of working for the Comédie-Française. But when that didn't pan out, she worked with Kenzo instead, with a front-row seat to the Kenzo boom of the late '70s. Bloomingdale's picked up his line but couldn't figure out how to sell it, so they persuaded Jayne to cross the ocean to show them the ropes. She and Anna, two English gals in the city, found each other quickly, and the rest is history. She was a godsend to have with us in Paris, one of the only Barneys people with fluent French—despite the Berlitz tutor that used to come to the office three days a week to do her best to teach me.

As for the contemporary market, the idea of showing cool, attainable clothes across all price ranges in one place—twenty-two-dollar T-shirts next to designer jeans, things like that—was still new, and Jayne was a mistress of it. She was the one who found Isaia, the young Black designer who for a time was like an entry-level American Alaïa, selling stretchy little going-out clothes we couldn't keep in stock. (They were so tight we called them the "sex pant," the "sex skirt," and so on. Sex really does sell.) Our contemporary department—we'd eventually call it the Co-op—would sell Basco, and the lower-priced Gaultier lines, and Stephen Sprouse, an Indiana kid who'd gone from the most clean-cut, all-American guy at RISD (this according to Chris Frantz of the Talking Heads, who met him there) to a kind of American Gaultier, a true-blue punk with a convert's zeal who was making great clothes in Day-Glo colors, many of them inspired by his muse and former neighbor, Debbie Harry. We hit it off pronto, and kept in touch for many years: We were both obsessed with rock. I loved the classics, like Zeppelin, and he loved the new guard. I never had a clue what he was talking about, so he used to send me albums, with giant labels Sharpie'd in his own hand, reading "Sprouse Approved." I still always went back to Zeppelin.

In 1984, browsing at the Designer Collective, a trade organization that sponsored group showrooms at one or another of the New York

With a young Anna Wintour at the New York Fashion Week shows.
I always told her she'd run *Vogue* someday.

hotels, I stumbled over a woman who would join the team and become a critical part of Barneys' growth in women's—stumbled almost literally, since when I met her, she was lying flat-out on the hotel floor, working away. She piqued my interest immediately, primarily because she looked so *weird*.

Connie Darrow was one of those fashion true-believers, like Anna Piaggi and Isabella Blow, who turn artifice into art. Connie rarely appeared anywhere without her greasepaint—she spackled her face as white as a Pierrot and rimmed her eyes raccoonishly in kohl. (We later learned at the Paris shows that her preferred wake-up call was at 4:30 a.m., to give her time to put her look together.) Her trademark was a Louise Brooks bob, which she frequently crowned with an actual tiara, the only person I've ever known who considered tiaras office casual. She adored jewelry—she wore a million tiny rings and stones on every finger—and armored herself in Chanel suits or evening wear (at any hour) by one of her discoveries, a New York designer named Andra Gabrielle. She could be fierce, often outright tyrannical, as we'd all come to learn: Her persona was as out there as her look. "I think she had spent her time as a child developing that," one of the other buyers opined to me years later. "She presented herself almost like a Diana Vreeland incarnate." Soon enough, Diana Vreeland was ours.

We needed the whole gang. A new wave of talent in fashion had fully arrived—after the transitions of the '70s, there was an energy in women's wear like never before. Thierry Mugler was putting on the most explosive shows of the season in Paris, filled with superheroes, aliens, bug women—dynamic, near-costume clothes. (Off the runway, his collection tended more to wasp-waisted suits and killer tailoring.) Claude Montana was remaking the silhouette, with a muscular, super-shoulder and more of those tiny waists. He wouldn't send out one model at a time—it would be twelve models, all together, all in some leathery armor, stomping down the runway like an army. (When those clothes reached real women, that spirit did, too—Barneys' PR chief, Mallory Andrews, used to wear them, and I laughed my ass off when one of her people told me years later, "I knew my life was going to be hell on the day she wore her Claude Montana suits.") Then there was Gaultier, Mugler's old assistant, like a pixie sprite, gleefully poking fun at any and every fashion piety.

These new guys were fearless. They referenced sex and S-M openly in their designs, played up their gayness in ways that the proper Yves Saint Laurent would never have dared. Montana used to hang out at Club Sept, a notorious Paris disco, with groups of leather men—he transmuted the leather look for men into a fashionable look for women, who eagerly snapped it up. Gaultier flirted with S-M, too: For one show, he sent out models in high-fashion fetish gear, walking each other up and down the runway on dog leashes. Of course, that happened to be the season we finally talked Fred into coming to see the women's collections on the catwalk. Poor Nancy had to sit next to our father through the whole spectacle, one that—for all his appreciation for creativity—can't have impressed him. He reserved his favorite word of complaint for it: "God*dammit.*"

Looking back today, it's amazing how many designers who became legend all started at just this time. (Or restarted—1983 was also the year that Karl Lagerfeld took over and totally reinvigorated the moribund house of Chanel.) Flipping through an issue of *Vogue* in 1983, you'd find spreads of the names to know: Gaultier, Azzedine, Rei and Yohji, Vivienne Westwood. We would go on to add many more. Punk-y, political streetwear out of London from Katharine Hamnett and Body-Map. Moody romance from Milan, by Romeo Gigli. A little later, the dreamy, intellectual so-called Antwerp Six, an ad hoc collective (they formed, loosely, in order to go dutch on shared London trade-show space, the only way they could afford to do the show) that included Ann Demeulemeester and Dries Van Noten. Bonnie and her team discovered Dries on the top floor of that trade show, with a slim rail of men's wear. It was mostly white shirts, schoolboy-ish, simple. But Bonnie saw something in them.

Despite being based in Belgium, Dries knew Barneys. He had visited when he came through New York, back in the days of the Duplex, and been amazed that Barneys not only carried the likes of Mugler and the Japanese designers, but even the most fashion-forward pieces by them, the runway pieces—the "strong pieces," as he called them. Barneys was "an iconic store," he told me years later. When Bonnie walked into his booth and introduced herself, he was so panicked that he actually ran away. "Luckily enough, I had a friend who was more business-minded, and she explained the collection in the first moments," Dries recalled with a laugh recently. "It was only after fifteen minutes that I cooled down and came back and was able to speak to them."

Bonnie, unflappable as ever, was undeterred by his nerves, by the fact that it was a modest collection of mostly shirts, or that it was mens-wear. "Just make us thirty-six knee-length skirts and thirty-six floor-length skirts to go with it and it's going to be okay," she told him. (The next season we bought the men's, too.)

Bonnie locked up an exclusive and we kept it for years and years. Dries became one of Barneys' proudest discoveries, and Barneys, his biggest single retailer.

.  .  .

In the winter of 1985, I was doing the rounds on the fashion-social circuit, and went to the opening of the Met's annual Costume Institute Gala. (They used to take place in December, not in May, as they famously do these days.) The Costume Institute was then under the direction of Diana Vreeland, the former editor of *Vogue* and one of the great fashion eccentrics. The exhibition was "Costumes of Royal

India," dripping in jewels and silks, not unlike La Vreeland herself. At the party afterward, I ran into a guy I knew slightly, John Bodum, who by day did sales for a company called Go Silk, but was better known by night as the ultimate social connector.

John looked like the Mama Cass of the East Village and he knew *everybody*: the schleppers of the Garment District, the party boys of the Pyramid Club, and every imaginable type in between. Another person he knew was a young installer on the Vreeland show, who had come from Los Angeles and was sleeping on his floor. In return for his services, Simon Doonan had been given two tickets to the party, and he gave one to Susanne Bartsch, the Swiss-born ga-ga club queen of downtown New York, and the other to John.

Out of my earshot, John elbowed Simon. "That's Gene Pressman," John told him. "You should really get to know him."

The name was familiar to me. Simon was becoming known at that time as a mad scientist of window display, equal parts Dr. Frankenstein and *Rocky Horror*'s Dr. Frank N. Furter. Born in Reading, in the southeast of England, a place he couldn't wait to leave, Simon was fashion-mad from birth. He escaped Reading for London, where he worked for Nutters of Savile Row, then decamped to Los Angeles in the late '70s, where he landed at Maxfield. Tommy Perse, Maxfield's founder, sold much of the same avant-garde European fashion that Barneys did, though doing so made him much more of an outlier in bad-style LA than we were in sophisticated New York. Maxfield, much more than Barneys, was known for black-everything—"Whatever Perse wants and can't find in black, he has made to order. In the past, that's included bicycles, combs, hair dryers, hangers and linens," the *Los Angeles Times* once reported—and all-black can be a drab downer. What Maxfield needed was humor to lighten it all up, and that was Simon's specialty.

"A window must be completely ambiguous so that the viewer can make up his own mind what the story is," Simon opined. But in his hands, ambiguous could be hysterical or insane. At Maxfield, he once filled the store's sole window with a coffin, corpse, and well-dressed mourners holding drooping lilies, a tableau odd enough that employees claimed it caused more than one car crash outside. Other times, he'd strung up stuffed, flying cats, or molded plastic urinals; the one that most stuck with me was a group of mannequins being set upon by a horde of fake rats. I remembered some of them; I usually made a point to stop by Maxfield, the city's best specialty store, when I was in LA. I liked anything with a little "fuck you" to it, and these windows were provocative but thoughtful. And now he was in New York—as I learned when Mallory Andrews brought me a copy of *Interview* with a page marked, a tiny article—a generous paragraph, really—with a photo of a bespectacled young guy in a Comme des Garçons shirt who was working for Diana Vreeland.

Simon came in for an interview. He was about five feet high, with a taste for Yohji Yamamoto and a madcap imagination that could out-Wonka Willy. Simon was, by his own estimation, pretty feral at the time, but that, to me, was a selling point. I told him I wanted him to shake things up. We bonded over film—we both loved Ken Russell's *The Devils*, a horror film about seventeenth-century French nuns that originally got an X rating—and allegedly, I told him I'd teach him how to enjoy all the finer things life hadn't yet thrown in his path, like eating meat (he was a vegetarian), smoking dope, and eating pussy. (I don't remember this, but Simon's memory is better than mine.) He arrived in January of '86, right around the time the women's store was set to open—and didn't, again.

Pressman projects are notoriously prone to delays; that seems to be our curse. Fred could tell you—the Southampton house he bought in the 1970s didn't even get fully underway until the early '80s, when a Long Island builder, working on his own initiative, decided that half of it was irreparably damaged, and demolished that half, rebuilding it to mirror the first. Fred was apoplectic when he discovered it. But like all building projects, if you get away with only major headaches—rather than complete collapse—consider yourself lucky. The women's store was the same way. We hit an underground spring during construction. We had furious tenants upstairs protesting for their apartments (we relocated them all, at our expense, and guaranteed their rents for life). The opening date lurched further and further back. No matter. We were designing for posterity. We were working around the clock to get the women's store ready, filling the warehouse, sampling with factories in Italy, buying from designers and showrooms—and then, when the store would be delayed another season, negotiating like mad to send what we'd bought back, since we'd have nowhere to sell it yet. It was a time of pure, constant chaos—and in the meantime, let's not forget, we had a flourishing store, mostly men's, but with two floors of women's, to run.

Undaunted by the delays, Simon and the rest of the team immediately set to work anyway, pulling together a summer exhibition dedicated to the Statue of Liberty, who in 1986 was celebrating her centennial. We invited artists, fashion designers, photographers, and a few locally notorious people to embellish Lady Liberty for themselves, to benefit the Cooper-Hewitt and the Smithsonian's National Museum of Design. Fashion and art were natural bedfellows, we felt, and it wasn't a bad way to underscore that Barneys had become every artist's favorite store. Roy Lichtenstein, Robert Rauschenberg, and Kenny Scharf all participated; so did Jean Paul Gaultier, Norma Kamali, Fendi, and Hermès. It ran that summer of 1986 and would have been a big enough undertaking for any store. For us, it was an appetizer. The long-delayed opening was, finally, nearly here.

# 16

# DRESSING UP
# DOWNTOWN

## 1986

On October 20, 1986, *New York* magazine splashed Barneys across its cover, underneath a giant headline that mimicked our own painstakingly redesigned logo: "Dressing Up Downtown." There we were, staring out at you from the newsstand, or up at you from the breakfast table, the Pressman boys, Gene and Bob, arms crossed to indicate serious business, me grinning in a brown and beige houndstooth cashmere jacket by Hermès, Bob starchy and buttoned up, with French cuffs and a white pocket square peeking out of his navy blazer. We were leading a charge: Behind us was a phalanx of the original mannequins Andrée designed for the opening of the downtown women's store, dressed in big-shouldered leather. "The Olympian Goddess," those mannequins were called, and they looked like they'd been freed from some deco department store of the '30s, with strong, chiseled, slightly androgynous faces and broad shoulders—not unlike Andrée herself. They made the usual mannequins look like scrawny waifs. The implication was clear: These goddesses, like us, were ready to go to war. The stakes were lost on no one, certainly not the magazine. "Barneys makes the big time," the cover announced.

Since first introducing women's in 1976, we had been building up quickly, but the women's store represented an exponential leap. The Duplex had been six thousand square feet of selling space. The new store, years in the making, was more than ten times that: seventy thousand square feet. We knew we had to make a statement to compete with the best, and we weren't shy about saying that that was exactly the goal. "The intimate ambiance, the personalized service, and the merchandising expertise which have made Barneys New York the foremost store for men will be applied to women's fashion to create the premiere women's specialty store in the country," Fred trumpeted in 1985, when he announced the new store officially for the first time. Everything would be expanded. Shoes. Evening wear. A four-fold increase in the size of Phyllis's Chelsea Passage, which would now have pride of place on the ground floor. Whole new departments for things we'd never carried before but that you couldn't have a women's store without, like lingerie and cosmetics. A beauty salon, helmed by Vidal Sassoon's right-hand man, Roger Thompson. A restaurant, much grander than the men's store's third-floor café. The contemporary department would get not just its own floor, but its own adjacent building, and finally, a name that would stick: the Co-op, befitting the building's original use (the apartments remained upstairs). Between the three stores—men's, women's, and Co-op—the little shop that Barney opened in 1923 would now take up an entire city block on Seventh Avenue, and halfway down Seventeenth Street toward Sixth.

The public got the triumphal version. Behind the scenes, things were a little hairier. That, of course, is what *New York* magazine captured for its cover story. "Though it's late August, and the opening of Barneys' Women's Store is just five days away, there's no store," the piece opened. "There's just a $25-million, six-floor construction site."

Oh, sure. Go to any construction project a week before it opens and see what it looks like—I guarantee you, not one will seem anywhere near ready for showtime. It *is* true that we were plagued by delays and unforeseen disasters, from layers of solid rock in the basement to cranky picketing tenant associations; they even created an advocacy group, Block-Eye on Barneys. "Everything that could go wrong did," was how one of the partners at our architects, Beyer Blinder Belle, summed it all up. The budgets were overrun, and then overrun again. As far as I was concerned, we had to do it and we had to get it right. And while women's was undoubtedly my baby, Fred was on board. "You're either in the women's business or you're out of the business," he told the *New York* reporter. "We decided to take the gamble." But the world had decided that it *was* a gamble. In a cinephile flourish I at least could appreciate, the same magazine that had decided we were making the big time couldn't help but give us a little jab on the way up. "Does the name Michael Cimino ring a bell?" it asked its readers, referring to the Oscar-winning director of *The Deer Hunter* whose follow-up had been a historic and costly bomb. "Will Barneys become the *Heaven's Gate* of retailing?"

. . .

You had to see this store. Elegant, but also clever. Tasteful, but also funny. So many ideas that we later implemented on a larger scale uptown began life on Seventh Avenue. We had scouted, and shopped, and flea-marketed, and haunted auctions for it, and nothing was box-standard. The display cases were by Ruhlmann. The hostess desk was Portneuve. The chairs were by Robert Oerley. The furniture was antique—I was at the height of my art deco/Wiener Werkstätte obsession, the turn of the century design movements. Andrée's staircase. A skylit atrium. Walls of glass. Peter Marino said it best: We were making a modern classic.

After a few years of shuttling through the men's store to reach the Duplex, women could now bypass men's altogether and enter the

$1.95 • OCTOBER 20, 1986

# NEW YORK

# DRESSING UP
# DOWNTOWN

**BARNEYS MAKES THE BIG TIME·BY PATRICIA MORRISROE**

store at its new entrance on Seventeenth Street. You could see in from the street: The windows opened directly into the store, luring in customers taken with the winding staircase within, the row of individual ground-floor shops meant to emulate Paris' rue Saint-Honoré. When you entered, Phyllis's Chelsea Passage dominated much of the front of the store, her collections of antique silver and china, Georg Jensen silverware, Porthault linens, Bonpoint baby clothes.

Down a few stairs was the apothecary, technically a cosmetics section. You can't be in the women's business without cosmetics. We did, a little begrudgingly, carry the Estée Lauders and Prescriptives for the working woman, the sort of stuff you'd see ladies applying on the subway during morning rush hour. But we sought out much more than that. We did natural beauty decades before "wellness" became a trend, bringing in Molton Brown and Neal's Yard from London and Kiehl's from New York. Bonnie went to Florence to find an order of nuns making the most beautiful smelling potions and fragrances, what the world now knows as Santa Maria Novella. François Nars, the most in-demand makeup artist, did his first beauty collection for us. We found a dealer with a collection of hand-blown antique Russian glass bottles and jars, just for display.

The rest of the floor was given over to accessories, an expansive, revamped department. Major labels had their own little sections, and the process of coaxing them in had taken years, sweet-talking Carla Fendi, one of the five sisters who ran Fendi with an iron fist; the Dumas family of Hermès; and the Wertheimers who owned Chanel, some of the Frenchest Frenchmen I've ever known, into selling to us. We had one for our own label—we started making Barneys bags before many of the other stores thought to do it, in the same factories as the big brands, but at a fraction of the price—and one for fine jewelry, which started out with about five pieces and became one of the defining features of Barneys. I thought it would be fun to display the jewelry around an aquarium stocked with live fish who swam right around the pieces. We'd come to be known for those aquariums, which we later brought uptown, too, and for their inhabitants, an ongoing source of both pride and headache for the staff. "Who fed the fish?" someone would always be asking in the office. "Did anybody feed the fish? Somebody needs to feed the fish!"

The second floor was business-friendly sportswear, anchored by Ralph Lauren, Perry Ellis, and Fred's old favorite Kilgour, French & Stanbury. There was some of our own label, like knitwear and blouses, some of it developed in Europe, the way Fred and his team had been doing for men's with Armani and Piattelli for a decade or more. These were Barneys "classics," tailoring for the contemporary working woman, who was a major part of the workforce like never before. At the back was all the lingerie. The third floor was American designers, like Calvin Klein and Ron Shamask.

On four were the emerging designer collections that customers flocked to, the new guard: Alaïa, Issey, Gaultier, Montana and Mugler, Anouska Hempel from London, Giorgio di Sant'Angelo from New York. Five had the established European designer collections, Armani, Basile, Ferré, Missoni, Rykiel, and the highest-end couture and evening wear, from Chanel, Valentino, Lagerfeld, and Saint Laurent.

All together, it was a magical mix. That's merchandising—the art and science of what you buy and how you show it. It's a puzzle you put together, a journey you take the customer on. When people today realize I was the guy behind the curtain at Barneys, what they all want to know is why there's nothing like it anymore. And there are a lot of reasons, but the real one, the truest one, is that nobody kills themselves to merchandise the way that we did. We wanted to give our clients an adventure. You had to seek out what you needed, and make what you couldn't find. You couldn't just bring in Hermès and rest on your laurels; you had to source the best *vintage* Hermès, from the great collector Didier Ludot in Paris, and display it in antique Ruhl-mann cases—even if Hermès got pissed about it, which they did, because they weren't making any money on the secondhand stuff. Who cares? It wasn't all *about* money. Many years later, when Barneys was in different hands, some bean counter ran the numbers and couldn't figure out why we had a little hat display on the ground floor. That was prime real estate, and no one wore hats anymore—with a slash of a pencil, they got rid of it. But sales all around that section started to slacken and sag. It wasn't about selling hats. It was about the charm of the experience, the old-worldliness of it; women would drift over and try on those hats, hats like their mothers and grandmothers wore. They didn't need to buy them. They loved them. And they bought elsewhere—a lipstick, a handbag, a Chanel suit upstairs. A hat isn't a line on a spreadsheet. A hat is a merchandising experience.

Merchandising is a trade-paper word, but the idea connects to everything. Everyone merchandises. When something is arranged perfectly, the seams never showing, the flow impeccable—that's merchandised. The second side of *Abbey Road*: merchandised to a tee. A great novel, a *Rabbit, Run* or *Portnoy's Complaint*: merchandised, too.

None of it just happens. To get it right, you need people attuned to every nuance, relentless in their pursuit of perfection. The ones who lived and breathed it, who'd work all night if they had to. And we often had to. A lot of people passed through Barneys, the best education in retail, in the almost thirty years I was there, but the best of them were the ones who were inexhaustible. The ones who would show up at the warehouse at 7:00 a.m. before the workday started to replenish the gloves in their holiday displays. The ones who loved walking the floor as much as Fred did, making the salespeople understand every stitch in the garments they made at a little factory outside

Florence, or what Katharine Hamnett's pop-punk political statements were really all about. These were often the wild ones, even the crazy ones. They were the Connie Darrows, who showed up to work every day in a ballgown and Brilliantined helmet hair. A customer might not want to dress like Connie dressed; she might not want to do a lot of things like Connie did. But she would reap the benefits of Connie's taste and dedication.

Not everyone had that level of drive. As the store was about to open, it was starting to look like Barbara Warner didn't. The women's store was a huge undertaking, and we couldn't afford to have any misses; the stakes were too high. I was particularly obsessed with the "classics" area, our own Barneys-designed, feminine interpretation of daywear, not Brooks Brothers for women, but fashion made in many of the same factories as our designer collections. Women in the workforce in the '80s were getting saddled with drab Dacron skirt suits, scrunch socks and Reeboks, carrying burgundy briefcases with little pop-up handles. We could do better for them.

Barneys classics didn't have the sex appeal of edgy European designer labels, but it did offer women what they needed. Our own label was and would continue to be a major point of focus for Barneys, not least because the higher margins you could make there by cutting out the middlemen helped float and fund the entire store. (If you want to have the wherewithal to stick with Jil Sander for several seasons before women get it, you'd better have a bestseller somewhere else.) A few months before the opening, I asked Barbara to walk me through the sampling she had done for this section. I did this with all the buyers and merchandise managers: I needed to make sure we were opening with all the ammo we needed. But the private label wasn't coming together. I didn't feel good about it, and what was worse, I felt like Barbara was yes-ing me about how she planned to fix it. My confidence was wavering.

It hadn't escaped my notice that Connie, though less senior than Barbara and a newer addition to the team, was executing her sections to perfection. They were about as different as two people could be. One of their buyers once whispered to me that if working for Barbara was like working for a hard-ass corporate executive, working for Connie was like serving royalty. Doors had a way of slamming when Connie was around, often by her own bejeweled hands. But she had thrown herself into the whole endeavor with an admirable verve. I took her aside. "I know you have your hands full," I told her, "but I want to give you this opportunity. Do you think you can get it done?" She didn't blink her raccoon eyes. Absolutely, she said. And she did. Private label can be very mundane, very boring, very tailored, very un-Barneys. She made it feminine and fabulous. Anything else would have been a disaster—it was on the second floor, unmissable on the way up. Falter there, and you're done. Connie did good. Better than good.

When the store was finally ready in September of '86, a sniping press corps couldn't help but point out the delays. "Barneys Unveils Women's Store (At Last)," wrote the *Times*. But even the snarkiest gadfly had to admit we had gotten it right. "The new Barneys is at least the equal of the best of its kind in New York," the paper wrote. The new store comprised several formerly individual row houses and a co-op apartment building that would become the Co-op, next door to the original men's store, which we, of course, were in the midst of entirely revamping. We couldn't let the men's store—the big brother, after all—fade beside its shiny new sister. We had announced that the women's store would reinvent women's stores as we knew them. Not too high a bar there. All it took was tens of millions of dollars of silver leaf and terrazzo, glass and steel, antiques from the world over. At the European shows leading up to the store's opening, we had stopped every time at the flea markets; I was shipping things back to New York by the crateload. It all came together—just. Construction crews were still hard at it on Sunday for the opening Tuesday morning. "I'm almost dead," I

The Pressmans—me, Fred, Barney, Bob, Phyllis, Liz, Nancy, Bonnie, and Holly—on the iconic art deco spiral staircase at Barneys' Seventeenth Street women's store.

apparently told the *Times* when they came on opening day. "I'm not nervous," Fred told the guy. "I'm a wreck."

By the time we finally opened, we had been eagerly awaited and anticipated for years. Going became an event—you had to see what the fuss was about. The store was busy all day. Women, unlike men, shop at all hours; the men's store got going at lunch breaks and in the evening after work, but women would come and stay. It gave the store a frenetic energy. Seventh Avenue no longer seemed so out of the way.

Looking back, the opening of the women's store on Seventh Avenue was a milestone in the development of Barneys, the place where Barney Pressman's old shop leaped into a new era. As the International House had been Fred's first major step forward twenty-five years earlier, now I had mine. Like Fred had, I intended to celebrate it. The International House, remember, had a street fair and a mayoral visit and all the local restaurants. This time around, we had something a little different in mind.

. . .

Slowly, and then all at once, HIV and AIDS had broken into the American consciousness. It had begun quietly. In 1981, reports began circulating in New York and San Francisco of a rare cancer called Kaposi Sarcoma afflicting gay men. KS, as it became known, usually affected men over fifty, and was rare enough that even dermatologists generally didn't recognize its telltale lesions. But men as young as their midtwenties were coming down with it, and in numbers that far outStripped any that had been seen before, the first inkling anyone had of the new disease that would become known as AIDS. It would be years before much of America was aware of it; President Reagan didn't even utter the word until years later, after tens of thousands had died. But those of us who worked with and among gay men learned of it much, much earlier than that, and by 1986, there was no avoiding it anywhere. With little research, little certainty, and no treatment or cure, AIDS was a plague.

I didn't know it at the time, but it was AIDS, in part, that brought Simon to Barneys in 1986. He had recently lost a boyfriend to the disease, one of many in the worlds of art, design, and fashion who were dying at a merciless pace. "It was just relentless," Simon told me many years later. "A lot of our friends were dying. We all thought *we* were dying." Tests were new, and not terribly reliable, and no one really got them at that point anyhow. They simply hoped for the best as well as they could, and lived like they were all going to die. Simon was grieving, and a friend—who later died—encouraged him to get out of town, try something new. New York was an escape for Simon. After the Vreeland exhibition opened, he went back to LA, held a garage sale of all his stuff, and came back to New York to start over. Why not?

Barneys was an effective distraction. The days were long, for all of us. Fred didn't like people to leave before the store closed at nine, so the workday could easily run to twelve hours. People worked like crazy. For the merchants who traveled, it wasn't unusual to work five straight days in the store, fly to Europe Friday night, and hit the ground running with shows and showrooms Saturday morning. But for Simon and others dealing with the onslaught, that was welcome. "It was a terrible, strange, horrible period," Simon says now. But for the most part I—and many of his colleagues—didn't really know. "People didn't talk about their personal lives at work," he says. "I didn't talk about people I knew who I was visiting in the hospital at weekends."

From the day I joined Barneys, gay men and women had been part of my orbit. Gay men were among our best customers when we began carrying serious fashion, early adopters and devotees. They were among our best salespeople. They were our neighbors, especially as Chelsea developed and became the "gayborhood" it is today, when gay guys moved in droves north from the Village, their previous enclave. New York's oldest still-going gay bar, Julius', was a few blocks south; and a few blocks west, the Chelsea piers, where gay men gathered to sunbathe and screw in the last years of prelapsarian innocence before the virus really took hold.

Fashion was filled with gay men. Gay men were the designers, the photographers, the retailers, the editors. Half the staff of *GQ*, the ones who helped create the new look for (and at) men—like the art directors Harry Coulianos and Donald Sterzin—gay. And though it didn't get much attention at first, not until gay men banded together and founded their own organizations, like ACT UP and Gay Men's Health Crisis, not until they protested and "died" on the steps of the FDA, these men began to get sick. The government refused to do anything. Reagan looked the other way. A lot of assholes were gleeful.

But anyone who saw AIDS at close range was forever changed. I'll never forget seeing Chester Weinberg, a fixture of the Garment District, getting pushed around in a wheelchair, looking like he was ninety years old—he was in his fifties. And once these men got sick, they began to die, one after the other after the other. The model agent Zoli—died, 1982. Klaus Nomi, the downtown-denizen performance artist who sang backup for David Bowie alongside Joey "Fiorucci" Arias—died, 1983. Joe McDonald, the first male supermodel—died, 1983. Closer to home, Sergio Galeotti, Armani's partner, whom Gabriella had squired around New York and who had broken bread with Fred as they hammered out Armani and Barneys' exclusive deal—died, 1985. Chester—1985. Perry Ellis, probably America's biggest menswear designer after Ralph Lauren—died, 1986, six months after his partner, Laughlin Barker. Willi Smith and Isaia, whose clothes we couldn't keep in stock—1987 and 1989. Francis Menuge, Gaultier's partner—1989. Charlie Suppon, a designer and a big, gay hulk of a guy who used to say hello by punching me in the chest—1989. Steve Rubell, my friend, my frat brother, whose funeral I attended in 1989. He had been the party king of New York City, the genius of Studio, but in the end, his goodbye was a small, mostly family affair.

Nor was Barneys itself immune. In the sales ranks, and in Simon's display department, a number of people were directly affected or had the disease themselves; a lot of them died. Display always had a fair amount of turnover—lots of freelance artists going in and out—and in their separate building, they worked removed from many of us. "They would start to get sick and then you wouldn't see them much and then they'd be gone," Simon says. "People didn't necessarily see that. I think that was sort of the nature of AIDS. If you were in the art world, the fashion world, and/or the gay world, you were like walking through hell. And if you weren't, then you weren't. It wasn't because people didn't care. It was because they just weren't dealing with it." Today, when people talk about "bringing their whole selves" to work, it sounds bizarre to say that these things weren't discussed. But generally speaking, they weren't, even at places like Barneys.

It was Simon who came up with the idea to partner with St. Vincent's Hospital, our near neighbor, down the road on Seventh Avenue and Twelfth Street and home to one of the city's only dedicated AIDS wards. We'd raise money, we decided, by holding a charity fashion show and auctioning off the clothes.

But what clothes? It had to be something anyone could wear and everyone could appreciate. We hit on a perfect piece of American sportswear, the Levi's jean jacket. I called up the Haas family in San Francisco, the owners of Levi's, and got them to donate the goods. Simon and Mallory Andrews and a brilliant woman named Anne Livet, who had her finger on the pulse of the art world, got many of our designers and the local artists who were Barneys' new fans, to customize them. "Artists loved Barneys, and they wanted to participate,"

Anne says. The great conceptual artist Felix Gonzalez-Torres—who himself succumbed to AIDS in 1996—once declared "Barneys is my bodega," at least according to his gallerist, Andrea Rosen.

Andy Warhol, Keith Haring, Jean-Michel Basquiat, Paloma Picasso, Robert Rauschenberg, and Kenny Scharf all did jackets. So did Azzedine, Karl Lagerfeld, Jean Paul Gaultier, Yves Saint Laurent, and Hermès. We called in friends and favors to book models. Madonna. Iman. Paulina Porizkova—soon to be Mrs. Ric "The Cars" Ocasek—from our new ad. Fran Lebowitz. Debbie Harry of Blondie and Kate Pierson of the B-52s. Nightclub It girls like Edwige and Dianne Brill. Nobody was paid. They came, they put on the jackets, and they did their turn down Andrée's centerpiece staircase, christening it right. They held up little numbered placards, like they would have at a couture salon presentation by Saint Laurent.

That event, held in November of 1986, was the biggest one at Barneys to date. "This is certainly the largest crowd we've had at any one time," Bob told *Women's Wear Daily* nervously. Eight hundred people crammed in: artists and friends and designers, socialites, money types like Levi's executive chairman Walter Haas. The models—nearly a hundred of them—came down the stairs high-kicking or shimmying or, in the case of Joey Arias, slithering on his stomach. There was even a little diva-off, when Madonna swerved in front of Iman just as she was preparing to do her walk. "The show was good," Andy Warhol told his diary. "Great jackets. Good ideas. Everybody was in the show— Joey Arias and John Sex and the girl with the shape, Dianne Brill, and Teresa Scharf." He took a photo with some nuns.

The fashion industry, even as many of its most high-profile participants sickened and died, had barely confronted the epidemic. There were a few little charity efforts—Kenneth Cole, the shoe designer, was an early supporter—but nothing on this scale. Bergdorf's or Bendel's, with their carriage trade clientele, quite simply wouldn't have done it—and the proof is, they didn't. It was an announcement by Barneys that we were in this community and of this community, that we wouldn't be bound by convention or history, that we were standing with our designers and coworkers and clients against the horror of AIDS. Not that we thought of it this way at the time. We just thought it was the right thing to do.

It was an emotional night. "There were many people like myself who were dealing firsthand with the AIDS epidemic, and we didn't bring it to work," Simon says now. But we had. Sister Patrice Murphy, a saint twice over—a nurse *and* a nun—who coordinated St. Vincent's hospice program for AIDS patients, came to answer questions. Madonna brought her friend and former roommate, Martin Burgoyne, a young English guy I had seen around before—he'd been a bartender for Steve at Studio. Now he was newly diagnosed with AIDS. Martin, who'd been well known in clubland for years; his party friends had given him a benefit of their own, at the Pyramid Club on Avenue A two months before, where he insisted he'd heal himself with more rest and a macrobiotic diet. But he came to the Barneys event with the telltale lesions of KS. Madonna wore the jacket he designed for the show, and aside from her turn down the stairs, didn't leave his side the entire night. It was a show of solidarity and support at a time of great fear and uncertainty—our own downtown version of what the world would see the next year, when Princess Diana was photographed shaking hands with an AIDS patient. Burgoyne didn't even survive the month. He died on November 30, all of twenty-four years old.

I don't mean to say it was only a sad event. In the face of it all, you had to insist on living, on having fun. And so we did. Get all those people in one room—probably around half of whom actually paid for their hundred-dollar tickets, and half of whom crashed—and there

When Barneys was brave enough to publicly support AIDS research, it got friends and family into the act, too. Here are just a few of the models in the Levi's jean-jacket fashion show we threw to raise money in 1986: Iman and Madonna.

are going to be some laughs, probably some tears. I think there were both for the evening's most shocking moment: When John Galliano, drunk as a lord, took exception to Kate Pierson's giant, tomato-shaped, John Waters–looking wig and leapt at her to rip it off her head.

# 17

# NEVER STANDING STILL

## 1986-1990

If there was ever a moment to rest on our laurels, it was this one. We had braved the leap, going from a few thousand square feet of women's selling space to seventy thousand. We'd corralled and tamed seven historic Chelsea row houses, calmed the picketing tenants, survived construction headaches and a dubious press. The awnings were up—beautiful lipstick orange-red, a color we borrowed, with great respect and affection, from the Plaza Athénée in Paris—and the reviews were in, and good. "Unexpected, understated, spirited," the *Times* wrote, not to mention "urbane, fun, stylish, and faintly '30s." If Fred (Astaire, not Pressman) and Ginger were to meet on Andrée's deco staircase, the reporter concluded, "they would dance." Even the downstairs Le Café was getting good notices.

But that would have been too easy. Onward we plunged. Within a few months, Barbara Warner had departed. There were always whispers that Connie outmaneuvered her, but the truth is simpler than that: Connie outworked her. Barbara had done a wonderful job in many areas, and had been an important player at Barneys, but when we were in the lurch, it was Connie who delivered. I knew she was hard on her staff, and on my staff, and that the Connie who kissed up to me wasn't the same one who was running the rest of the store ragged—I'm not an idiot. But Connie was firing on all cylinders, and so was Bonnie—in the wake of Barbara's departure, Bonnie picked up a ton of the slack, and was now managing cosmetics and accessories, too.

"Connie" and "Bonnie" only sounded alike. They couldn't have been more different, and they couldn't stand each other. Connie, whose temper was legendary, was awful to Bonnie, snubbing her at every opportunity and refusing to speak to her. I think she was jealous, and rightly so—Bonnie was turning into an excellent merchant. You'd think Connie would've been smart enough not to make an enemy of the boss's wife, but that wasn't the way her mind worked. Bonnie had excellent taste, and Connie had excellent taste—that was enough to drive Connie up the wall.

We kept hiring, furiously. Now that we had a dedicated women's store, we were able to lure in dedicated women's merchants, many of whom would have a huge influence on Barneys' direction in the decade that followed. Women like Sandra Constantine, a no-nonsense former Bendel's buyer who came in to do accessories, and Judy Collinson, a former *Glamour* editor whose la-di-da vintage boutique, Reminiscence, had been a staple of '70s Greenwich Village, who was hired to buy for the Co-op. The Co-op, half complete by the time the store opened in 1986, soon had to be given a total face-lift anyway—the Japanese architect's chilly, brutal vision being a terrible match for the shop's young, fun, inexpensive spirit. It reopened in much better form in the spring of '87, sunny and cheerful and stocked with Pucci scarves and beachy straw hats, Levi's jeans and Anna Sui dresses, and little bits and bobs we made all over the world to fill in the gaps. We found the greatest Italian factory to make perfect little T-shirts, which we sold for $8. Eight bucks! And people say Barneys was elitist.

Despite all this, we were still just one store—a downtown store at that. Our presence was huge; our reality, sometimes less than that. We lured Bloomingdale's top personal shopper, a no-nonsense Queens gal named Louise Maniscalco, down to work for us, and her uptown colleagues told her in no uncertain terms that she was making a huge mistake. "They said, 'You are going to fail,'" Louise says now. "One client said to me, 'You might as well move to Europe, I'm never coming down to you.'" Undaunted, she came anyway . . . and moved into an office at the store barely the size of a desk. "I think I was in a fire hazard," Louise laughs. "The fire chief came a few days after I had started to do an inspection and they were like, 'This is not good.'" Nevertheless, it was Peter Marino–designed. And the wallpaper was from France.

Within a few years of opening, the women's store downtown had developed a reputation for excellence. They might not have been the fullest stores in the world—Louise was shocked, her first weekend in the store, to hear that ten women browsing through the racks constituted a lot of activity. Bloomingdale's on a Saturday? It was like the BQE by comparison. But unlike the Bloomingdale's rubberneckers, these women were there to *shop*. What's more, it could be hard to tell them apart from the staff. On her first day, Louise walked in behind a woman in a beautiful suit and cape, carrying a Hermès Kelly bag. And she walked into the employee entrance. Louise assumed there was some mistake and hurried to tell her. But there was no mistake. She was a manager on the designer floor.

Stylish men were populating the men's store, too. The hip downtown magazine of the moment, *7 Days*, was serializing a novel in monthly installments, and Barneys had a way of popping up to signify sophistication—the kind that delighted some and terrified others. "They sat there smoking, watching the crowd in the gallery," one passage ran. "Who are all these people? Heath wondered. He thought he saw the salesman from Barneys go in, but then he realized all the men looked like Barneys salesmen."

.   .   .

Bob, the money guy, was itching to expand. Business was what turned him on; it wasn't the merchandise he loved, the way Fred and I did. He and Holly were living in Greenwich with many of the other Masters of the Universe, and I wonder if it was competitiveness with them that inspired his expansionist urge; I've never known for sure. But he was bullish on the idea of going big. He'd already been working real estate deals, buying up neighboring properties in Chelsea, including our office building and the building Basco's showroom was in. But he wanted more. He felt Barneys itself could move beyond its New York origins, an idea that had been floated and then batted away for years. I had to hand it to him, it was an obvious pitch. And though with the clarity of hindsight, I can see that Barneys should never have tried to build a zillion small stores in second- and third-tier markets, I will be the first to confess that at the time I thought it was a good idea—as long as we got OPM (Other People's Money) to do it, and kept them relatively small, just in case.

Bob engaged Goldman Sachs to shop around for investors. It was 1988, and the economic situation in America wasn't all that rosy. After years of flying high, in October of 1987, the stock market had crashed in the most precipitous slide since the Great Depression. The gains of a five-year bull market, driven in part by increased foreign investment in the United States, suddenly sank on a new Black Monday, October 19. The US financial sector had developed new ways to bet on risk, making free use of derivatives and options, which hastened sell-offs when things turned bad. The Fed stepped in to avert disaster, but the recovery was challenging. By 1989, the city (and then in 1990, the country) slumped into a recession.

The immediate effects of the '87 crash were felt throughout the world, but in some places more than others. In Japan, it was relatively light. In the 1980s, the country was going gangbusters. The Japanese were flush. Goldman asked us if we cared if they sought the money abroad. We already loved Japan's culture and fashion. Sure, we thought—perfect fit.

Besides, the Japanese were on a spending spree. They loved American culture, and even more than that, they loved *owning* American culture. One by one, they scooped up trophies: a controlling interest in Rockefeller Center in 1989, Pebble Beach in 1990. When we got into business with the Japanese a short time later, I floated the idea of buying 50 percent of the New York Giants, then on the block—and they thought about it!

So when Goldman suggested looking to Japan for funding, we agreed. They put together a selection of retailers to go to for investment, Tokyo-based department stores that were at that time making a killing. Thus began our Goldilocks moment. There were three stores on their short list. Seibu was modern and cool, with huge open floors and hip displays—it kind of had a Bloomingdale's-in-the-'70s vibe. Mitsubishi was the establishment, the Japanese equivalent of Bergdorf Goodman: old, powerful, but snobby. The third I knew the least. It was called Isetan. But it had two powerful arguments in its favor. For one, it wasn't the largest, but it was the most profitable of any of them. For another, it was, like Barneys, a family business, then being run by its fourth-generation family heirs.

We flew to Tokyo to meet them. I loved Kuniyasu Kosuge, the president, a cool guy about my age with a gorgeous wife and a spread that seemed to be about a full acre of real estate right in the middle of

Tokyo. (Even his fish pond was stocked with the most designer koi available.) Bob hit it off with his number two, the bean-counter. They owned twelve stores throughout Asia—not just Japan, but Singapore and Hong Kong, too—and we began hashing out a plan to spore Barneys across America. Bob negotiated what even I have to admit was a wild deal: $12 million initially, that would grow to many millions more, in investment capital for the opportunity to license the Barneys name, with our guidance and direction, across the Far East. The Pressman family would be the minority owner in these Japanese businesses, and with their investment, the Kosuges would be a minority owner in a new US venture called Barneys America, which would open up smaller Barneys nationwide. Even better, we'd get a license fee from all the businesses they would build in Japan, and they made a commitment to build several large stores there over the next few years. Dollar signs danced in our eyes; these Japanese stores would be throwing off profit like mad. Even Barney, on one of his regular calls from Miami, was salivating at the prospect. "In 1941, they b-b-b-bombed us," said my grandfather, who was born well before the age of political correctness. "And in 1989, we b-b-b-bombed them!"

We had already been tiptoeing outward. A new commercial development in New York, the World Financial Center, was set to open, on the site of a former landfill by the Hudson River. With founding tenants like American Express, Merrill Lynch, and the investment brokerage Oppenheimer, it had enough office space in spitting distance of Wall Street to become an instant hub for the kind of customers Fred coveted: big-spending, suit-and-tie guys. The WFC developers were bringing in retailers to make the new mixed-use space a destination, and offering unbelievably good rent deals—opening there just about paid for itself. Barneys took its first step beyond Seventh Avenue down by the West Side Highway, with a ten-thousand-square-foot menswear mecca that would open in the fall of 1988. It was a beautiful space, with giant windows right out onto the Hudson. Fred was in heaven. The way he could coddle a shoe or the sleeve of a jacket and rhapsodize about it for hours, he did with that whole store.

It came at the right time. Men's retailing was in the beginnings of an arms race to serve the high-powered, high-spending Wall Street guys with their ballooning incomes and lust for power suits. The "store wars" that would come to dominate my attention in the '90s, when I faced off against uptown women's, actually began with Fred and the *men's* stores, a competition that came to a head in the late '80s. The same fall that Fred opened in the World Financial Center, Murray Pearlstein of Louis Boston, New England's best men's store, planted a flag at Fifty-Seventh Street and Lexington. Bergdorf's announced its intention to build a thirty-thousand-square-foot men's store on the site of the old F.A.O. Schwartz, across the street from its women's store on Fifth Avenue, to open in 1990. Saks expanded its men's section. Bloomingdale's expanded its men's section. The press was eating it up. "The battle lines have been drawn and the guns are blazing," *DNR* blared.

While Fred was fighting the men's war, Bob and I were gearing up to launch Barneys America. The initial plans were ambitious. With Isetan's cash plus more to be raised on the strength of it, we'd open five stores a year across the United States, beginning with three the following year: in Boston, Long Island, and Short Hills, New Jersey. The stores would be smaller than Seventh Avenue—6,500 square feet apiece—and carry a 75/25 mix of women's wear and menswear. (Sales at the main store were still weighted just about the opposite—business was about 70 percent men's.) And anchoring both the men's and women's would be the Co-op departments, the incipient moneymaker and big driver. By the time the first three Barneys America stores opened, contemporary women's wear accounted for more than half of all the women's wear Barneys sold.

. . .

Who would have said no to the Barneys America deal? Who could have? We built the coolest store in New York—or the world, if you asked me—and people came from all around the world to visit it, like a holy pilgrimage. That "Out-of-Towners" ad from a few years back—"A Japanese diplomat brought home English tweeds by Burberry"—wasn't a fiction, it was a fact. It seemed like nothing less than our due for some more Japanese diplomats to want to visit us, even to want to throw piles of money in our lap. America was suffering, Japan was prospering, and cash was raining down on us, as if from the clear blue sky. The Kosuges believed in the partnership, we believed in the partnership, and we had no shareholders to demand immediate results, a point Bob would make to the press every time a reporter noted that the warning signs in American retail at the time were, in fact, not good. The strategy was long-term growth. "We fit well together," Kosuge told *The New York Times*. "We have good hopes for this project."

In 1989, we started opening the first Barneys Americas, all of which were at that time in shopping malls. That itself should have been a red flag. I hated the crass commercialism of malls; it was antithetical to the unorthodox charm that was the essence of Barneys. But malls were hot. American shoppers were thrilling to the idea like never before—turn on the TV in the late '80s and you couldn't escape mentions of the mall, whether as a setting on prime-time shows or in advertisements for "Mall Madness," a best-selling board game that got kids hooked on the idea even before they could drive themselves there. So I swallowed my antipathy and trusted the idea. These weren't just malls, they were the best malls in America: The Mall at Short Hills, The Shops at Chestnut Hill outside of Boston, and Americana Manhasset on Long Island, an outdoor mall complex that was like yenta paradise. For decades, these suburbanites had to come to us if they wanted Barneys. Now we'd go to them.

We might have been putting Barneys where Barneys had never been, but we were adamant that we were staying true to ourselves. "We don't think of this with a chain store mentality," I told *The Wall Street Journal* at the time. "We won't try to be watered-down New York." But maybe we could've tried, at least a little. A normal retailer would've reflected the local community. "I don't think we ever took that approach. We were more, 'Sometimes people don't know what they want, until you present it to them,'" said Kevin Dyson, the leather-jacket-wearing, motorcycle-riding Bostoner we hired to manage Chestnut Hill. At the beginning, we brought in every designer you would find on Seventeenth Street: Comme, Yohji, Alaïa. There were some stylish people in Boston, but were there enough? The women of Boston evidently thought so. We'd held a focus group before opening, where they sniffed at the prevalent Boston stereotypes: "Why would you want to do anything different from what they do at Barneys New York?" they said. "This is not *Cincinnati*." But even *The Boston Globe* had to acknowledge the truth was a slightly different story. "Some Boston women admit that they keep their trendiest outfits in the closet until it's time to take a trip away from Boston," the paper wrote when Chestnut Hill opened in 1989. "Only out of town will they wear their miniskirted Donna Karans and Calvin Kleins, while they keep their longer skirts and baggy cotton dresses for New England."

Was Barneys America ahead of its time? In retrospect, probably. A time-traveler from today to 1988 or 1989 would probably think they'd landed somewhere in the Victorian era. Most households didn't own a computer. Email was still a government secret. If you were a big shot, you might have a car phone. Everything traveled slower—planes, cars, people, news. Today, everyone can find out everything, instantaneously, everywhere. But back then, there were still such things as local knowledge and insiders' secrets. Generations of New Yorkers knew Barneys; they'd grown up with it, and in many cases, so had their fathers or even grandfathers. But in Chicago, Houston, Orange County? Not so much.

Among the plugged-in of New York and Los Angeles, Barneys was beyond a known quantity. Celebrities loved shopping with us, and would bring their friends; our personal shopping team had to grow to keep up. At one point, poor Louise, the personal shopper, was paged away from working with Danielle Steel to help Michael Jackson, who was waiting in her office. Another time, she was fitting Robert De Niro for a suit when she got word that his old friend and costar Al Pacino was coming in. "Let me be his fitter," De Niro told her. "I'm going to come in when you're fitting him and be his tailor." And Louise will never let me forget that time I insisted that she go down to the restaurant after my lunch with two new friends to offer them her services: Tom Cruise and his then-wife, Mimi Rogers. They were in a clinch, basically on each other's laps at that point—Barneys had that effect on some people. "He's my friend, go interrupt them," I told her. And because I was her boss—and for no other reason—she did. "And they both looked at me," Louise remembers, "Like, are you *nuts*?"

But even into the early '90s, we were finding that our name didn't carry quite as far afield as we had envisioned. Planning for a huge Beverly Hills store was well underway when we opened a Barneys America in 1990 at South Coast Plaza, the nicest mall in Orange County, in Costa Mesa. "No one knows what Barneys is," Kevin Dyson told me, after he shipped out from the Chestnut Hill store to Costa Mesa to triage when it sputtered in its first year or so. "Barney" was a term for a loser in California slang, which didn't help. "I hear it all the time," Kevin said. "That's what they call guys who can't surf. So that's . . . *interesting*."

· · ·

What was it about my foot and the gas pedal? I couldn't stop. I think if we'd had years to tinker with Barneys America, we would have eventually gotten the mix right. But there was so much else going on. I was back at Peter Marino's office several days a week, working on the design of the first Tokyo store, which was to be thirty thousand square feet right in the city center. The Japanese were sending over young buyers to get steeped in the Barneys mentality, to learn from our merchants how to buy with a Barneys' eye. And not just buy—how to live like we lived at Barneys. Recently, I found a card one of the Japanese buyers sent to my mother. "Dear Mrs. Pressman," this Satsuki wrote, "When I visited you at the New York office for the first time in 1990, you taught me a very basic rule of table setting by your hand drawing. Since then, I have learned a lot of positive things from you." She mentioned one in particular: the "magic mix."

We were planning major stores, and opening an increasingly national chain of smaller ones. We were going back and forth from Tokyo to make deals with the Japanese, and then hosting them here and in Europe when the deal was made. Did I mention that this was also the time that I got into the restaurant business? Despite the fact that restaurants are famously money pits, impossible businesses that no one in his right mind would attempt.

It made sense to me. Restaurants and stores are similar. They're offering you what you want, not what you need, so they've got to make that offering enticing and unrefusable. (Be honest: You've got a closet full of clothes and a fridge full of dinner at home.) They need both the best product and the best service to survive—no one's eating at a restaurant with bad food, and no one's eating at one where the waiter treats you like shit. I knew how to deliver both in the store. Why couldn't I do the same in a restaurant?

We had the space. Bob had been busy making real estate deals, and we now owned an incredible redbrick building on the corner of Seventh Avenue and Eighteenth Street that had, in the old days of "Ladies' Mile," when the area was one of the city's first retail destinations, been the stables for the R. H. Macy family. A carved horse's head on the building attested to that. We had the money, thanks in part to all

In expansion mode: The Barneys team in Japan during the
construction of our first Tokyo store. Bonnie is second from left;
Connie, two to the right of her; Nancy Klein, who worked on
Chelsea Passage, right behind her; Phyllis and I are center,
with Liz Pressman to my right; Sandra Constantine, far right.

those real estate deals, and to the profit that Barneys was throwing off every year. We had the architect, Peter Marino, who was already doing most of Barneys' store designs, and many of the family's own homes besides. And we had the nerve. We were used to spending big and trusting it would all come out in our favor; everything we touched turned to gold, or so it seemed.

Once upon a time, the pickings for dining in the area had been slim. I loved going for big plates of veal in almond sauce and shrimp with garlic at El Faro, an ancient Spanish joint that had been going since the '20s, policed by surly, ancient waiters who seemed like maybe they'd been going since the '20s, too. Fred's favorite, the Old Homestead Steakhouse on Ninth Avenue, with the giant steer hanging over the entrance, was even older—it had been there since 1868. But the ongoing development of Chelsea had given the old places company. The longest lines were at Nell's, a restaurant and club co-owned by Keith McNally and Lynn Wagenknecht of The Odeon and the eponymous Nell Campbell, an Aussie actress (she'd been in *Rocky Horror Picture Show,* as well as in our jean-jacket show) who used to descend every evening and serenade her guests. It became the hottest new spot in years, when it opened its doors in an old electronics shop on Fourteenth Street and Eighth Avenue in 1986.

With the space in hand, all we needed was a restaurant to fill it, and I had one. I'd been going to BiCE since my earliest trips to Milan. They did northern Italian food right: bright golden risotto alla Milanese, rich with saffron, deep-fried, bone-in hubcaps of veal. I'd become friendly with Roberto Ruggeri, one of the BiCE family's sons. He was like an Italian version of me. He loved cars, like his '53 Corvette, and would do anything for a good time—once, he took me to his family home in Sardinia, where he brought me to a pig roast on the beach . . . at three o'clock in the morning. I was the only person there who wasn't a chef that had just clocked out for the night.

In the mid-80s, Roberto said to me, "Would you want to open a BiCE with me in New York?" We cut a deal: a 50/50 partnership on the worldwide rights to BiCE everywhere. (And they now are everywhere: Milan, New York, Florida, the Middle East—but I'm getting ahead of myself.) I set Peter to work renovating the building, putting in beautiful vaulted ceilings and opening it all up. And then, one day, I was in the office with Fred when Miss Terry walks in. "Gene," she said, "*Women's Wear Daily* is on the phone and they want to speak with you."

When *Women's Wear*, the main trade paper for the women's fashion industry (its brother paper was the men's-focused *Daily News Record*) called, it was generally to cause trouble. They were hoping to either tell you about some controversy or, even better, start some. This was the latter. "Mr. Pressman," some reporter said over the phone, "we wanted to ask you about your partner, Roberto Ruggeri. He is currently in jail in Rome, indicted as part of a car ring that stole over a hundred vehicles—Mercedes, Ferraris, Porsches. Do you have any comment?"

I did not. I told the woman it was the first I was hearing of it and I was sure it was a mistake, and quickly got off the phone. But Fred and Bob, both there with me, looked ready to lose their minds. The receiver was barely down before Bob declared that we had to cancel the contract immediately. "Hold on a minute," I said to him. "He didn't murder anybody. We don't know the facts here. Can't we wait and find out the whole story?" Privately, I was thinking to myself, the whole country of Italy's basically corrupt anyway—no one there will pay attention to this. It's just another day for them!

Then the phone rang again, and in came Miss Terry. "It's Roberto, calling from jail," she said. "It's not my fault," he sobbed. It was the usual story: He didn't know what he was getting into. The police targeted him. It was a shakedown. He didn't do anything. I half believed him. I mean, the Ruggeris were a major family in Milan: Stranger things had happened. Then again, it wouldn't be hard to believe he'd done something a little silly and hoped not to get caught. He did love that '53 Corvette.

Tearful calls from Italian jail were too much for Fred. He was as straight an arrow as they come, and Italy was probably the country closest to his heart—he wasn't interested in getting mixed up in anything like this, whether Roberto was at fault or not. When Fred put his foot down, it was law. I had to tell Roberto, who was devastated and furious—he didn't speak to me for years afterward. The more pressing matter was that we had a restaurant-to-be and nobody to help us run it.

Fred had his own idea. He'd been a regular at a little Italian place, Il Cantinori, for a few years. It served Tuscan food—good, simple, also pretty rich—on East Tenth Street, and was overseen by a feisty little Toscano named Pino Luongo. Pino wasn't a born chef. He'd been an actor in Italy, but came over in 1980 to avoid military service and found himself starting at the bottom of the restaurant world, as a busboy at the popular Sixth Avenue Italian place Da Silvano. He worked his way up there, from busboy to manager, and opened Il Cantinori ("the canteen owner," but misspelled for ease of American pronunciation) in 1983. Pasta with truffles, Tuscan farmhouse decor—it was all very Fred, who had a taste for the finer things when he wasn't lunching on tuna salad. He wanted Pino for the restaurant and Pino, whose ego was ripe for things like rapid expansion, readily agreed. He had a great concept, he told us. Ask any Italian who the best cook on earth is and he'll tell you in a second: It's his mother. New York didn't need any more chef-y types reinterpreting Italian cuisine; it needed more mammas. Le Madri ("the mothers") was born.

Pino did bring in three Italian women, though they weren't all mothers. One was all of twenty years old. Another was a Sicilian woman living in Brooklyn. A third had been cooking in a tiny restaurant in

Piemonte. And there *was* a chef, a youngish guy who'd been at New York fine dining spots. No biggie! Pino loved the romance of his concept, the rest was details. He was like an actor that way—he'd take the bare outlines of a part and fill it out to make the scene.

We all had a part to play. Le Madri was going to be a de facto Barneys cafeteria, and we weren't going to leave anything to chance. Phyllis sourced the china and silverware. Lance and Basco designed the waiters' uniforms. When it opened in 1989, it was a great success. It had Barneys across the street to funnel in customers—maybe you bought something at the store and your salesperson happened to mention it would be a great local spot for lunch. But Le Madri would have done fine even if Barneys shoppers hadn't beelined there. Da Silvano and Il Cantinori had both been clubby, insider's spots, and Pino learned the lessons there of how to give a place heat. That might mean giving preferential treatment to friends and known quantities, but that's how the restaurant business works. Soon enough, everyone was Pino's friend, or wanted to be, and the rich and influential were lining up at Le Madri. "The summer of '89 belonged to Pino Luongo," the *New York Times* reviewer informed his readers. "For the last three months, Le Madri, his Tuscan restaurant on West 18th Street, has been the coolest sanctuary of the bronzed and fashionable set, its weeknight West Hampton." You could always tell when Malcolm Forbes, the playboy publisher of *Forbes* had arrived: You could hear his motorcycle roaring into the parking lot from the restaurant, his blond boyfriend on the back.

# 18

# A CONSPIRACY OF TASTE

I was fed up with the advertising agencies of Madison Avenue, and they were fed up with us. We'd worked with the best—one after another—but as the fashion quotient of Barneys got higher and higher, the more we needed marketing to match. Agencies were great for consumer goods: supermarket chicken, toothpaste, IBM computers. But the ads were starting to look, to my increasing chagrin, like something for a department store. Putting together our own in-house agency made sense. I don't think they were too sorry to see us go. Young copywriters and art directors fought to work on the Barneys account, which always brought awards and recognition (and, often enough, trips to Paris), but the sheer volume of our output meant we were nearly impossible to make money off of.

Barneys was now incontrovertibly a fashion destination, and we had to think like one. We brought in Neil Kraft from Epstein Raboy, one of our last agencies, who had the industry know-how to keep the trains relatively on schedule, and with him to handle administration, I was free to bring in whoever seemed most creative to take our message to the next level. People like Paula Greif, who directed our lo-fi TV spots, and Fabien Baron, a Frenchman in New York who was working at a now long-forgotten magazine called *New York Woman*. Fabien picked up where Marc Balet, our previous art director, had left off. Fabien wanted to push things in a fashion direction—half the reason he took the job at all was that he wanted to work with people like Steven Meisel, who was already shooting for us. Fabien came on board and soon was producing incredible shoots with people like Annie Leibovitz and Meisel. Not every photographer Fabien wanted said yes. Helmut Newton said no. So did Richard Avedon, most likely because he was competitive with Meisel, who he was sure was knocking him off.

Who needed them? Fabien's campaigns were great. It was a whole new look for Barneys, and people began noticing. Fred was slower to get it—"What the hell are you doing with those ads? What does it mean?" he used to shout at Fabien—but customers loved it. For a men's campaign in 1988, we decided to have Annie shoot handsome, sepia-toned portraits of real New Yorkers who were actual Barneys customers. We had plenty to choose from. Joseph Papp, the brains behind the Public Theater and Shakespeare in the Park. The editors of *Spy*, the coolest new magazine taking the piss out of New York society. John Malkovich, the actor's actor. Kirk Varnedoe, the director of painting and sculpture at the Museum of Modern Art. That one was a little controversial—the ad ended up running in the *Times* the same day as a news article about his MoMA appointment. But we were always ahead of the curve.

For the women's campaigns, we could really push fashion. For one shoot in those first few years, we wanted Lauren Hutton. Hutton had been one of the top models of the 1970s, then a Hollywood actress for a while; she had a lead role in the Armani-costumed *American Gigolo*. But by the late '80s, she was no longer top of mind in fashion or in film. But she *was* very Barneys: smart, sexy, a little off-kilter, that great gap in her teeth. . . . Steven got it, and I loved it. So what if she was in her midforties? More concerning was that "a little off-kilter" in her case meant "well on the way to full-blown nuts." Her short hair in the ads—which counted as national news to *The Washington Post*, who wrote a whole story about it—was the result of her accidentally setting her hair on fire roasting a Thanksgiving turkey. ("In the apartment at the time were her gynecologist, her German director and her 'punk rock 'n' roll' house cleaner," the newspaper dutifully reported.)

When the ads came out, they were a sensation, and Lauren thought she deserved a little extra credit. She came into the store one afternoon, scooped up armfuls of clothes, and demanded to take them all as her due. When the salespeople politely told her that wasn't really how it worked, she screamed bloody murder to get Gene Pressman on the phone immediately. I wasn't around, but Nancy was, so good old Nance had the pleasure of telling Lauren Hutton we didn't give freebies and we didn't give discounts. I imagine facing down the Medusa would've been easier. Finally, after much back and forth, Nancy offered her a small discount: 10 percent. Clearly Lauren thought a woman of her stature deserved more. Newly aggrieved, she stormed out, vowing never to return. Did she? Who knows. The photographs, at least, are forever.

• • •

The smartest people know that advertising, properly done, is an art. And a good number of them passed through Barneys' little agency in those years. One of the most notable was Glenn O'Brien, whose long career in advertising started at Barneys; he'd been a pal of Paula's (she used to date his best friend, Jean-Michel Basquiat), and she'd thrown him a little cash to write the copy for one of the TV ads she did for us.

Glenn joined up around the time of the women's store opening in 1986. He had a great sensibility, one that was perfect for Barneys: He loved beautiful things, but he was a wise guy about them. He'd wanted to be an artist, but he found his real medium in advertising and, befitting a guy who got his start in Warhol's Factory, was smart enough to realize that advertising could be art, and art could be advertising. He described ad work as the "demilitarized zone between art and commerce," and he was right. He grew to become one of the great admen of his generation, while keeping up with all his other projects. He even wrote a column *about* advertising for *Artforum*, called "Like Art."

Glenn was a character unlike any I'd ever met. He had foxy little features on a giant head, and he projected a kind of fuck-you cool, with his close-cropped dark hair and permanent sunglasses. His background wasn't so unusual: He grew up in Cleveland, went to Georgetown, came to New York to study film at Columbia. But once he got to the city, any vestige of his Midwestern past quickly faded away. He found his way to the Factory, where he modeled himself on Fred Hughes, Warhol's dapper business manager, and wrote a music column for *Interview*. But Glenn wanted more, and in 1978, he and Chris Stein, the guitarist for Blondie, launched their own public-access TV show, *TV Party*, a send-up of late-night talk shows that turned into a pretty real talk show when all their friends came on it. David Byrne of the Talking Heads, Debbie Harry, Robert Mapplethorpe, Mick Jones from The Clash—they all showed up for a chat on his low-budget couch.

One of the great wits, he was a genius of concision. He could boil down a message into the perfect one-liner, achieving more with that sentence than the old ad guys could in thirty seconds of voiceover.

He had a real flair for understatement, for cutting through the bull-shit. In the late '80s, we hired the photographer Timothy Greenfield-Sanders to shoot a series of large-format Polaroid portraits that we turned into a campaign that ran in the *Times* magazine. Greenfield-Sanders shot terrific portraits of a variety of real New York geniuses—Spike Lee, Harvey Keitel—and a few out-of-towners we loved despite that shortcoming. (I'll always be proud we got Tom Jones—you know, "It's Not Unusual"—into a campaign.) Glenn's copy completed every shot. "There are actors' actors," ran the line on a photo of John Hurt. "We have the tailors' tailors, from Savile Row." Or the perfect line for Sandra Bernhard, the raspy comedienne, who we booked last minute when someone else fell out. A woman in a men's campaign? Some of our more conservative elements were worried people wouldn't get it. Glenn, unruffled, supplied the exactly right line: "Barneys, Fine Clothes for Men Since 1923." No more, no less. And no confusion.

Or take the famous vintage-photo campaign we did. I'd been paging through an old book of Elliott Erwitt photos and loved them—I suggested that we build a campaign around them. The team took the idea and ran. We convinced photographers and their estates to let us use their work, and soon we had incredible images, by Erwitt, Roy De-Carava and Garry Winogrand. Glenn hit on the perfect line for each. For the Erwitt picture, a photo of a family of nudists, he reprised Steve Gordon's old line from the famous "Men of Destiny" ad: "You'll All Need Clothes." For the Garry Winogrand shot of four handsome young guys huddled over diner coffees, deep in conversation, "A Conspiracy of Taste."

Within a few years, the Barneys ads were once again winning awards. It wasn't all smooth sailing. Glenn could be fiery, especially if he felt underappreciated. In 1991, *Adweek* suggested that it was Neil who made Barneys the advertising genius that it was, and named him print copywriter of the year. Glenn, in a rage, stormed out of the office, threatening never to return. He did, of course, the next day.

But he was right. Anybody who knew anything about it, inside or outside Barneys, knew that it wasn't Neil writing those ads.

. . .

Neil got too big for his Comme des Garçons britches quickly after that. He was a classic example of right place, right time, but he believed that he had made Barneys everything it was and more. (As one of his Barneys colleagues, who I'll let remain nameless, told me, "He could have ended up at another place and no one would have ever heard of him.") Instead, he took credit for everything the Barneys team did—*as a team*—and walked out the door to a series of jobs he'd never have secured otherwise. I wasn't sorry to see him go. We'd been close at one point, but the more successful Barneys' advertising became—successful enough that, by 1988, we had set up our own shingle within the company and were doing not only our ads, but ads for others, too, with projects for Morgans Hotel, Glacéau water, and amfAR, the AIDS nonprofit—the more obnoxious Neil became. It's one thing to be rude to me (though I don't recommend it). It's another to be, as he was, disrespectful to Fred, whose opinions he increasingly discounted and rolled his eyes at. That was it. I was ready to kill the guy, though that wouldn't have been professional. I got my little revenge other ways. In the gym I built in the office, where I'd spend early mornings sparring with my trainer, I inscribed the name "Neil" on the one-pound weights. That got a good laugh from all the staffers I let use the gym alongside me.

Mega companies had a way of keeping our agency fresh—by poaching our people. First Fabien had left to redesign Italian *Vogue* in 1988, then Neil went in 1991, to Calvin Klein. We brought in a young guy named Doug Lloyd, who was with us for a couple of years before he, too, caught the eye of the Gap and we were back to the job search. Then *Details* magazine closed, *Interview*'s closest competitor for downtown bible. It had been a scrappy little magazine, but punched well above its weight: Bill Cunningham, who later became a decades-long fixture at *The New York Times*, did its fashion-show reportage, Patrick McMullan, who later became the biggest party photographer in New York, did the party pictures, and every downtown club kid was dying to be in the social column of its man on the street, Stephen Saban. (Saban was a good friend of Nancy's from out and about. He wrote up her wedding in his column over her objections: "The very pretty Jewish-princess bride pledged her troth to the good doctor in a lovely white gown designed by Giorgio di Sant'Angelo.") *Details'* fashion director was a gal named Ronnie Cooke, and when Si Newhouse, the publishing magnate whose family owned Condé Nast, bought the magazine and shut it down, she was out of a job. She can't have taken it too personally—she later married Si's cousin Jonathan.

I knew Ronnie a little bit from the show circuit, and realized she'd be perfect for the job. I called her up. "Cookie," I said to her, "you're the only one who hasn't called me about this job." "That's because I don't want it," she told me. "Also, what job?" "Just come in here, Cookie," I told her. "Come in and see me."

She joined the team that year. She and Glenn became instant friends, and despite her fashion background, she wasn't a diva—*Details* had been run on a shoestring, and she was used to doing anything and everything, writing, organizing shoots, picking fashion, working on page designs. (As she once put it to me, "If you were working on something, you did it and you swept the floor afterward.") She had a great eye and a great fashion sensibility.

We'd been using Meisel for a few years at that point, since Marc Balet first had to rent him the camera he used to shoot, and he developed an incredible rapport with a Canadian model named Linda Evangelista. Linda had risen to become one of the first-generation quote-unquote supermodels, and after some newspaper ads with Fabien in the early '90s, she and Steven shot a series of ads, first with Doug, then with Ronnie, that are still talked about today. Linda became our de facto Barneys mascot: She had that perfect combination of beauty and wit that was so Barneys. When she had red hair for a while, she leaned into the character, and became, for a time, our own Lucille Ball. "It's probably the work, besides a couple of editorials, I'm most proud of," she says today. "People remember those ads and still approach me to this day about them. If I'm signing an autograph, for example, it'll be one of those pictures."

She could channel the vibe of a 1950s cover girl but look totally modern, too; she could convey more emotion and thought in the cock of an eyebrow than most models could with their entire bodies. She was game for anything. In one famous picture, she's kissing a chimpanzee right on the lips. "The chimp, she was fabulous," she says. "She was so entertaining. She was a little older than a toddler, so very mischievous. I remember them saying, 'Don't let her go.'" The reason why soon became clear. "She kept looking up—she was looking at the exposed pipes on the ceiling," she says. "Her intentions were to go for a good swing. I held on to her. I had to try and keep her attention. But she kept looking at the pipes. Eventually, I put a candy in my mouth from the craft service table, and she got so excited. And she took it from me very, very, very gently and it looks like she's kissing me. That is how we got the shot."

The chimp wasn't her only Barneys paramour. "Ronnie did bring me good props," she laughs now. "Including the men." On set for us, Linda danced with Gregory Hines (or next to him; he refused to dance himself) and crooned with Tony Bennett. ("He must be deaf, because I'm the worst singer ever.") And it was on set for Barneys that she met the *Twin Peaks* actor Kyle MacLachlan. In short order, she'd left her husband and the two of them became an item, eventually engaged.

Ronnie brought new photographers into the fold, too. She became obsessed with a young English girl she wanted to use for a campaign.
She was a game changer, Ronnie swore—this girl was going to be big.
"Fine," I said, "bring her in, I want to meet her first." The kid was so
green she didn't even have an agent; she wouldn't fly to New York
without her grandmother. "Listen," Ronnie told me, "you complain
about agents all the time. Now I have a photographer with no agent,
and all she wants is to bring her nan. What's the problem?" So she flew
them in. The girl clearly had something. She was a force of nature
with a squeaky little voice and an elderly grandmother parked in the
corner of the meeting. I figured, Barneys is a family business, what
the hell, but I warned Ronnie: This better be fucking good. "Let me
do this," she said, "and if it's not good, you can fire me."

That was the sort of no-bullshit approach that endeared Ronnie to
Fred, and vice versa. This was no Neil redux. She wasn't intimidated
by Fred's toughness, she just rose to the occasion. Fred could test people. Some days he'd call Ronnie and complain that business was down
33 percent yesterday and demand to know, what was wrong with her
advertising? She would say, Fred, there was a snowstorm and they
closed the city. And he would go, *That's no excuse!* Ronnie used to call
it "Jewish yelling"—like, "What kind of answer is that?" She got that it
was banter, and she wasn't scared off. Fred couldn't abide boasting.
You had to be fine with him coming into your office and sitting there
for hours, rhapsodizing about the seventeen possible shades of black
for a sock. But Ronnie was.

Ronnie was right about Corinne Day (and never boasted about it—at
least not to Fred). She became one of the key photographers of a new
movement that was beginning in fashion and fashion photography
both, a new minimalism stripping away the froufrou excesses of the
'80s showmen. The crashes of the late '80s had reminded everyone
that no party lasts forever. The rising '90s generation wanted to

strip away the gloss. The signs were everywhere. Perry Ellis, who epitomized the polish if not the froufrou of the previous generation, was gone and his namesake label was now being designed by a young Parsons grad named Marc Jacobs whose grunge collection, with its mismatched pieces, wool ski hats, and combat boots was such a scandal that they fired him for it. "We're over the superstar model thing," Marc told *WWD*, while he still had a job. The new models were the type to go to Frédéric Fekkai and ask him to make their hair look greasier, not cleaner.

There was a toughness to it all. It felt like a refusal to play pretend. It could still be pretty, or feminine—just look at Corinne's famous photos of Kate Moss, whose star quality she saw long before most, and who would become the movement's supernova, eclipsing, for a time, even the super-est "supermodels." Kate the Great. Whatever "It" was, she had it. She was shorter than the other models, couldn't have been more than five feet seven inches or so, painfully skinny, kind of ragamuffinish. But look at the pictures of her with her little crown on the beach that Corinne did for *The Face*, the British magazine that everyone in London ran to the news kiosk to buy. Or at the photos Kate did with Corinne shortly thereafter for Barneys.

That 1993 campaign, "How to Be Good," was one of our best. It introduced Corinne to America—after we shot with her, Gap and Banana Republic swarmed her, as did many of the magazines. Ronnie likes to tease me about how I couldn't resist racing up to Anna Wintour at a fashion show and bragging that we were shooting with the greatest photographer no one was using here. Ronnie feared that Anna, who's as competitive as I am, would swoop in and commission her.

Corinne's portraits were light-years away from Steven and Linda's stylized shots. There was a charm in their simplicity; half of the models weren't even professional models at all. (A Chicago newspaper gleefully reported that Corinne liked unspoiled naïfs so much that she'd found one of her models in a McDonald's, and a second renting a go-kart. "Leave it to Barneys New York," the paper wrote, "to be the first in this country to hire a young British photographer who is getting so hot she's taking over some of Steven Meisel's territory.")

The clothes were simple but charming, too. A disparate group of new designers were rising to prominence, united more than anything else by the purity of their approach. It wasn't all grungy or punky. There was Jil Sander, a stern but fabulous German woman whose cuts were so perfect, and so deceptively simple, that for several seasons, many of our customers didn't understand why they should pay high prices for them. Miuccia Prada, who for several years had been quietly updating her grandfather's leather-and-luggage line and introducing clothes that the fashion editors were going gaga for in Milan, and which season after season got better and better: strange, sometimes purposely tacky, strongly influenced by vintage, but with an off-kilter slant no one but her could have imagined. They sold so well that in short order she introduced a second younger, more affordable line, called Miu Miu, after her childhood nickname.

Designers who had been working away for a few years already were coming into focus in this new context. Martin Margiela was a reclusive Belgian—so shy that, like Pynchon, he refused to be photographed and to this day, almost no one knows what he looks like—who had been staging Paris's most avant-garde shows, in subways and abandoned warehouses, using his real-life muses rather than models. Helmut Lang, a stiff but cool Viennese with an uncompromising vision, who a few years later would shake up New York fashion when he moved to the city from Paris. Helmut would later take credit for being the first fashion brand to advertise on New York City taxi tops—but he wasn't. Barneys was. As Ronnie likes to remind me—and I know has reminded Helmut—that was her idea, when we were moving up to Madison.

In those days, no one would be caught dead advertising on the little placards that sat on top of taxis. The ads that ran there were for things like Virginia Slims cigarettes and Off-Track Betting. Our ad space buyer was horrified even at the thought. But what's more New York, New York, than a yellow cab? Ronnie brought the idea to me, expecting that I'd balk—taxi tops were no place for a high-end store. But I loved it. "Go for it," I told her. It was true then and it's true now, it's not just what you say, but where and how you say it. As Fred had wrestled Barneys' ads into the pages of *The New York Times* when the uptown stores considered Barneys less-than, as I had secured the back cover of the *Times* magazine for Timothy's portraits in the days when everyone read it cover to (back) cover over Sunday-morning coffee, here again it was location, location, location—even if other people couldn't see it. Taxi tops were as perfect a calling card for Barneys as any of those other placements. And Ronnie and Glenn, together with Jean-Philippe Delhomme, the illustrator whose trembly, urbane caricatures are associated with Barneys to this day, came up with the perfect campaign for it: "Going uptown, going downtown," the ads read, like the drivers themselves would ask you when you flagged them down.

And then, as always, we moved forward. Ronnie was laughing recently, remembering her offer to be fired if Corinne Day didn't work out. Obviously, that didn't happen. "I think you said something like, 'What the fuck you gonna do next, Cookie?'" she recalled.

Monkey business. Linda, "our Lucille Ball," on a hot date
for a Meisel-shot Barneys campaign, early 1990s.

Our cheeky sensibility: Fashion advertising without any clothing at all. We ran this famous image by Elliott Erwitt, taken at a nudists' colony, with a reprise of the famous tagline from the 1970 "Men of Destiny" ad: "You'll all need clothes."

Another great ad, this one by Timothy Greenfield-Sanders, starring Barneys superfan and customer, Sandra Bernhard. The copy for this one read, "Fine men's clothing since 1923."

# 19

# I FEEL GOOD

## 1990-1993

In January of 1993, on the occasion of Fred's seventieth birthday, the family all came together for a major holiday trip to the Caribbean. He was now the undisputed patriarch; Barney had died, peacefully and at the advanced age of ninety-six, in Miami a year and a half before. His had been a short illness. As Bob recalled in his obituary, he'd continued calling the store daily for sales reports up to a few weeks before the end. He had lived long enough to see the store he founded become an international symbol of style, a long way from the early days when, as Fred remembered, customers used to cut the Barneys name out of their suits so that their friends would think they'd bought them at Saks.

The Pressmans had grown into a formidable clan. Fred and Phyllis, four kids, each with a spouse and at least one kid of their own. Bob and Holly had Ned, Will, and Meg. Bonnie and I had Keith in 1989, and Wallis, in 1992. Two years before, Nancy, the youngest, had tortured her older sister by getting married first. Ken Dressler was Phyllis's dream: a

Jewish doctor with a Harvard MD. Liz followed suit the next summer, marrying a doctor of her own, Seth Neubardt, an orthopedic surgeon with a side hobby in videography. Now Nancy had Andrew and Danielle, and Liz had David and Seth. We were a gang of seventeen. What could go wrong?

Seth always had a video camera handy, and captured the Pressmans for posterity—captured, in many cases, more than we bargained for. Watching these videos now, you see a large, bumptious, loving family, but also one starting to strain under the pressure of many different personalities living, loving, and working together. We're all, for better or worse, true to ourselves. Liz and Nancy are fighting. "Oh, I can't handle this!" Phyllis moans, holding her baby grandson David. Bob is being Bob: He sallies up to the camera and blows a kiss, with both middle fingers up as he does. Bonnie has receded quietly to the sidelines, playing with little, bowl-cutted Keith as chaos rages around her. I am, customarily, unbothered and unhurried, as everyone else carps and complains. "Who are we waiting for?" someone asks. "Let's all guess," Bob says. (The camera comes and finds me: I'm in the shower.) "It's not fair," Liz wails. "It's all for Gene. It's always been grouped around Gene. No, really, Gene, this has all been grouped around you."

Was that my fault? I was just doing my own thing. If only everyone could have taken it in the spirit Fred did, Fred who saw the humor in it, and who accepted it all with a shrug. Fred wasn't going to raise his voice. He made light of it instead. "This is to assert his authority," he jokes when I appear in a towel. "This is to make no doubt where the authority lies. He's getting beautiful now . . . the body beautiful just got inside . . ."

Fred is doing his best David Attenborough, explaining the scene to all the curious viewers at home, grabbing a rare moment in the spotlight. "This is your typical outing of this family here," he narrates to

Seth, who trains the camera on him. "Fighting is just about to begin. I would say that in about five minutes, everybody will be primed up, normally primed up, and everybody will be doing their thing. Screaming, arguing."

"Is this part of the magical mix?" you can hear Seth asking from behind the camera.

"This is part of the magical mix that the Japanese bought," Fred says. "The only problem is they never saw it on TV."

"Is it the magical mix or magical myth?" Seth says.

"It happens to be both," says Fred. "This the magical mix and also the myth. And it's a total mix-up. This is what they bought, and if this film ever got out, we're *rooooooned.*" He's joking, drawing out the word for effect. Isn't he? "Ruined," he repeats. "Don't ever let this film out—make one copy and keep it in a vault somewhere."

With Barneys now in business with the Japanese and expanding fast, the press was taking more of an interest in our goings and comings, the scene behind the scene. It would be a few more years before they caught wind of the screaming and the arguing, the complexities of being a Pressman. But in private, as Fred refereed between two very different sons presiding over a very different business from the one he'd inherited from his father, the cracks were starting to show.

. . .

Tension was inevitable. Barneys was expanding explosively. Looking back now, it's hard to fathom how we managed it all. The pace was frantic. The plan was to have twenty-five stores by 1994, and we were working furiously toward that goal.

The growth was happening on two parallel tracks. Barneys America, the mall stores that were Bob's baby, were multiplying. The first store had opened in Chestnut Hill in 1989. By the end of 1990, it had been joined by a half dozen more: Beside South Coast Plaza, suddenly we were in Seattle, Dallas, Westport, Manhasset, and Short Hills. Each one required a flurry of planning, not just to find the real estate and negotiate the deals—that was more Bob's area—but to ship in the window displays and teach the new sales staff how to talk about the merchandise.

The buyers traveled around the country constantly, taking the temperature of local markets, trying to figure out what would work where. Sales appointments got longer and longer, and buys got bigger and bigger—we were gaining clout with our vendors as we snapped up more and more merchandise to fill out what was becoming a national network of stores. The logistics became dizzying. Buyers would travel to Europe with suitcases full of Polaroid film, to snap photos of every piece that interested them—before email and digital photography, there was no other way, unless you were prepared to sketch. Back at night in the hotel, after long days of appointments, they'd spread all the pictures out on their beds and deal them like cards, or maybe it's more accurate to say arrange them like puzzle pieces. This dress would work in Short Hills and Chestnut Hill, more of this one in Manhasset or Seattle.

The PR team worked to make sure no one could miss our arrival. There was the courting of local socialites and local newspapers. There were opening parties and sponsorships of local charities. The parties were legendary. When we got to Dallas—Neiman Marcus country—we knew we'd have to go *big*. I told Mallory Andrews and our PR shop not to tell me what would happen, just to be sure I'd be surprised and amazed. She did. After a cocktail at the new Dallas store, in the Highland Park shopping complex, helicopters took seventy people for dinner—shuttling them over in small groups, the choppers descending and ascending on repeat like in *Apocalypse Now*. We zoomed over the city until we finally touched down . . . on the 30-yard line of the Cotton Bowl, where the Cowboys had played all through the '60s. Mallory had thought of everything—except a football. It's every Dallas boy's dream to play in the Cotton Bowl, and there was no way we were gonna make it this far and not play. She found a ball in the locker room and after dinner, the guys took off their ties, the girls took off their heels, and we had a game, whose players included my sister Liz, our architect Jim, and Richard Marcus, as in Neiman. We out-Texas'ed Texas. And let's not forget, Neiman's owned Bergdorf Goodman, our number-one competitor in my mind.

For all our work to ease ourselves into the local markets, and in with the local customs, some friction was inevitable. I was on vacation, sitting on the beach, in early 1991 when I picked up a copy of *The Wall Street Journal* and learned from the front page that Roger Thompson, the hair guru who we had talked into opening a salon in Dallas with us, had infuriated the ladies of Texas by refusing to do the big hair they loved. "Mr. Thompson doesn't think that's any reason for the women of Big D to hold their heads high," the paper snarked. "He thinks their heads are too high already—with hills of hair, bleached, lacquered and stiff as a board."

Was this really front-page news? It was definitely a headache. Dallasites were only too happy to fight carpetbagging New York arrogance, and Thompson had dragged us right into the middle of it. His stylists had to basically go into hiding, the newspaper reported, quoting one colorist at the salon who'd taken to telling people he was a construction worker when he went out on the town. "This is a pretty cliquish town for hairdressers, and the Thompson salon has offended it," a rival salon owner snapped. The Thompsons dug in their heels, which didn't help. "The Dallas 'do will go out of style before we lower our standards," Sara Thompson, Roger's daughter and business partner, said. If it hadn't been for Barneys, she added, they'd never have come to Dallas at all; they'd have preferred "a more sophisticated" city.

We considered these growing pains, and kept going. In 1991, we opened in Cleveland. Then Houston, where we opened the store by having voguers from the House of Xtravaganza perform in the windows ("What is it? Rapping?" Christophe de Menil asked), followed up by an epic party at her mother's Menil Collection to celebrate a Robert Rauschenberg exhibition. We'd flown Rauschenberg's favorite Zydeco band in from New Orleans to perform, and the artist and honoree got so drunk, stumbling across the dance floor with a bottle of Jack in his hands, that at one point he grabbed me by the lapels—whether to kiss me or punch me in the face I've never known.

In 1992, we added Troy, Michigan, and then Chicago, another huge flagship. Donna Karan was the hottest designer going at that time, and we gave her the kind of entrance even she wouldn't have gotten on her own: A motorcade of thirty Harleys cruising up Oak Street, with Donna on the back of one. We had spent months recruiting all those bikers, haunting bike bars in parts of Chicago you wouldn't want to find yourself in at night. It was worth it. We sold $65,000 worth of Donna Karan that opening weekend.

In parallel to all these Barneys America stores, we were also working on bigger flagship Barneys stores in key markets. If Barneys America was Bob's pet project, these stores were mine. They were everywhere I wanted to be. And in 1990, we were planning and opening three at once.

In August, we announced our intention to break ground in Beverly Hills, bringing me back to the West Coast for long stretches for the first time since the early '70s. Almost as big as Seventeenth Street, the

With Robert Rauschenberg at the party celebrating our
opening in Houston. Must've been a great conversation.

Wilshire Boulevard Barneys would be a major flag planted in Los Angeles.

Peter Marino had come a long way since his time as a "baby draftsman" (his words) on the earliest iteration of Phyllis's Chelsea Passage in the '70s. In the intervening years, he did homes for the Agnellis and Valentino, as well as the renovations of Barneys' women's Penthouse into the Duplex, but even so, when we approached him to work on the women's Seventeenth Street store, he told Fred, "I don't want to waste your time—I've never done a store in my life." Fred, wisely, told him that he just wanted someone with talent—Fred knew enough about doing stores for the both of them. And he was right. After the women's store opened downtown, about a third of his business became retail. Peter himself admitted that he had Barneys to thank for that.

Now we kept him and his office busy. He was our guy for Beverly Hills, and for Tokyo, the first Japanese Barneys store, which we opened in November of that same year, with another Japanese store in Yokohama to follow. The Tokyo store was shaping up to be beautiful, an eleven-story, thirty-thousand-square-foot space in the heart of Shinjuku that would carry a ton of Barneys' private label, as well as American labels like Donna Karan and Zoran, European labels like Alaïa and Dries, and Fred's beloved Italian tailoring, from Zegna and Luciano Barbera. The whole crew flew to Tokyo in 1990 to merchandise the store in record time, working night and day: Simon on the displays, a bow-tied Marino on the decor, Phyllis with her number-two, Nancy Klein, on Chelsea Passage. Schreier was there for the men's sportswear, Rizzo and Tommy Kalenderian for the men's tailoring and furnishings, Bonnie for women's, Mallory to handle the press, Fred to preside over everything, and Bob and Holly and Ken and Nancy and Liz and Seth, with his ever-present camera, taking it all in.

"This for the PBS special, *How to Make a Store in One Week*," he cracked, as he panned over all of us attending to the billion little details that go into making a store a success. There's Phyllis, in her best WASP-y pitchwoman mode: "We're having a *maaahvelous* time here, it's the most beautiful store in all of Tokyo." There's Fred, leading around a Japanese sales guy and caressing every individual shoe: "See how beautiful they are?" There's Bob wandering through the background, being Bob. "I *like* litigation of assholes," he says, apropos of god knows what. "I'm looking forward to killing this guy."

When Tokyo opened, it was another huge success. Besides all of the merchandise, the store had an art gallery, two restaurants, and a bar. Crowds thronged the building, and a thousand people came to the pre-opening party, including eminences like Hanae Mori, the queen of Japanese fashion. Seth brought his video camera to that event, too. "The store's open now," you can hear him telling Fred, who's still inspecting every last item on display. "You can stop looking at the merchandise." We did $450,000 worth of sales in its first three days.

Tokyo hadn't been open two weeks before we were on to the next major undertaking. We opened another restaurant with Pino Luongo on East Seventy-Fourth Street: Coco Pazzo, "the crazy cook," which proved to be truth in advertising. But that could barely compare to the other news that month. On November 16, 1990, we announced the biggest Barneys opening yet, one that I had been privately plotting and planning on for years. Having established ourselves in women's, we were going to take the fight to our biggest competitors in their own neighborhood. The major battle of the store wars was about to begin: Barneys was going uptown.

Bob had spent the last fifteen months negotiating over the purchase of a huge space at 660 Madison Avenue, nine floors (and two basements) of a midcentury building originally designed for the Gettys. With Isetan behind us—the real estate portion of the deal was 50/50, with Barneys retaining complete control over the merchandising—we bought the space in cash. There was no question it was a shot across the bow at the local competition: Bergdorf's was just down the block on Fifth Avenue, Saks and Bendel's a bit farther still, Bloomingdale's to the east. "It took me by surprise," Arie Kopelman, the president of Chanel, told *Women's Wear Daily* when they broke the news. "It's as if one is looking at the triangle—Saks, Bloomingdale's, and Bergdorf Goodman—and Barneys says, 'I think I'll go somewhere in the middle of you guys.'" That could pose a problem, he noted, for brands used to selling to both us and the uptown guys without ruffling too many feathers. "It won't be an easy and fun process" negotiating distribution, Kopelman said.

The competitors noticed, too. "It sounds like an ambitious program," Bergdorf's stodgy chairman, Ira Neimark, said dryly, "and the Pressmans are very professional merchants."

Now we had two or three years to get it together before a projected opening in 1992 or 1993. Game on.

. . .

In 1992, Steven Meisel (at the time, Barneys' house photographer, more or less), Fabien Baron (Barneys' former art director), and Glenn O'Brien (Barneys' copywriting genius) teamed up with a local celebrity who wanted to make a book of photographs with a little clever, Glenn-ish text. She used to call up Glenn at Barneys to discuss the project, invariably reaching the receptionist, who assumed she was being pranked. "Yeah, right, you're *Madonna*," she'd say, and hang up. Glenn had to sit her down and set her straight. It really was Madonna, he promised her. She had to put the Material Girl through.

Madonna at that time was at probably the height of her fame. If you needed proof that the biggest movers in culture were watching what was coming out of Barneys, here it was—Madonna was hiring our people. She had a long association with Barneys herself. She'd brought a ton of attention to the newly opened women's store when she walked in the AIDS-benefit jean-jacket show right after its opening. After that she was a customer, and a regular. Her friend Sandra Bernhard told me that when Sandy was doing her one-woman show, *Without You I'm Nothing*, off-Broadway, she and Madonna would meet for dinner in the Barneys' café before going off to their respective evening performances.

Madonna loved fashion, and fashion loved her. She had a special feeling for Jean Paul Gaultier, who Barneys had been carrying for years; she called him up two days before one of his shows to ask him to design costumes for her world tour. That *Blonde Ambition* tour, in 1990, changed everything for him: When she wore those famous cone bras (which he'd been making and showing since the early '80s), and his sexy, corseted, men's style suits, he went from famous to world famous. She did him one better when he hosted his own AIDS benefit for amfAR in Los Angeles in 1992, with a runway show that featured the elderly sexologist Dr. Ruth (in a rubber nurse's uniform), Billy Idol, and Faye Dunaway. Madonna wasn't going to let herself be outdone by any of her fellow models. She made her runway walk in a Gaultier suit, then tore off the jacket to reveal not a cone bra, but a frame bra: Just a few straps around her bare breasts. That's one way to raise $700,000.

For most people, that moment—it's a photograph, Madonna and Gaultier hand-in-hand on the runway, that still circulates widely today—would be enough infamy for a year, if not a lifetime. But that wasn't even Madonna's most controversial outing of the quarter. In October, the book she made with Steven, Fabien, and Glenn hit the market, in a print run of three-quarters of a million. It was called, none too subtly, *Sex.*

*Sex* was a sensation. It was billed as a collection of Madonna's fantasies, which included everything from S-M to a bisexual three-way with Naomi Campbell and Big Daddy Kane to hitchhiking in the nude. There was Madonna applying lipstick in bed to Daniel de la Falaise, the son of Saint Laurent's muse and collaborator, Loulou. There was Madonna spanking dancers at the seedy Times Square gay burlesque The Gaiety. It didn't matter that the critics didn't think much of it at the time. ("The Empress Has No Clothes," wrote *The New York Times*, though its photography critic did note that "Fabien Baron designed the book with great invention, somehow managing to vary the layouts for a daunting quantity of tongues and breasts.") The run sold out; it remains a cult collectors' item, if you can get it. The Yves Saint Laurent company reprinted it for the first time in 2022 in a special luxury edition, and in 2023, Christie's held an auction of forty-two prints from the book's 128 pages. (Legend has it Meisel originally shot eighty thousand pictures.) The most popular ones went for over $100,000 each.

I don't remember getting a copy of the Madonna book, but in 1992, my media diet was more *Sesame Street* than *Sex*. Keith was three, and that year, he was joined by Wallis, as beautiful a blond baby as you could ever hope to meet.

I was just happy for Steven, Fabien, and Glenn. Successes like this confirmed Barneys as an incubator of the best talent out there, not to mention that we had a good track record of spotting these people young and early. Fabien had only spent a year at *New York Woman* before I grabbed him for Barneys; he honed his eye and his work at the store and was quickly noticed and snapped up by others, like Italian *Vogue*. By 1992, he was back in New York and was taking on the biggest jobs at brands and with magazines. He was working for Calvin Klein, and redesigning *Harper's Bazaar* to better compete with *Vogue*—its launch issue that September is still one of the most famous magazine covers of the '90s, an elegant Patrick Demarchelier picture of Linda Evangelista with one hand in front of her eye. I hardly need to say that Linda, too, was another Barneys person—in the summer of

1992, she was still our campaign girl. Anyway, Fabien has always been gracious about Barneys and what he learned there. He calls the store pivotal to his career.

So I was glad to see our people go out into the world and make their own names. We had plenty more in our stable. Ronnie was doing a bang-up job with our ads by that time, and all of my focus was on preparing for Madison.

By the time the next round of shows rolled around in the spring of 1993, we were buying *big*. "A Barneys Binge," announced a report from the European collections in *The New York Times* that March. "I woke up singing James Brown's 'I Feel Good,'" I had told Amy Spindler, the *Times* critic, at lunch. "No wonder," Amy wrote in her article. "During last week's showings of fall and winter ready-to-wear, Mr. Pressman was the king of Paris—a retailer with money to spend and an itch to gamble—as he prepared to fill up the racks of the company's Madison Avenue store, scheduled to open Sept. 8." We bought Givenchy and Xuly Bët, an African designer, and Margiela and Ann Demeulemeester and Dries Van Noten, who'd recently expanded his label to include a proper women's collection, too.

We were driving hard bargains. Designers had long managed to keep from having to choose between the department stores and us by pleading geography: They were uptown, we were downtown, and the client, they reasoned, was different enough to justify distributing to both. An uneasy peace reigned. But now we were moving up the block. The uptown stores were pressuring their favored brands not to sell to us; we were pressuring them to sell *only* to us. Alaïa, of course, was loyal, and cut off Charivari when we moved uptown, to their irritation. "I felt hurt because we worked so hard to represent him for so long," Barbara Weiser sniffed to Amy. "We don't have fourteen stores like Barneys."

The press, naturally, went to town: spreading rumors, calling up designers and stores, stoking resentment and gossip. Armani, in a stunning show of disloyalty to the man who had made his name in America, tried to refuse to sell us uptown. But Fred, whose preferred style of combat was tuning it out, wasn't about to take that lying down. The terms of his original contract with Armani seventeen years earlier had been clear: He had the right to sell Armani in New York as long as the conditions of Barneys were no worse than they had been when the contract was signed. There was no arguing we were worse off than we were then—Barneys had gotten better and better. He ended up taking the dispute all the way to a Swiss court tribunal, a three-judge panel that found, unanimously, that the contract was ironclad. Armani was coming with us uptown whether he liked it or not. And he didn't like it—in retaliation, he stopped selling us in Houston and Dallas, which the contract didn't cover, claiming he didn't care for the stores. But where it really counted, he was stuck. Whenever I would see him after that, I used to have one word for him. "Giorgio," I'd whisper. "*Forever.*"

Other brands didn't have those kinds of contracts and could sell or not sell as they pleased. Their loss. Stores like Bergdorf's pressed hard for their advantage, and Chanel and Ralph Lauren declined to sell with us on Madison. That is, if you believe everything you read in the papers. As I remember it, we did have Chanel (though only the shoes), and Ralph (but only the men's). Thirty years later, it's hard to remember exactly where the truth lies. And really, who cares?

We were getting fashion by the armloads. The best designers were getting their own designated areas: Jil Sander. Prada. Hermès. Alaïa. Comme des Garçons. Issey Miyake. Donna Karan. Gaultier. Romeo Gigli. Christian Lacroix. Armani. And on and on . . .

The designers always loved Barneys, because we loved them.
Bonnie and I are here with Vivienne Westwood, Azzie, and John Galliano.

# 20

# POWER TOOLS AT FIVE,
# COCKTAILS AT SIX

## 1993

On Tuesday, September 7, 1993, we opened Madison Avenue. "We" being the operative word. Though it was the Pressman family that tended to be named in the press, like a celebrity clan or a benevolent Mafia, and the Pressmans who everyone whispered would either soar or crash down to earth in a blaze of hubris, Barneys had always been a group endeavor, and never more than with Madison Avenue.

The job took everyone. Like all construction projects, this one looked like it might never be finished up until the moment it was—which was approximately one minute before we opened the doors. "I remember walking through that morning, and thinking there's no way," Roman Alonso, one of our PR guys, told me recently. "Six hours earlier, before the police put up their barricades outside the main door, the store was the architectural equivalent of a Martin Margiela dress," quipped Cathy Horyn, the toughest critic in fashion, in her report on the opening night events. "It was thoroughly deconstructed." We were loading in clothes at the same time as we were finishing painting—always a great idea. Giant pieces of furniture and display were being moved in and around at a hectic pace. At one point, some curved glass vitrine from Europe, hand painted with gold or silver leaf, was dropped onto the mosaic floor, where it smashed into a million pieces. A giant construction worker literally burst into tears.

The staff was working night and day. Alex Koo, a young designer buyer, remembered working into the early morning night after night, going home so exhausted that he fell asleep in the middle of making himself a few dumplings for dinner. "When I got up, the fire alarm in the apartment was going off," he says now. "The kitchen was filled with smoke. My dumplings had turned into stones. For a week, I smelled like smoke. Everyone was like, 'What is the smoke, something smells smoky?' And it was me." The night of the opening, Alex and a number of his colleagues ended up stuck in a women's dressing room upstairs, still in their work clothes, when the party started before they had a chance to run home to change.

The PR team had killed themselves putting the opening event together, in total secrecy, working on it for over a year. That could never happen today, that not a word was leaked. But Mallory Andrews ran her department with an iron fist. From the Mrs. John L. Strong invitations down to the gushers of champagne, not a detail was missed. I let the team know: This had to be huge.

In those days, we didn't give a lot of thought to what people now call "work/life balance." Life was work, work was life, and if you were lucky, you loved both. The *Times* magazine had sent a reporter to trail us for months leading up to the opening for a big, splashy story—a friend inside the paper told me it was meant to run on the cover, though we were ultimately bumped for a story about the sexual harassment scandal of some Oregon senator—and Phyllis put it plainly to him, maybe more plainly than she should have. "I have no idea what other families talk about," she said. "We talk about business."

It was a multifront war. The team worked through the night; we put half the staff up in rooms at the Pierre to ease the burden. We had to finish constructing and merchandising the store. We had to plan for and arrange the party. We had to steward a flotilla of preopening press, a complicated dance of waltzing in journalists to see the space, but only what they were meant to see: small corners jury-rigged up for photographs while construction chaos raged just out of frame, competing reporters kept far from one another. And by the way, we still had fifteen other stores to run, and Japanese partners to be kept abreast of every development.

The night before Madison opened, I took Vera Wang for a tour. Vera was an old friend—she'd been an editor at *Vogue* for years and years before she launched her own collection, which at the time was all bridal. I called her up a few months before Madison opened and said, "Vera, the evening wear out there is shit. You've got do some evening wear for us." She protested and protested; she had only recently gotten bridal up and running, she couldn't do any more. But I insisted, and we bought a tiny capsule collection of eight pieces based on a few quick sketches Vera did. I wanted to show her where they'd go. We went through the whole store—the whole wreck, at that point—and she was shocked at the size and the scale. "Oh my god," she said to me, "what if this doesn't work?"

"Then it's going to go down with the biggest fucking bang anybody ever saw in fashion," I said.

. . .

That Tuesday night in September, the store opened its doors and the guests arrived—at least those who could make it past the velvet ropes.

Bob and me in front of the Madison store construction in 1993.
The entire façade was sheathed in French limestone—just one
of the factors that added up to a $100-million-plus final bill.

In streamed Bianca Jagger, Barry Diller, Barbara Walters, Joan Rivers. Designers flew in from all over the world: towering Hubert de Givenchy and Christian Louboutin from Paris, Rei Kawakubo from Tokyo, Jil Sander from Germany. The locals: Calvin, Donna, and Vera. The uptown contingent, the society gals who the skeptics said would have to be chiseled away from Bergdorf and Bendel's with a pick, came in force: Anne Bass, Gloria Vanderbilt, Edgar Bronfman Jr., Mayor David Dinkins—mayors had long had a thing for Barneys, ever since John Lindsay came to the store's fiftieth anniversary and Ed Koch to the opening of the downtown women's store seven years before. Speaking to the press, Dinkins struck a diplomatic note: "It's a vote of confidence for our city by very smart business people," he said.

New York needed votes of confidence. Though we weren't worried, there was plenty of reason to be. The mood in the city was the grimmest it had been since the near-bankruptcy of the 1970s. The recession that had begun in 1989 hit harder here than it did nationwide: Though the economists diagnosed the national recession as officially lasting only eight months, in the city, the pain was more acute and ongoing. If we were acting like we hadn't noticed, plenty of others had. "This is 1991 and the feeding frenzy of the last decade is a memory," the restaurant critic of the *Times* wrote about Coco Pazzo a few months after it opened, but "behind the narrow, discreet facade on East Seventy-Fourth Street, the recession hasn't happened. . . . The little black dress and the large black turtleneck are still in fashion. Eight o'clock dinner reservations require connections." By the spring of 1992, unemployment in New York City was at its highest rate in fifteen years.

So plenty of eyebrows were raised by Barneys' megascaled expansion plan. The opening was greeted, one observer later wrote, "with the kind of feverish excitement the city normally reserves for triumphant baseball teams and mass murderers." "Damn the economy! Full speed ahead to designer shoes on 4! That's the Pressman family cry," was how *USA Today* put it that September. The headwinds were already starting to blow. No one could miss the stakes. Fred himself put it bluntly to that *Times* magazine writer: On the line was "our whole future," he said. Between the Madison Store and Beverly Hills, which we were working on in tandem in anticipation of a spring 1994 opening, we were effectively doubling our size in two years. We were doing it our way. Or, as I put it at a press conference to announce the store opening: "We only know how to be Barneys." "One suspects he is exactly the kind of person to shake up the old B-line, from Bergdorf's to Bloomingdale's," Cathy Horyn wrote. "And all this, at a time when most retailers wished they owned stock in the Gap."

I was confident—maybe more than confident—but I was also backed up by Bob, who handled all of the numbers, and our incredible deal with the Japanese. "Let the consumer speak," I told reporters when they prodded me. We could afford to take the long-term view: recessions are temporary, and our Madison Avenue agreement with Isetan was a partnership for 499 years.

Who could stop to worry? The party was too huge. If it had just been a cocktail at the store, with this store, it would have been enough. The merchandising, the mix, the custom-made furniture and fixtures, the gorgeous materials, from the French limestone cladding the building to the forty different types of wood inside—it was a marvel. "It's like a movie set of what retailing is," one designer said. Twenty years after leaving Hollywood, I was in the movies at last.

But it wasn't just cocktails at the store, not that anyone knew that at the time. From inside, we led guests, about a thousand of them, through an unmarked door off to the side. We'd discovered it during the renovation. Staff brought guests through it, and into a long hallway. "Where *are* we?" Anna Wintour asked, confused. She, like all the guests, had been led through a secret passageway into the Pierre Hotel, whose ballrooms had been taken over for the occasion.

The teams had spent months designing them to be unrecognizable. We had turned the place into an elegant, time-out-of-mind supper club, inspired by old haunts like El Morocco. Everything had been painstakingly reupholstered in blue velvet—hundreds of vintage chairs and settees, chandeliers were fitted with blue velvet tassels, even the custom cigarette boxes we made with Nat Sherman, distributed by retro cigarette girls, were blue velvet. There were baby lamb chops and caviar omelets, but this was no stuffy seated dinner—everyone ate wherever they could park themselves. Not everyone loved that—Joan Rivers and Hubert de Givenchy, obviously used to stiffer affairs, were annoyed not to be formally seated and left. But everyone else got into the spirit of the thing. We may have finally arrived uptown, but we were doing it our downtown way. We put down a black-and-white checkerboard dance floor and had Johnny Dynell, the DJ from the Pyramid Club and the Limelight, spinning records. Everyone was dancing, everyone: The society dames and the designers, the artists and even a few crashers. I'll never forget looking across the floor and seeing Rei and Jil dancing together. Where else would that ever have happened?

And again: It would have been enough. But it wasn't. A little after 11:00 p.m., the records came to a stop and the orchestra struck back up. And there on a stage built for the occasion was Barry White. We not only booked Barry, but we reconvened his forty-piece Love Unlimited Orchestra, who'd barely been heard from for a decade. Everyone had Barry White top of mind that summer, because the cute pop star Taylor Dayne had re-recorded his '70s classic, "Can't Get Enough of Your Love, Babe." But to have Barry there, Dr. Love himself, in a satin pajama suit and that same old satin voice? The people went insane.

And then (always another "and then"), a woman popped up out of the audience, as if spontaneously. It was Taylor Dayne. She got up onstage and the two of them duetted, his original song and her refurbished hit. It was the most incredible moment. And you'll never see

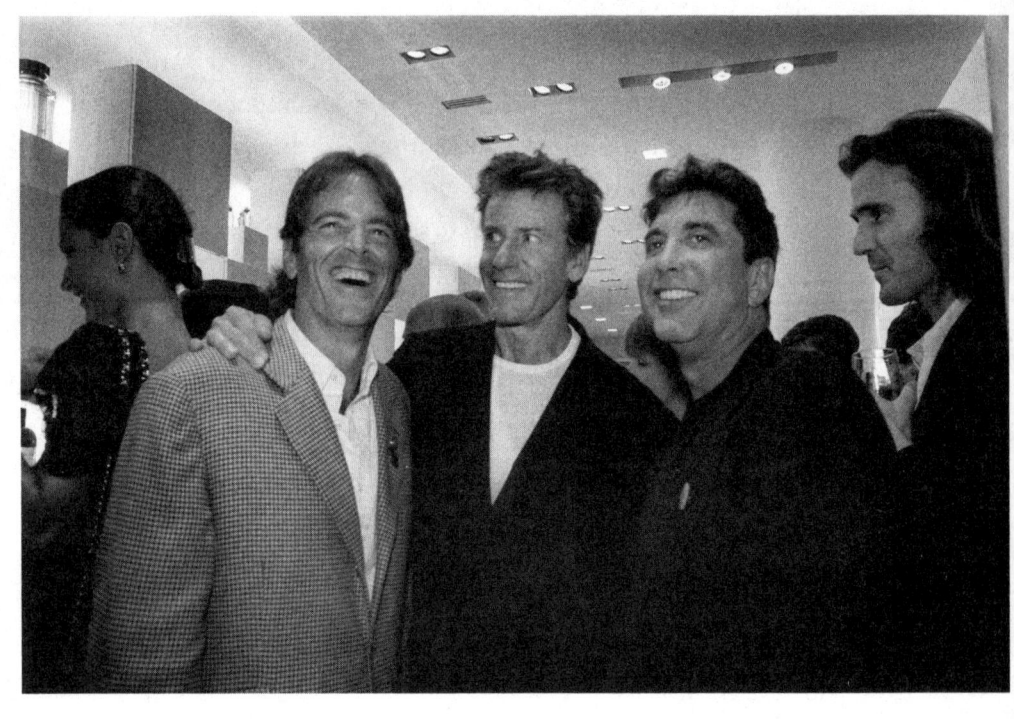

With Calvin Klein and Sandy Gallin, manager to stars like
Dolly Parton and Barbra Streisand, at the opening of Madison Avenue.

Wilt the Stilt hobnobbing at the fragrance counter.
You never knew who you'd meet at Barneys.

Barry White performing at Madison's grand-opening party. We brought in the Love Unlimited Orchestra for this, and surprised everyone with a secret passage to the Pierre Hotel ballroom right from the store.

it. There aren't any pictures of it, none that endure to this day. There's a good reason for that. We dressed Taylor for the occasion in Donna Karan, a gorgeous, sexy gown. But it was sexier than we realized. In regular light, it looked totally normal—slinky, very Donna. No one would've batted an eye. But when flashbulbs went off, it showed up totally transparent on film. She wasn't wearing a bra, and only the tiniest little thong underwear—all of which (and all of the rest of her) could be clearly seen in every photo the few photographers there managed to get. There would have been a scandal. And so, like so much of Barneys' magic, you just had to be there.

. . .

The store was amazing. It sounds conceited, but it's hard to be humble knowing stores just didn't look like this—not anymore. We had gone back to the past, to the grand department stores of the late nineteenth and early twentieth centuries, back when they were glamorous, with their hand-painted counters and ornate fixtures. The old Lord & Taylor (originally founded in 1826), not the mumsy later version. The old Saks (which came to Fifth Avenue in 1924, after being founded in Washington). Bonwit Teller, founded at the turn of the twentieth century. And of course, Fred's favorite of all time, Harrods, the oldest of them all by a hair: founded 1824.

We had the greatest designers and architects working in tandem, long before every Chanel, Dior, and Tiffany were hiring top architects— Peter Marino chief among them—to make their boutiques into luxury palaces. The place was just beautiful, or it was after we made it that way. The building itself, a 1950s Emery Roth office tower, was stripped down and reclad with French limestone. Marino put in bright, open, ten-foot windows—none of the casino-like cluttered claustrophobia of the current-day department stores, designed to keep women shopping like prisoners. Our words for the store were "light" and "airy."

And "fun." "Let's face it, it's got to be fun to shop," Peter opined when *Vogue* came to preview the space before we opened.

The other stores were scared. You could tell. Not because they said so, not in public (though rumor had it that the pressure from the department stores' advertising teams was responsible for getting the *Times* magazine to boot us off the cover). You could tell because they spent the year leading up to our opening frantically renovating and refurbishing their own stores. Bloomingdale's replaced the fifteen-year-old staircases on their ground floor with new ones in white marble. Saks renovated its men's store. And Bergdorf's, or as I took to calling it, Berger King? They affected a sneering non-concern to anyone who asked—"The bulk of their business is being done at price points below ours," Burt Tansky, their chairman, told a reporter—but actions speak louder. Bergdorf's had spent a year redoing floor after floor. The fifth floor was ripped up entirely and rebranded as "5F," a younger, cooler space with trendier clothes, which would have looked to anyone with a brain in her head like a knockoff version of the Co-op.

Who could blame them? This was *big*. Barneys would be the biggest specialty store built from the ground up since the Depression—in fact, since Bergdorf's itself in 1928.

At the front of our main floor, individual boutiques shared space with jewelry. Right up front was one of our great discoveries, the Japanese American jeweler Kazuko Oshima, who wound fine gold wire around what she considered to be healing stones. They were the opposite of mass-produced: Every piece was unique, handmade by Kazuko, who had been a filmmaker before turning to jewelry, and who insisted that each stone had its own vibration and needed to be designed accordingly. Women to this day still tell me how much they treasure their pieces by her, exactly the kind of things you would never find at that time in Saks or Bergdorf's. Kazuko represented Barneys' own spirit.

There was another reason you'd never see her in Saks or Bergdorf's, of course—we had her collection exclusively. She would come to the office multiple times a week, insisting on selecting healing stones for her buyers and checking in to see how they were working. The terrible irony is that Kazuko herself died far too young, in 2007 at the age of sixty-five.

In the back was fine jewelry, in custom glass cases that also housed our famous fish tanks. We thought nothing of sending a member of our display team to Boston to work with an aquaculture company to make sure every piece of coral, every saltwater fish in those tanks was just so. People lived for those fish. (Don't get me started about the time our night-cleaning crew used Windex on the tanks and the ammonia seeped through; we came in one morning to thousands of dollars worth of fish floating at the top of the tank.) Farther back still was the cosmetics section, against the backdrop of a custom mosaic of thirty-two Byzantine-style portraits, offering exclusives like Shu Uemura from Japan, Face Stockholm from Sweden, Stila, and Nars. It was controversial to put cosmetics in the back; usually when you walk into a big store, you're attacked by a perfume spritzer first thing. I *hate* that. Cosmetics is a big money maker, but if people are going to go to it either way, there's no reason to put it front and center (and there's never any person to blast them with a perfume they don't wear five seconds after they walk in the door).

A level below, but open for gawking, was Pino's Mad.61, his new restaurant concept. Lean over the main floor railing of Barneys and you could take it all in, the power-lunchers or the evening suppers, a forty-foot reflecting pool in the center of it all. "It's not seasoned yet," Gael Greene, the famous *New York* magazine food critic wrote when it opened, "But we're all here anyway. Gianni Versace at lunch, Beth de Woody, Vera Wang at a high-voltage table for dinner, Ron Perelman back again, Christie and Billy." (Brinkley and Joel.) Gael loved

The beauty of Madison Avenue. This is the ground floor, where customers could gawk at more customers over the railing at Mad.61, the bustling restaurant downstairs.

the roast chicken with shoestring fries, and focaccia with truffle oil. I preferred the pizzas. Ruth Reichl of the *Times* gave us two stars. "Eating here is fun," she wrote, comparing the restaurant to the "town square of a particularly chic city." "And the food is terrific."

Go up from the main floor, and on two, Phyllis's Chelsea Passage had expanded to the better part of a full floor, filled with Lalique crystal, Georg Jensen silver, vintage hotel and restaurant china, Clarice Cliff ceramics from England, the surrealist faces of Piero Fornasetti. From there, the designer floors began. On three, the more classic designers had their own mini boutiques. Prada. Jil Sander. Hermès. Christian Lacroix. Armani. On four, Alaïa, Donna, Issey, Dries, Gaultier, and Romeo Gigli. A career-woman's floor on five, anchored by Barneys' own label and Calvin Klein—plus a hearty helping of Andra Gabrielle, a Connie discovery she was pouring energy into. Six was sportswear, with DKNY and CK Calvin Klein. On seven, the Co-op.

On eight and nine, we were planning a whole new offering. There'd be a Roger Thompson salon—a new and improved version of the one on Seventeenth Street—and joining it was a Susan Ciminelli day spa, and the part that excited me most: A full-scale gym, developed with Cindy Crawford's trainer, a muscled Romanian named Radu, complete with a sixteen-by-sixteen-foot boxing ring, like the one I had installed in the Barneys' offices for my morning workouts. Barneys didn't have to just be a store, I had decided. It could be—not that we ever used this word at the time, but since everyone does now—a *lifestyle*. It was wellness before wellness. It seemed clear to us, if not yet to everyone else, that the future of style would go deeper than clothes.

Fred's men's store had its own entrance on Sixtieth Street, but it connected to the women's store on several floors, including the main one. You wanted that interaction between the men and the women, who often shopped together. Everyone wants to look at everything, you learn quickly, even if for the women that means looking at the men's clothes, and for the men, looking at the women. I hadn't forgotten my salad days in the early '70s, going to Bloomingdale's on the weekend to pick up girls. A mix of men and women gives energy to a place. Why would you ever separate them?

The men's store, more than the women's, had a feel of a place out of time. Merchandise stretched from the floor to the ceiling, as at the pre-twentieth-century English tailor's. On the main floor, the ceilings were so high that we were able to install a mezzanine, where we did all the made-to-measure shirts. It had the feeling of a private back room, with the zip of a busy store—you could still feel all the traffic on the ground level below. One thing we'd learned from long experience is that a store has to feel lively. Without people bustling around, even the best store just feels dead.

On the second floor was Armani, six thousand square feet of it: Armanipalooza, one of the largest spaces. ("Giorgio, *forever.*") Almost twenty years after Fred had first discovered him, Armani was still a major driver for Barneys, and we prided ourselves on our selection. Above that, more men's clothing and the designer labels. Sportswear and men's Co-op above that. Classics above that—the old Madison Room stuff—and at the time, the best of Italy, Brioni, and Zegna, with some of Ralph Lauren's Purple Label in the mix.

The response was immediate. People flew in from all over the country to see what we were doing. You don't have to take my word for it. Reporters swarmed the store in its early weeks, picking up customer responses. *The New York Times* happened on Shari Applebaum, an art dealer from Los Angeles who "had flown in from her spa week at Canyon Ranch for the store's opening." (Nice life.) "I love the openness," she said, "as opposed to the Bloomingdale's claustrophobic feeling." Or two actresses from California who were "shopping the Co-op floor with an abandon usually reserved for carnival rides." *Women's Wear Daily* clocked shoppers from Chicago, Forest Hills, Millbrook, New

York. Our first day in business, Wednesday, September 8, two hundred people were waiting outside the doors for us to open at 10:00 a.m., and by the end of the day, we had taken in almost $1.5 million. That wasn't a huge surprise; you always get a first-day bump. But sales continued to climb from there. Sales on Saturday jumped up about 30 percent from our day-one high. In our first five days, *Women's Wear Daily* announced to its readers from the cover, we had done $6 million in business, 55 percent ahead of projections.

· · ·

Growing as fast as we did, on as many fronts as we did, it was inevitable that problems would arise. Throughout the whole process, the only disagreement I ever remember us having was about how much space men's should have, relative to women's; Fred wanted more, more, more, more suits than even I thought we could sell. I don't blame him. We each had our own fiefs, and though Fred, Bob, and I were nominally overseeing everything, there weren't enough hours in the day for us to review what the others were doing. In some ways, that was good. When a family works this much together, they need to *not* work together—everybody needs their own niche. But it was all incredibly intense. We didn't have time to supervise anybody else's domain. We certainly didn't have time for personal lives. Bonnie and I were each whirling like dervishes, intersecting only when we'd knock into each other. She was also managing things at home with Keith and Wallis, trying to stay on top of their school projects, keep every ball in the air. I didn't even make it home half the time; I stayed over in the city when late nights became early mornings at the office.

Juggling so many projects—and by the way, under the direction of Bob and his number two, our CFO, Irv Rosenthal, we were *also* opening outlet stores—we found ourselves overextended and our resources strained. The big flagships, Madison Avenue and Beverly Hills, were overrunning their cost projections, as all major building projects do, and leading up to the opening of the store, we had payment problems.

In retrospect, I should have been more aware. Fred was a true left-brain/right-brain genius: He could do Barneys' financials down to the last nickel *and* buy the most exquisite sport coat Italy could make. Bob and I each focused on our lane. I was merchandising. Bob was numbers, and probably wouldn't have cared if we were selling toilet seat covers—it was the sales, not the product, that he loved. How else could you explain his never, not once, coming with me to Europe to see the collections, to tour the showrooms, to see the stuff that made Barneys Barneys? I never understood it. Who doesn't want to go to Europe? But that was his choice, and I decided not to question it.

As Bob and I took on greater leadership roles at the company, we began working more in parallel with less insight into what the other was doing. Our offices were next to each other, and I had a door put in between them in an attempt to connect; Bob had a lock installed on his side that night.

In the middle of construction on Madison, it became clear that costs were spiraling out of control. We had never nickel-and-dimed with expenses; it wasn't the Barneys way. A buyer might fly to Paris to see Azzedine—for an afternoon. We didn't do it to be extravagant. We did it because when people are treated like the best, they behave like the best. Besides, we had always turned a robust profit, so the ends seemed to justify the means. The Madison store might have been our biggest undertaking ever, but I don't remember attending a single meeting laying out a construction or operations budget; Bob and Irv negotiated all the costs. Should I have been more involved? Absolutely. But I assumed they were watching the ball. There was trust there.

Fred, congenitally more cautious than I am, could sense everything wasn't going well. He went to Bob, and reamed him out. "Nobody's watching," he told Bob. "I want Irv Rosenthal to get off everything he's doing. His *only* job from now on is going to be watching the construction expenses of that store." Bob, who hates more than anything on earth to be embarrassed, who would rather sink the whole ship than admit he was wrong, said to his father: "Irv works for me, and it's none of your business." And he slammed the door in Fred's face.

It was a bad omen. And it was about to get worse.

It wasn't that we didn't try to adjust. In 1992, clearly seeing that you couldn't run a global empire of this many stores like the kitchen-table family business Barneys had once been, we brought in a corporate guy to try to institute some order. Though Barneys' financials had always been tightly guarded, Bob agreed to hire an accounting firm to perform an audit. We chose Coopers & Lybrand, a "Big 8" firm, where we were put in the hands of a partner named Charles Bunstine II (formerly Chuck Bunstine). Bunstine had some retail experience—he had started his career at The Limited, and for a time owned a Ralph Lauren Polo franchise—and he'd done well at Coopers. He seemed like a natural fit, and we lured him away to become our chief operating officer.

Things weren't looking so hot for the Japanese, either. A few months before Madison opened, Japan's economy was tanking. Isetan's sales were going down with it, and its largest shareholder was trying to sell its billion-dollar stake in the company to a supermarket chain. Faced with all this, Kuniyasu Kosuge, who had been instrumental to the Barneys deal, resigned. Still, we were bullish. "All projects are proceeding according to plan and we look forward to opening the Madison Avenue and Beverly Hills stores very shortly," Bob told the press. "Nothing has changed," Isetan's American president, Takeshi Inouye, said with significantly more understatement. "We have a contract." Very encouraging.

We did open the Madison store on time, and it was celebrated like the second coming of retail. But within weeks, rumors started to circulate that all wasn't as well as we'd said.

*The New York Times*, which had noted Madison's having to "fight to keep people away," about-faced and, in November, published an investigation alleging that some of Barneys' vendors were complaining of late payment. Keep in mind, we had at that point more than seven thousand of them. Store space had grown exponentially, as did our buys, both in breadth and in depth. None of that is an excuse. Barneys was a major champion of fledgling designers, but those are also the designers who have the most trouble keeping the lights on. Any cash flow issues can be a significant problem for them. And Barneys, which had been run for decades like a small family business as it was becoming a much bigger and more corporate one, had always delivered.

Now we were hitting choppy waters. "Barneys buyers, who are known for discovering fresh talent, are fielding calls from designers seeking payment," the *Times* reported. "The designers say the buyers have become negotiators and apologizers for an unresponsive accounts-payable department." These numbers weren't huge—one designer who was willing to risk her relationship with us by complaining publicly was owed $2,200—but that doesn't make our delay right. We had, in retrospect, become overconfident . . . okay, arrogant. "They've taken an attitude about paying their bills that they pay when they want to pay," one factor, a company that extends credit to designers and manufacturers and then receives payment on their behalf, said. The *Times* reporter had found more than two dozen small companies who had been paid later than thirty days after bills were due.

Two dozen among more than seven thousand is not a huge percentage, but Barneys had an obligation to our vendors and we'd taken our eye off the ball. In a perfect world, they might have extended us a little more patience where possible; a few ornery vendors sued us for payment, which we promptly delivered. But it should never have gotten that far.

Once they smelled blood in the water, other reporters began to circle, even if the story did not seem to hold up on further inspection. "Is it a case of bad cash flow, bad management, or simply bad manners?" *Women's Wear Daily* blared across its cover in December. The paper had to acknowledge that our first-quarter results indicated financial health *and* beat our own projections, but we were nevertheless "haunted by horror stories of slow payments." They dredged up angry creditors—from people who did color work on Barneys ads to the air conditioner supplier for the Madison store—to give colorful, irritated quotes about us. Not everyone would take the bait. Azzedine's sales manager in Paris told them "Barneys is a good client and always has been." Patrizio Bertelli, who ran Prada and was married to Miuccia, can breathe fire when he wants to, but not in this case: "I think the story about Barneys being slow to pay its suppliers is more slander than anything else," he said. But the moral most readers took away from it all could be summed up by one factor's response: "Until I see the checks, I'm holding up orders."

We had to clean up this mess, and fast. We took the rare step of issuing a lengthy statement, explaining that as part of our year of growth, we had hired an accounting firm to audit all of our business practices, and they had found them out of step with many of our competitors— so far, in fact, that we essentially capitalized the businesses of some vendors. We had brought our terms more in line with the industry standard—that is to say, paying later—but you can't expect the companies on the receiving end to welcome that, and we probably didn't communicate the change as clearly as we should have.

Over the next several months, we did everything we could to reassure both our vendors and the business community at large that we were doing fine. We shared updates from our quarterly reports publicly, despite the fact that, as a private company, we had no obligation to do so. Behind the scenes, our lenders and insurers went over everything with a fine-tooth comb and found us shipshape. It wasn't our finances that were the problem; it was that our expansion had pushed our management capabilities to an impossible degree, a situation that took several months to remedy. (Over which time, the press continued to publish tetchy barbs from vendors chasing payment.) The only way forward was contrition. Even Bob, who has rarely apologized for anything in his life, said publicly that he was ashamed and truly sorry. I told the world the truth as I understood it then: We were pulled in a hundred different directions and a few things fell through the cracks. "I was totally dizzy for the last two years," I admitted to Amy Spindler, the *Times* reporter who had published the original story, when she followed up six months later. "The pressure to get this all done was incredible. The whole experience was excruciating."

It didn't matter that even at the time, many companies sprang to our defense. The Barneys-doesn't-pay story had taken root. "They had a lot of difficulty as they changed their accounts receivables system but they are more considerate today than ever because they have gotten so much flak," Barry Schwartz, Calvin Klein's president and business partner, said in December of that year. The same month, Connie announced she was leaving Barneys after almost a decade, to move to Milan and work for Prada.

It would be a change, but probably a good one. Connie was a major talent, but she had become impossible—even the coworkers who shared her office said she'd barely speak to them. Bonnie, who by this time was overseeing all shoes, accessories, and cosmetics, was ready to step up and assume her responsibilities. It wasn't losing Connie that drove me nuts. It was that the reports of her departure didn't miss a chance to twist the knife: "Designers describe Ms. Darrow as instrumental in getting their late invoices paid."

# 21

# LA LA LAND

## 1994-1995

We should have taken more pictures. Thirty years later, that's one of my major takeaways. It always seemed cooler not to. In those days before iPhone cameras and omnipresent social media, when people got together to let their hair down, they really let their hair down. I wasn't going to be the one who stuck a camera in their face and published them the next day on the front page of *Women's Wear Daily*. The only photographer who reliably came to Barneys' parties was Roxanne Lowit, the late, great documentarian of every good party and backstage, who snapped the famous picture of Naomi, Linda, and Christy in the bathtub—she knew everyone, everyone loved her, and only she could get photos like that. Of course *she* came to Barneys' events—but she came as a guest. If we had been more attuned to posterity, maybe we'd have brought in others. We would've committed more of our memories to film. You think at the time you'll remember them forever, but they go so quickly; lightning flashes and then vanishes if you don't catch it in a bottle.

We had an amazing party to bring Barneys to Beverly Hills before the store opened in 1994, thrown by Lisa Eisner, one of my oldest friends in the business, and the fairy godmother of all fashion aspirants in LA. Lisa had been a *Mademoiselle* editor; she and Lyssa Horn, Steve's daughter, worked together there and were like sisters. In the '80s, they both ended up in Paris, where Lisa worked for *Vogue* and Lyssa ran Barneys' Paris office, the advance guard for all of our activities in France, from setting up showroom appointments with fledgling designers at their little garrets to booking out Chez Omar, my favorite Lebanese restaurant in the Marais, for the dinners we'd throw during the collections. There, too: discretion. You'll never find pictures of a Lebanese belly dancer gyrating on top of a table with Azzedine, or sticking her boobs in Rei Kawakubo's stony face. Live and learn.

By the nineties, Lisa (though not Lyssa) was back in the States, having settled in LA with her husband, Eric. They lived in a kooky, rambling mansion high in the hills of Bel Air, higher even than the Bel Air Hotel. Lisa has worn many hats in her day—jewelry designer, photographer, art-book publisher, Ashley Olsen's mother-in-law—but as much as any of the others, she's an incredible connector. She hosted a great party to introduce the Pressmans to the LA crowd in a Moroccan tent set up in her backyard, where all the guests sat on pillows on the ground. Barbra Streisand was there. Diane Keaton. Jerry Bruckheimer. Wayne Gretzky, then with the LA Kings. That part everyone remembers, because he was sitting on one of Lisa's ground pillows, and she accidentally stepped on his hand walking across the room. A few centimeters over and she might've ended his career a few years early.

I was so excited about the store we were building in Beverly Hills. Eric remembers me dragging him out of a dinner we held at Mr. Chow nearby—another "meet the Pressmans event"—after a few too many drinks to see the construction site on Wilshire. I was even more excited because it was freaking out all the department stores there. Our landlord owned both Saks and what would be the Barneys' location next door to it; Saks was about to move out and take the new space, but when they got wind of our interest in the West Coast, they tried to pressure the landlord into not renting us their old one. Big mistake: The guy, pissed off at the attempted bigfooting, sold us the lot next door instead, which we designed and built from the ground up. He could've been a Pressman.

Los Angeles was finally getting cool. The style out there still wasn't on par with New York—and still isn't—but now they were hungry for the good stuff. There were some great boutiques in LA, like Maxfield, where Simon had worked, and a good-enough Neiman Marcus. But nothing like what we built for Barneys. To this day, Bonnie calls LA the prettiest Barneys we ever made. We had been designing three huge stores in tandem—Madison, Tokyo, and Beverly Hills—even before we had any idea whether any of them would be successful. Madness? Probably. But that was how we worked.

I had the idea to do the Beverly Hills store in a Spanish style, as a nod to LA's Spanish architectural influence. But the last thing we wanted was the Disneyland version, so I dragged Peter, none too unwillingly, to Sevilla for an inspiration trip. When we pulled up to the Hotel Alfonso XIII, originally designed in the 1920s, we had an epiphany: This is it. We built the new Barneys in its image, going to insane lengths to get it right. Peter actually put manure on the roof as we were building it so moss would grow, just like it does in Spain. Cascading water features on mosaic walls on either side of the entrance gushed into mosaic fountains. Mission accomplished. It looked like it had been there forever. But we didn't forget where we'd come from, either. In Barney's honor, I made a deal with the Greengrass family of Barney Greengrass, the best appetizing shop in New York, to open an outpost at the store, where all the deli fans and homesick New York expats could go for their bagels and sturgeon. I never forgot my grandfather's upstairs fridge stocked with deli and appetizing, and his regular trucking to the "other" Barney's across town (Greengrass, unlike Pressman, was on the Upper West Side). At Barney Greengrass in Beverly Hills, we had handmade matzah on every table.

In the months leading up to the opening, in the spring of 1994, the whole town seemed to be paying attention. "Wilshire Retailers Brace for Arrival of Barneys in L.A." blared the cover of *Women's Wear Daily* in the fall of 1993. The department store I. Magnin nearby spent that fall renovating and adding younger, cooler designers ("I don't want my organization to become obsessed with Barneys, just with becoming a better store," its chairman told the paper—yeah, right). Saks was struggling through its own renovation. Our name was on everybody's lips. At a Todd Oldham show at Neiman Marcus in Beverly Hills that December, a news reporter overheard someone saying that the audience was "more Barneys than Neiman Marcus." We already had plenty of LA customers who'd fly in to visit Barneys in New York; as Bob pointed out, 10 percent of the population of Beverly Hills had Barneys credit cards.

When the store was finished, in March of 1994—down, once again, to the wire—it was a beauty. Five stories high, spanning almost the full block of Wilshire, right in the "Golden Triangle" where Wilshire, Rodeo, and Santa Monica meet. At 125,000 square feet, it was smaller than Madison, but larger than the downtown women's store, though it resembled its Seventeenth Street cousin, with a majestic spiral staircase climbing all five floors to a grand atrium skylight. If there's one thing Angelenos dream of, it's stardom, and anyone who walked down that staircase felt like she was Scarlett O'Hara in *Gone with the Wind*. A balcony off the men's section looked straight out onto Hollywood. There were Barneys touches everywhere. The mad genius Ruben Toledo, who had worked with us for years on displays, made a sixty-square-foot mosaic for the cosmetics section, cousin of the one on Madison, only instead of medieval portraits, this one had fifty portraits of his muse: his wife, Isabel, one of the designers we carried. Having learned the lesson in Manhattan, we opted for light and space, doing away with walls and installing floor-to-ceiling windows to let in the light. There was a turret like on a medieval castle where we put the VIP department, a literal tower with thirty-foot ceilings. This was the Tinseltown dream of Barneys. We'd arrived.

So had customers. We'd sent out small black Barneys New York boxes filled with coffee beans and a note: "Wake up and smell the coffee." It was a message to shoppers, but also, as a few magazines noted, to the competition. And it worked. On a Saturday morning not long after we opened, two hundred shoppers were lined up by 8:45 a.m., the gossip columnist Suzy reported. Before the day was done, Winona Ryder, Rosanna Arquette, Heather Locklear, Harry Hamlin, and Donald Sutherland had all passed through. (To put it in terms Angelenos could understand, *L.A.* magazine characterized it this way: "By late afternoon, Barneys' army of valets had parked more than 3,000 cars in lots as far as five blocks away.") Within a few weeks, early signs remained positive. "Barneys' black has struck gold in Southern California," *Women's Wear* trumpeted in April, and sales were 20 percent ahead of plan. Barneys California—it almost had a ring to it. Bunstine started telling people we were looking up and down the coast, and thought we'd open in San Francisco within the next five years.

· · ·

We'd gone LA. Can you blame me? Los Angeles was a city I'd always wanted to conquer, having passed through many times on my way back from Hong Kong with Lance. I had even started to think again about trying my hand at making a film. I spent a good while with Ray Manzarek, the keyboard player for the Doors. I'd taken him to see the Hagler/Leonard fight on the big screen, trying to sell him on a feature about The Doors—eventually, Oliver Stone beat me to it. Ray told

The exterior of Barneys Beverly Hills, our most beautiful.

The ground floor at Beverly Hills, and the stunning staircase that let every client feel like they were getting their Hollywood entrance.

Let the light shine in.

me a story about when he and Jim were film students at UCLA. Jim gave him a bunch of poems he'd written and asked him to perform them. Ray told him, "You wrote 'em, you sing 'em."

Los Angeles was no New York, but it was very amenable to Barneys. Years later, many of the town's biggest fashion people—the stylists who dress up stars for the red carpet—revealed that in that often fashion-challenged town, it was at the Wilshire Barneys where they'd first discovered this or that designer. Young stylists would come to the store just to experience the best European clothes up close, to see them and touch them for the first time.

We did adapt a little to our new environs. Glenn came up with new, LA-ified lines for our local ads, which we put up on billboards on the Sunset Strip: "For Lucy, meditation was not enough." "Cliff wanted understanding but he would settle for residuals." Some of the local flakiness may have set in. In those days, the thing to do when opening a new store is partner with a local charity to host a big event: Make nice with the hometown grandees, bring in some likely customers. But we accidentally irritated the wealthy do-gooders of LA by dragging our feet on picking one. I guess we ended up pissing off a few people—I learned as much from the *Los Angeles Times*. "Not even a note saying, 'It was very nice meeting you,'" a local charity worker told the paper.

Whoops. We had too many options, and I wasn't exactly unhappy about being the hot new commodity in town. I remember running into Barbara Davis, who was one of the big society matrons of LA, at a restaurant, the fall we opened. I was with two new friends of mine, Bret Michaels, the long-haired frontman of the rock band Poison, and his girlfriend, Pam Anderson. (This was before she was with Tommy Lee.) We were having a good time—Bret asked me to come on tour with them, and if I'd been twenty years younger, I would've. But when I saw Barbara Davis sitting nearby, I knew I had to go over and kiss the ring. She immediately started in on me about partnering with her

Carousel of Hope ball that she threw to raise money for juvenile diabetes. Everyone told me, if you don't play ball with her, you'll never survive in Beverly Hills. But I never was into her, and as she looked over at my table, between Bret and *Baywatch* blond Pamela, I had a hunch the feeling was mutual.

We couldn't stay long to chat. We had places to be that night: Specifically, the Playboy Mansion, for an AIDS benefit at the mansion organized by the New York club doyenne Susanne Bartsch. This was quite possibly the gayest party ever held at the mansion, before or since. It was a bunny fashion show, called "The Hoppening," at which most of the bunnies were men in drag; only a few, like Pamela and Roseanne Barr, were women. Local designers created bunny costumes for them, and a judging panel—Phyllis Diller, Cheech from Cheech and Chong, Debi Mazar, and a very pregnant Elvira, Mistress of the Dark—eventually crowned Roseanne the winner. She wore a gray silk bunny suit by Richard Tyler, the red carpet designer. Judy Tenuta played the emcee. "Are there any straight people here tonight?" she asked from the stage. "Pick up the courtesy phone!"

There were two, at least: me and Hef. I'd sometimes wondered what it would be like to party at the Playboy Mansion—every boy has—but when I got there, the reality left something to be desired. The Grotto? More like a cesspool. Every infection that ever lived and died must've taken a dip in those waters. ("You can smell history in there," one drag queen quipped.) If amoebas could talk. . . . Hef himself was no better. I took my seat for the fashion show, and found myself next to Mr. Bon Vivant himself. Paisley bathrobe, velvet slippers, greasy hair, and smoking a pipe. I *hate* pipes, but live and let live—it's his house. But I was smoking a cigar—I never was without one, in those days—and he had the nerve to say to me, "Could you please put that out?"

"Sure," I said to him, "when you put yours out." I never did get invited back.

. . .

In short order, Barneys Beverly Hills was going full throttle—this was not a piddling Barneys America, but a major flagship like Seventeenth Street or Madison that extended Barneys' reach in a major way. This was the "shot heard round the Golden Triangle," as one local magazine put it. "I take Barneys very seriously," the general manager of the LA Neiman's, told them. The store was a real boon. Designers who had been loyal to us for years, and appreciated Barneys' particular POV, now had a way to build their businesses in Los Angeles. Store events that had at one point been one-offs became national tours.

In the fall of 1994, Rei Kawakubo launched Comme des Garçons' first perfume, and selected Barneys as the exclusive US store partner. True to Rei's essential weirdness, the perfume—unisex, a new idea at the time, just like Calvin Klein's ck One, which also debuted that fall—came in a squished-looking bottle modeled after a whiskey flask, that couldn't stand up and had to lie flat. It was also a peculiarly pissy shade of yellow. We launched it twice, first in New York, then in Beverly Hills, each time with parties, and Kawakubo herself in attendance, as well as a number of oversized clear-plastic bags filled with yellow perfume as decor. ("They resembled mastodon-sized bags of urine," Simon recalled.)

It was an unusual evening in Beverly Hills. The party at the store had been a typical Barneys mix of all and sundry. Peggy Moffitt, who'd made Rudi Gernreich's breast-baring swimsuits famous back in the '60s, came. So did Harry Dean Stanton, the Bassett-hound-looking character actor, who Rei had cast in some of her menswear shows. And so, Simon remembers, did Kato Kaelin, uninvited. This was November 1994, in the midst of the O.J. trial, and the world—and most especially LA, where the whole thing was unfolding—was obsessed with the tawdry details, not least thanks to the blockbuster testimony of Kato, O.J.'s deadbeat couch-crasher turned star witness for the prosecution. For one brief second, Kaelin was about as big a star as you could find in LA at the time, and here he was—not that Rei seemed to have any idea who he was, or care.

Afterward, we gave her a dinner at Chasen's, whose red leatherette booths had been a cheap-and-cheerful Hollywood staple for decades. She loved it—and she loved Simon's suggestion for the remainder of her stay in LA. Something gave him the insane idea to send her to Frederick's of Hollywood, the old lingerie shop on a trashy stretch of Sunset Boulevard. He later heard that she stayed there for hours, pawing over every bra and garter.

We were getting a foothold. The next February, we brought the Warehouse Sale to LA for the first time, filling up a hangar at the Santa Monica Airport with deeply discounted stock. "The most famous sale in New York and possibly the world is now in Los Angeles," our ad in *The Hollywood Reporter* informed Angelenos. "It's so enormous it's in an actual airplane hangar. Thousands and thousands of hangers hanging in one hangar." (In classic LA style, we provided driving directions: "Take the 10 or 405 Freeways. Take Western. Take Pico. Or take a plane.") Bargains weren't all that was on offer, either. "It's the best place to meet single men," a woman who'd been a New York Warehouse Sale shopper told the *Los Angeles Times*, advising readers to hang around the ties to offer single guys fashion advice.

Ritzy LA types are no different from their New York counterparts: They all love a bargain. The LA Warehouse Sale never became the legend that New York's was, but thousands of people used to tromp to it all the same. By the second one the following year, the papers had gotten the idea to send reporters to see who was sniffing around the thirty-thousand-square-foot hangar, and they spotted Paramount boss Sherry Lansing, Linda Evangelista, Liv Tyler, and Al Pacino.

We kept hosting great events, too. The July premiere of Isaac Mizrahi's doc *Unzipped* that summer, for example, with Isaac receiving compliments with Cindy Crawford on his arm, Sean Penn chatting up Dennis Hopper, and a mad rush to secure and destroy the security camera footage of . . . well, let's just say a few famous guests misbehaving in the back office. Isaac absolutely refused not to smoke indoors—he smoked *everywhere*—and once he did, everybody else did, too. Roman Alonso clearly remembers Parker Posey walking up the grand staircase, sniffing, and asking, "Is that smoke I smell?" He braced himself for a meltdown as he said yes. "Great," she said, and pulled out a cigarette. Our laissez-faire attitude had a way of adding up: We were fined by the Beverly Hills Fire Department for that party, *and* we had to power-wash all the brand-new limestone floors.

Back in New York, where the books were kept, I'm sure some eyes were rolling at our excesses. Isetan had essentially written us a blank check to buy and build the big stores on Madison, in Beverly Hills, and in Chicago, and in exchange, we would pay them rent. But the store projects got bigger in the building of them, and not always because we had to have mosaics or forty types of wood. Met Life pulled out of the upper floors of 660 Madison Avenue, leaving us on the hook for the whole building. The city of Beverly Hills demanded that we build a five-floor subterranean parking structure for the store once construction had begun. We had to keep spending to get it all done. But we were riding so high, we didn't care. Besides, the Madison store was off to a great start, and LA was, too. I was sure money wouldn't be a problem.

More than a year after opening, we did finally host a major black-tie event: the annual Fire & Ice Ball, benefitting one of LA's top cancer hospitals. The ball was the brainchild of two LA heavies, Ron Perelman and Lilly Tartikoff, whose husband, Brandon, was an NBC exec—he's the one who originally signed *Seinfeld*. (And he would die of cancer a few years later, much too young at forty-eight.) We loaned them the Beverly Hills store for dinner and dancing for twelve hundred people. Wolfgang Puck served salmon; Olivia Newton-John gave a speech about her recent diagnosis of breast cancer.

Though no one knew about it yet, it was a cause that hit close to home. Earlier that year, Fred's customary tirelessness had finally started to fail him. He had always had stomach trouble; he'd never complain, but you could see things were churning. We always assumed it was because he was a thinker, and a worrier. But his stomach began bothering him more and more, and he was losing weight. A few visits to the doctors revealed the terrible truth. In early 1995, in the midst of major expansion, Barneys' greatest champion and innovator was diagnosed with pancreatic cancer, whose five-year survival rate was then around 4 percent.

# 22

# CHRISTMAS FROM HELL

## 1994-1995

Back in New York, we hadn't anticipated anything out of the ordinary for the holiday season. Holiday windows are any big store's biggest canvas, and one of the biggest marketing expenditures of the year. Back when everyone shopped in person, rather than online, the holiday season was when you had the most bodies through the door, most eyes on the windows, and most sales at the register. (For retail, it's still generally the most important quarter of the year.) Every year, Simon had to outdo himself on the holiday windows, especially once they became a destination in their own right.

With his excellent team—especially his trusted deputy, Steven Johanknecht—he made the most surreal and hysterical kind of magic. Most store windows are mannequins wearing dresses. Simon's were political commentary, guerrilla theater, high comedy. The windows were his canvas, and he was an artist—probably the greatest window artist the world has ever known. The windows were, as people would say, "very Barneys." Tourists would visit them like any other museum.

Simon working his magic in the windows,
hanging with "Prince" and "Madonna" in 1992.

In the early days, I think Mallory would approve window displays, but within about six months, Simon had carte blanche. Nothing was off the table—which I loved. In 1988, there was a "Twelve Days of Christmas" theme, which in Simon's mind meant Nancy Reagan leaving the White House (two American Airlines tickets in her hand) surrounded by geese a-laying (one of whom was laying a Dan Quayle egg). Another, four "calling birds" on bright telephones, running up a huge phone bill. Another, twelve bongo drummers drumming.

On and on it went. There was the Halloween window with the guillotine, a clever play on the fact that many mannequins are (already) headless. Another with a glamorous lady in evening wear being chased by zombies. One spring, a combination *Edward Scissorhands*/Lorena Bobbitt window—maybe not a reference that resonates with people today, but one of the biggest news stories of 1993, about a distraught housewife who got revenge on her asshole husband by cutting off his schlong. To Simon and Steven, that suggested a gardener (it was spring!) with enormous shears pruning the "twig" from a man-shaped topiary.

None of it prepared us for the shitstorm of Christmas 1994. As Barneys became more known, not only downtown, but now uptown, across America, and around the world, we found we could become notorious as well as renowned. Barneys' success could put a target on our backs: People were watching what we were doing, and not everyone liked what they saw.

That year, we'd come up with the idea to turn the windows over to artists, who had long been Barneys inspirations, customers, and collaborators. The theme would be red, and we'd ask artists—visual artists, fashion designers, more than three hundred in all—to make any piece they chose, as long as it incorporated red and was (at least, by their lights) holiday appropriate. We partnered with Christie's to do a silent auction of the artworks that would run through the holidays and conclude at the end. To bid, shoppers would go into either the uptown or the downtown Barneys and pick up a red telephone. The proceeds would go to the Little Red Schoolhouse, a historic school nearby—anything for the theme—and to the Storefront School, in Harlem.

Artists had been pivotal parts of Barneys' displays and windows before—think of the artist-designed Levi's jean jackets we auctioned off for St. Vincent's, or the Statue of Liberty windows we commissioned while the downtown women's store was still under construction—and nothing seemed to raise red flags here. By late summer, the artworks were beginning to arrive, from the likes of Brice Marden, Francesco Clemente, Alex Katz, and Nan Goldin, not to mention our old friend Robert Rauschenberg.

Also included was an up-and-comer called Tom Sachs. Today, Sachs is a major blue-chip artist, who shows at Gagosian and sells out Nike sneaker collaborations. But at the time, he hadn't even had his first gallery show; he was a twenty-eight-year-old who Simon and the visuals team sometimes hired to work on displays or installations. (He had previously made racks for Barneys' Alaïa section, welded with 23,000 pennies.) Sachs was obsessed with consumer culture—a good fit for Barneys, you'd have thought—and the way that we all worshipped brand names like gods. For his piece, he created a crass, commercial Nativity. Playing the part of the three wise men were three little Bart Simpson dolls. The McDonald's logo featured prominently. And standing in for the Virgin Mary was a doll Sachs had made that combined Madonna (the pop star, rather than the Holy Mother) and Hello Kitty . . . legs spread, nipples (six of them) exposed. It had a profane bite, but it felt silly enough to be harmless. It was Pop Art for a new generation, a piece that Warhol would've recognized and probably loved, had he not died years before.

All the earlier controversies had boiled down to basically nothing. Maybe we had a few complaints about the condoms on the Christmas tree in the Magic Johnson holiday window. For all the politics involved—ah, the Christmas where Simon cast Senator Jesse Helms as "Censor Claus" with Bigotry, Homophobia, and Censorship as his loyal reindeer—most everyone got the joke. The worst of it was the occasional letter, some of which did get pretty nasty: "Dear Mr. Doonan, I would like to see you fired from your present position and rehired as the men's room attendant. . . ."

Not this time. This wasn't even Simon's doing—he was a curator, not the designer—but Sachs's window caught the attention of the local, and then not-local, Catholic zealots. A conservative radio host, Bob Grant, took to inveighing about it on the air, and in no time, TV stations and networks were sending camera crews to Madison Avenue. We set up a war room in the PR department, which was fielding constant calls. Fred parked himself in PR with the rest of us, listening nervously and demanding constant updates as they all tried to convince the press that the whole thing was a nonstory.

We found ourselves in the midst of a First Amendment battle. Should we stand by the right of artists to express themselves—we didn't feel we were endorsing anything, after all—or bow respectfully to the strong feelings of the devout? Letters were one thing, but then the phone rang with a credible threat: Some wackjob said he was going to bomb the store. I made the call—we had to act. We removed the offending Nativity from the window—just in time to make the cover of the *Daily News*. ("Reaction to Nativity is frank, incensed, not mirth": I hope some headline writer got a bonus that day.)

Half of the reactions seemed to be coming from people who had never heard of or seen Barneys, let alone this window; now we were getting the aftershocks of these cranks' hell-raising. We took the rare step of buying a full-page ad in the *Times* to apologize and explain: This had been a charitable project, the artwork was one of 309 donated, the cause was just, and our intent had never been to offend. "We wish you a most joyous holiday season," it concluded.

Naturally, it didn't end there. A number of artists were furious that we'd pulled the piece and accused us of everything from cowardice to censorship. Andres Serrano, who had likewise run afoul of the religious right when he made his famous work *Piss Christ* (basically what it sounds like), was more measured than most when he opined in the pages of *Newsday* that our "capitulation to outside pressure from a small but vocal minority is unfortunate but not without its precedents." (He did get Tom Sachs on the phone, who called us "wimpy" and accused us of wanting the "glamor of art without taking the responsibility that goes with it"—a little stronger than the meek apology he offered when the *Times* had called him a week or two earlier.)

The storm eventually passed, but I think it shook Simon up pretty good. If only it were the worst of our problems. Though we didn't realize it at that moment, going into 1995, Barneys was about to enter its annus horribilis.

·  ·  ·

In January of 1995, we announced major news—though we left out the real news. That was Fred's pancreatic cancer. You don't want any kind of cancer, but you *really* don't want pancreatic cancer: It's a relentless beast, totally merciless. Fred still walked the floors of Barneys, petting the jackets and buttonholing anyone who would listen about ticket pockets and canvas linings. But the family business was now bigger than the Pressmans alone: It was a multinational, nationwide empire of flagships, Barneys America stores, and outlets, with two thousand employees, doing millions in business every year. Barneys would live on after Fred, just as it had lived on after Barney, and we had to prepare for that. To begin the new year, what we announced was the promotion of Charles Bunstine to president. What we didn't announce was why.

I think the promotion was Fred's idea. He was tiring more easily than he used to, and the baton was—without so many words to this effect—

# HE DOCTOR IS OUT

**nton fires Surgeon General Joycelyn Elders**
**sex-in-school remark – SEE STORY ON PAGE 2**

# DAILY NEWS

SEVENTY·FIVE·YEARS
1919·1994

## NEW YORK'S HOMETOWN NEWSPAPER

Saturday, December

# AWAY WITH A MANGER

BILL TURNBULL DA

cene in Barneys holiday display window portrayed the Virgin Mary and Baby Jesus as cats and the three Magi as Bart Simps

## rneys yanks tasteless Nativity from windo

### SEE STORY ON PAGE 3

quietly being passed. More and more he was limiting his presence at Barneys to roaming the traffic-heavy floors of Madison Avenue, doing what we joked was a hit-and-run: Swooping in to help a men's floor customer, never introducing himself as the store's owner, then disappearing as instantly as he'd appeared. But he knew that Bob and I weren't getting along, and if he wasn't going to be there to keep the peace, he wanted assurance that someone would be.

This was a sea change. Bunstine's appointment marked the first time in Barneys' history that a nonfamily member was near the top of the food chain. He not only was meant to referee between me and Bob; he was also supposed to insulate us from the day-to-day operations so that we could think about the big picture. All of the company, including all of the merchants, would now report to him, and he would report to us. People who used to have unfettered, direct access to me or to Bob suddenly had a new boss.

That included Simon, who had been almost my right arm, hashing out details of displays or installations as we jogged together around the Tuileries during the Paris collections. It included Peter Rizzo, who ran men's merchandising and was nearly a son to Fred—he would one day give one of his eulogies. It even included Phyllis, Mrs. Pressman herself, who was not exactly used to explaining herself to outsiders. Still, we put a responsible spin on the whole thing. "I think family businesses make the mistake too often of not realizing that the family can't do everything itself," Bob said at the time. "We've done that ourselves sometimes. But the family really needs to have other partners they can trust working with them, and Charles really meets that need for us."

The problem was, Charles just wasn't "Barneys." He hadn't been raised in it the way we had—dyed in the wool, as it were. If Fred's word for Barneys was "charm," with all the ineffable, unquantifiable aura that implies, Charles's was "efficiency." He was an accountant type, and he was going to run Barneys like a business. But Barneys—though it was responsible for millions in sales, and plenty of careers—wasn't anything as staid as that. Department stores were only businesses. Barneys was Barneys.

Charles wasn't afraid to jump in headfirst. But he had neither the feeling, nor the experience, to take on as much as he did. He eliminated senior executive meetings, blocking off the access to the Pressmans that Barneys executives had always appreciated—that was one of the signal differences between us and Bergdorf's or Nordstrom. (Ira Neimark, may he rest in peace, was not exactly approachable.) He even got involved with our vendors, negotiating without the finesse or understanding that had always characterized those relationships. We may have driven tough bargains with many of the labels we carried—plenty of snide things have been written in the press about me demanding certain margins or whatnot—but we always did it with great affection and respect, as well as the absolute knowledge that these people were great talents. Suddenly they were sitting across the table from a bean counter.

We were—it seems clear in retrospect—drunk with the possibilities of expansion. We couldn't believe the amount of money still being thrown at us, all without any equity position in Barneys, Inc., separate from Barneys America. The Japanese were drunk, too—on ambition, it seemed. That had been the fellow feeling I recognized in Kosuge when we originally were negotiating the deal. Like me, and like Bob, he had inherited control of a multigenerational family company and was eager to modernize and expand it, looking to the United States for direction. Did he have the same fire I had, to take his birthright and make his own mark on it? Those are deeper conversations than you have on the golf course, where the deal was done. But if I had to guess, I'd say he did.

But Kosuge was no longer in charge of Isetan, not since his resignation in 1993, and it was becoming clearer that it was less a resignation and more his being strong-armed out of day-to-day operations by the board. The Japanese stock market was down by double digits, and we weren't the only US acquisition that was costing more than anticipated—the Japanese ended up having to take a haircut on Rockefeller Center, too. But whereas before we had been dealing family to family with the Kosuges, now we were dealing with a bank. Banks, in my experience, don't care all that much about charm.

Add to this that we were experiencing significant cost overruns across the board—construction issues, real estate issues, the still-frosty retail market—and the Japanese partnership became a little less handshake-between-friends than it had been. Bob had always dealt with a Japanese counterpart he called "Panda," because of his looks—he and Bob could've been brothers—but Panda had been shown the door at some point. He'd inadvertently overseen some very expensive mistakes having nothing to do with us, I think. I stayed out of it. I was marketing and merchandising a newly national (and growing) network of stores, and Bob, as ever, worked removed from the rest of us. We still sent Isetan our requisition bills, and they still got paid, without comment as far as I knew.

I did know that our cash flow needed shoring up. For over a year at that point, Bob had been taking out a series of short-term loans from the Japanese to keep the gears turning. Isetan realized it had a vested interest in giving us what we needed, even if it was none too pleased to do so, but they did demand one thing in return, as I learned with a cold shock when Bob summoned me to our lawyers' office one day. The desk was piled high with reams of paper, a contract it would have taken a week to read. "Just sign it," Bob told me. I don't sign things without reading them, I told him, so he summarized it for me: As collateral for this loan, we would be giving personal guarantees—pledging our own personal fortunes.

I hit the roof. "I am *never* signing this," I seethed at Bob. "This is total bullshit. Business is one thing, but I'm not going to jeopardize my family." But Bob was icy calm. "Don't worry," he told me. All of our assets—our shares in Barneys, the real estate—were protected in trusts and had been for years. We could sign personal guarantees, but the Japanese would never be able to break into the coffers. Besides, he told me, we really have no choice.

I'm not proud of this, but I signed the deal. The money started flowing again—for a time.

But the debt continued piling up faster than we could pay it off. It was a toxic mix of our rent bills (the form our debt was taking to the Japanese), overruns, expenses, and interest on top of that, and it was a recipe for disaster. Sometime in the spring of 1994, Bob had begun speaking, maybe more ominously than he intended to, of a "global solution" that would solve all our problems with our new partners at Isetan. He'd conceived of an arrangement to swap our debt for equity.

This was a Rubicon. We had never wanted to give up equity in the mother ship, and the Japanese, by some miracle, had never asked for it. But we had to steady the ship. We believed in the value of the company, and so did the Japanese. This was a way for them to buy into that belief. So when Bob started to float this idea to his counterparts in Japan, they were interested. We started to feel a sense of relief, thinking there was light at the end of what had become a darkening tunnel. Giving up part ownership of Barney's business was a growing pain, to be sure, but we figured it was better to own a percentage of a thriving company than the entirety of an untenable one. Fred's position, as I recall it, was a sad but resigned, "Let's get this done."

Deals like this don't get done quickly. Both sides bring in their bankers, their accountants, their highly paid advisers. And in a point that would turn out to be the linchpin of a multiyear legal battle, Isetan agreed—whether they agreed to *negotiate* swapping the debt, and our future rent, for equity, or whether they agreed to actually swap it depends on who you asked. We would check in with Bob from time to time to ask, how's it going? When are we going to close this deal? He always indicated that it was going well and just takes time. I allowed myself to believe that—and for all I know, it may have been true. But as 1994 turned to 1995 without an agreement, I began to grow uneasy. Why was this taking so long?

. . .

Over that year, many of Barneys' most loyal employees began taking the headhunter calls they received constantly more seriously. Ultimately, many of them chose to leave. It was a hard time in the business, and a hard time at the company, and that's not entirely on Charles. The burnout rate at Barneys could be high, given our celestial expectations, and opening Madison, LA, and more had put all of our staff through the wringer. Many of them had been with us for years, and were ready for a change. Cycles are regular in the business. But many of the people who had made Barneys what it was began to drift away.

Mallory Andrews, who had overseen the publicity department, resigned in September, when Charles promoted Simon, adding publicity and store design to his already significant portfolio. Ronnie Cooke left us for London in December of 1994, moving to be with her new boyfriend, Jonathan Newhouse, one of the scions of the Newhouse family that owned and ran Condé Nast, the publishers of *Vogue* and *Vanity Fair*. (I'm convinced I introduced them; she's not so sure. Either way, she soon became, and remains, Ronnie Cooke Newhouse.) In March, Glenn made for the exit. He'd been with Barneys for a decade, and had been responsible for some of our greatest campaigns, and of all the people who have made their mark on the store, his imprint was one of the most durable. "I wanted to do some different things," he shrugged to *Women's Wear*.

Simon, bullishly, opined that "Change is the essence of this kind of business. I'm looking for new blood to replace both he and Ronnie Cooke." He did note that Glenn's final campaign was "marvelous": our return, after several seasons of only Delhomme illustrations, to photography, and to non-models who were real-life Barneys enthusiasts. That was the spring we had a young, pre-*Daily Show* Jon Stewart in our ads ("So, you found a salesperson you like," the headline reads, as he browses ties with an absolutely gorgeous girl). We also had Richard Johnson, the Page Six gossip impresario. Who else would've? His fellow columnists had a field day. "I've been thoroughly corrupted now," Johnson told the *Times*. "I don't think you'll ever read a bad word about Barneys in this column." (He clarified that there was no real conflict, because he didn't cover retail.)

During Charles's tenure as president, the departures continued: top-tier merchants as well as marketing execs and divisional managers. Barneys had been built on people being clever and finding ways to make a lot with a little—Charles's attempts to institute order put a stop to a lot of that. The PR department, for example, had the genius idea to get Barneys' name out there *and* generate some income by allowing the store to be used (sparingly) in film and TV, like the *Seinfeld* episode that aired to millions of people in December of 1994. (Elaine shrieks that Barneys has "skinny mirrors"—could there be better press than that?) Previously, the PR department had been allowed to keep the money they made from these bookings. They worked hard for it, spending all night at Barneys with the *Seinfeld* team, since we weren't about to close a section of the store during shopping hours, and eventually, spots like this provided much of its annual budget. Now Charles was taking that money away.

Through 1995, the negotiations with the Japanese continued. Bob was going overseas more frequently, but no resolution had been made, even as the interest on the debt kept accruing. In November of 1995,

Bob headed back to Tokyo, and this time, unable to ignore the problem any longer, I went with him.

Relations between us and Isetan had cooled, and there was no mistaking it from the treatment we received in Japan. At our first meeting—I don't think we even went to our hotel first, it was straight to their offices—we were ushered into an enormous boardroom. We were faced down by a room full of executives, many of whom we barely knew, who scolded us like children. The next day, still jet lagged, we were back to their offices to meet again, where they ushered us into a tiny office—it reminded me of a dentist's waiting room, so small you basically had to open the door to change your mind—and left us there on our own for hours, like a kid's "time out." We waited and waited. They brought us soda and crackers, like prisoners. It was absurd; if we weren't so fucked, it would've been funny. Bob was used to that kind of treatment—on one visit, he'd been made to sit on his own for twelve hours, from 9:00 a.m. to 9:00 p.m.—but I wouldn't stand for that, even from people who could put a heavy thumb on the scale of our fate. I didn't want to go nuts—the walls were thin—but how could Bob have let it go this far? I walked out and played tourist in Tokyo, checking out department stores instead. We were there to work, and to me, scoping out the competition was more work than whatever we were meant to be doing in a tiny Isetan office.

That trip ended up resolving nothing. The Japanese decision was a nondecision: "We have come to an undecided position," they told us. I celebrated my forty-fifth birthday that month with my fate hanging over me.

Still, I was sure we'd pull it out in the end. Barneys was Barneys and always would be—these were accounting details, embarrassing to be sure, but footnotes to history. (As I've always said, accountants are 99 percent right, and 100 percent useless.) I couldn't square this existential crisis with the customers that still flocked to Barneys' stores, customers so attached to Barneys' name and what it represented that they used to steal our monogrammed paper towels from the bathrooms.

Back home, it was business as mostly usual. After a year of searching (every step of which was covered by the trades as tea leaves to be read), we were about to sign a lease in San Francisco. In New York, we kept up our busy schedule of events—we honored Helmut Newton in September, for some reason or other that I can no longer remember—and made headway even with the most recalcitrant holdout. Ralph Lauren, who'd let it be known publicly that he wouldn't be selling to Barneys uptown before Madison opened, had thought better of his opposition. Fred had wanted Ralph Lauren for years before he finally cracked him, then we'd undergone a two-year hiatus, and now, in December 1995, we were able to announce that we'd become too good for Ralph to refuse—again. His highest-end men's collection would come to the store in January and women's would follow soon after that.

The Japanese, it seemed clear, would also come to realize that we were too good to refuse. Wouldn't they?

# 23

# NOT SOMETHING FOR EVERYBODY, BUT EVERYTHING FOR SOMEBODY

## 1995-1996

For Christmas 1995, I took my family to Hawaii. We all needed to get away. Bonnie and I hadn't been getting along, and as if that weren't bad enough, she'd been diagnosed with breast cancer. The treatments, though successful, had put her through hell. But I was so focused on keeping the company going that—despite an outward show of bluff confidence—I could barely pay attention to anything else. The ongoing talks with the Japanese had totally broken down—they were keeping us in a holding pattern, the sword above our heads—and work was like a constant migraine. I'd clearly been neglecting Bonnie and the family, and I'd prepaid about a zillion nonrefundable dollars for this villa in Hawaii. So we treated it as an opportunity. We brought the kids—Keith was six, Wallis three—and three other couples. None of them knew what I knew: That a few days earlier, the Barneys board had voted to file for bankruptcy right after New Year's.

I felt like shit, but I didn't show it. I've always been able to compartmentalize—I'm probably better at it than is good for me—and no one knew what was going on. I golfed my way through the holiday as usual—my old friend Tomio Taki, the co-owner of Donna Karan, who would become one of our bigger creditors, had no idea anything was amiss when we played a few holes in Honolulu. In between golfing and beaching, I spent every day on the phone with Bob, who had spent Christmas in his war room, strategizing, trying to figure out what the hell would happen next. I think some part of him even *liked* this shit. He didn't just want to declare bankruptcy. He wanted to sue Isetan, too.

On New Year's Eve, Bonnie sat me down. "It's not working out," she told me. "I think we should get a divorce."

I wasn't shocked. We needed more than a Hawaiian vacation could fix. We had been growing apart. I loved Bonnie, but work had slowly supplanted our marital relationship. When it was good, it was great, but as things began to turn, the hot water we were in boiled. It was difficult to be stressed out together at work and stressed out together at home. We tried to keep it going as long as we could. But we had run out of road. I was heartbroken and also, to be totally honest, a little relieved.

It felt like the capstone to a terrible year. I'd always been lucky—absurdly lucky—but the fabled Pressman luck was starting to turn. My marriage. Bonnie's breast cancer. Fred getting sicker and sicker. The stores. The press. The Japanese. Even our *dogs* died, for Christ's sake.

But it was New Year's Eve on a beautiful island a thousand miles from our problem. We went out for dinner, blew the horns, wore the hats. I'm sure it was incredible. I barely remember it. The worst was still to come.

· · ·

"Bombshell by Barneys," read the cover of *Women's Wear Daily* on January 12, 1996—bright red letters over a black-and-white photo of

Though we kept up appearances—like some party in the Hamptons we attended in 1993—Bonnie and I were drifting, and our marriage was coming to an end.

the Madison store. Inside were no fewer than three articles about the shock of the year. (Granted, the year was only twelve days old.) We made the front page of *The New York Times*, too.

We filed for chapter-11 bankruptcy protection in the Southern District of New York. It was literally an eleventh-hour filing—down to the wire, filed at the home of the bankruptcy court clerk just before 11:00 p.m. We had missed January rent payments to Isetan, and the grace period built into the loan was set to expire Wednesday, January 10. Had we not filed that night, Isetan could have started foreclosure proceedings on Madison, Beverly Hills, and Chicago.

Bob and his team had secured debtor financing with Chemical Bank to put $100 million into the business while we hashed it all out in court, and we insisted—honestly and correctly—that the business itself was sound. Sales were good. We had some $350 million in debt, yes. But I'm proud that despite the significant sums we owed to banks and insurers, we owed much, much less to the designers and labels whose work we championed. And as many people as complained about us, plenty of others supported us. "Their sales, sell-throughs and margins, appear to be that of a healthy company," the president of one of our many vendors told a reporter who came calling, no doubt looking for blood. "Their business appears to be solid going forward. It's more a matter of difficulties with their Japanese partner." "Everyone on the street should take up a collection for Barneys, for what they've done to retailing up there—look at Madison before and since Barneys opened," said the president of Christian Dior. And we didn't even carry Christian Dior!

The hope was that this filing would allow us to renegotiate our partnership with Isetan, to force them to stop dithering and proceed with the debt-for-equity swap they had been interested in for months. But Bob and his team went one step further, suing Isetan to recoup $50 million in payments that had already been taken out of Barneys. The intention may have been good, or good enough—our cash reserves had been dwindling—but it would have been hard to infuriate Isetan more. They turned around and immediately countersued us for repayment of the emergency loans, $168 million in all—the ones we had personally guaranteed.

The Japanese were apoplectic, and any veneer of civility they'd once shown us dissipated overnight. "The attitude of Barneys management up to this stage is totally deplorable," was their official statement, released to the press. Soon enough, commenting duties were taken over by an Isetan vice president named Michio Jomori, who had a real way with cutting remarks. "We believed our partners in a family-run business were talented and serious, but they turned out to be lacking," he told one journalist. "Thinking back on it now, we did make a mistake."

It didn't matter that the wave of Japanese investment in American companies from Japan's hyperprosperity in the late '80s was now running aground everywhere. Mitsubishi Bank, now pulling the strings at Isetan as its managing team (it had been one of Isetan's largest shareholders, and our new "friend" Michio Jomori had been a director at the bank), had already sent Rockefeller Center, another American trophy turned albatross, into bankruptcy. Matsushita, the Japanese electronics giant, who had bought MCA (which put out records, movies, and books, and ran theme parks) for $6 billion in 1990—at the time, the largest Japanese buyout of an American company—had basically washed its hands of MCA and walked away. Sony, the Japanese company that had bought Columbia Pictures for $3.4 billion in 1989, had been losing money for years and was telling anyone who would listen that they'd overpaid.

It also didn't matter that we still had a business to run. Basically the only thing Barneys and Isetan agreed on was that Barneys had to keep going: We had declared bankruptcy to get out from under impossible obligations, not to tank the company, and Isetan, which still had the license for Barneys in Japan, had a vested interest in keeping that brand strong, even before the $616 million we owed them. And we had every intention of continuing on. We had a network of stores to keep stocked, and a die-hard customer base that counted on us to stock them. I hated that the merchants, who had always been pretty well guarded against the finance side, were getting panicked calls from their vendors, many of whom were as shocked by the news of the bankruptcy as the merchants themselves. (One of my great regrets is that they had to find out about it from the papers, not from us.) We were many of our vendors' single biggest accounts. It wasn't only bad news for us if we went under.

I became very familiar with the truth of the old expression, "when it rains it pours." The pile-on was immense. Anyone who ever had a gripe with us aired it publicly, and anyone who'd ever had even a passing interest in anything we had, took the occasion to pounce. People I thought were friends started calling up our employees, offering exit plans.

More than I'd ever realized, there was an underside to Barneys' insistence on the finest of everything, the joy we found in seeking out and offering our customers the most beautiful things in the world. It was selective by design—remember, "Select, don't settle." That was a world away from Barney Pressman's own motto; he used to say, "Sell to the masses, not the asses." (That one never made it onto the radio.) I knew which side my allegiance fell on. But there were, I came to understand, some people who took Fred's and Barneys' relentless pursuit of the best for elitism.

We never really minded that. Barneys' buyers bought for Barneys' customers, not for everybody on earth—you don't have to be all things to all people, you just have to be the best things for *your* people. "We didn't really care if you wanted to shop with us," Sandra Constantine, our brilliant accessories buyer, says now. "You either were a customer or you weren't. My husband was an attorney, and we would have to go to these attorney dinners. I would be talking with the people and they'd say, Oh, are you an attorney, too? And I'd say no, no, I'm not an attorney—I wouldn't go any further because I didn't want to go down that road." But eventually, she'd get badgered into telling them what she did, and they'd shriek, "Barneys? I can't find anything in that store. Everything's small and everything's black." And Sandra, bless her, actually said to them, "You know what, maybe it's not the store for you. Maybe you'll do better at Saks. They'll have a better selection for you." I love that woman.

All of a sudden, anyone who had ever felt un-Barneys had their own bully pulpits to explain why we were the problem. To the editors of *Chain Store Age*, we were insufficiently respectful of the shame that should attach to bankruptcy. ("If ever there was an example of how bankruptcy filings have lost their ability to stigmatize a company, but rather are used as proactive strategies, the filing last month by Barneys New York was it.") Any customer who had ever felt poorly treated could find a receptive audience for his message. We were targets personally—all winter, a *Vanity Fair* correspondent was asking everyone I knew about me, and *Crain's* had a reporter who seemed to have a particular bone to pick with Bunstine—and we were targets collectively. No one seemed more gleeful about it than the *Times'* hotshot columnist Maureen Dowd, who took a break from skewering the Clintons (Bill was running for reelection that year) to skewer us.

"I had always been a little intimidated by Barneys' imperious manner," she wrote. "But emboldened by the news that it handles money with less skill than I do, I headed to Madison Avenue to gloat." Gloat she did. She needled the sales staff, demanding to know why Prada wallets cost so much, and what the words on certain ID bracelets we were selling meant. (Granted, this explanation is coming about thirty years too late, but "Reir" means "to laugh" en español, Maureen.) I don't think she was ever much of a Barneys customer, but that didn't stop her from coming by to be nasty in the biggest newspaper in the country, maybe the world. "I no longer needed to pretend that I wasn't appalled by $1,345 Comme des Garçons brown jackets covered in black netting that don't make you look at all Comme des Jeunes Filles," she wrote. Maybe it's just not your style?

Barneys' devoted partisans sprang to its defense. One woman wrote a letter to the editor explaining that Dowd had misunderstood Barneys and why so many, in the letter writer's own word, "worship" there. "It is not a question of cachet," she went on. "Barneys carries original, inventive and appealing clothes and shoes that defy description. For shoppers beaten down by the bow blouse and pastel parade of 'mid-level' designers who populate major department stores, Barneys is an oasis of renewal. . . . Barneys regulars are praying that it survives." Lynn Yaeger, the fashion columnist for *The Village Voice* and a devoted Barneysite (right down to the Connie Darrow-ish rouge roses on her cheeks and little bob, though Lynn's is more Mamie Eisenhower than Louise Brooks), wrote a whole page on how at Barneys, the "most imaginative clothes in the world—Westwood, Gigli, Gaultier, Alaïa, Margiela, et al." are all "just hanging there, not even chained to the racks, waiting for you to feel them up and try them on as many times as you want, without ever having to buy a thing." Barneys was an ecosystem and a library—if you wanted to know what was happening in fashion, whether you ever put down a credit card or not, Barneys was the place to go.

But if the *Voice*, that scrappy downtown rag that had been the bible of the avant-garde, was David, the *Times* was still Goliath, and Dowd's reach was far greater than Yaeger's. All of the merchandisers and marketers on my team were fuming: We were working as hard as we could to keep Barneys going, and some Washingtonian (Dowd lived in DC) was helping herself to cheap shots. She had complained about the prices, and someone at the store came up with an idea: Send her a list of the many things we offered at rates she might find more reasonable. She had complained that if Holly Golightly had come to the store with her ten dollars to spend, she'd be laughed off Madison Avenue, so we enclosed a ten-dollar gift certificate. We invited her to tour the store with Simon, one of our most charming ambassadors, and hear about our traditions of quality, of innovation.

That was a mistake.

"Barneys is disappointed in me," Dowd wrote in a follow-up column in February. "Barneys thinks I'm a philistine. But Barneys is not without mercy. The emporium of hip was willing to take me in hand and educate me." She wasn't impressed by Simon, though she did call him "slyly funny." But she wasn't laughing at the printed list he gave her of 2,197 items we sold for under ten dollars. She felt like "Holly Gocheaply," she wrote, sneered at the Miyakes and the Gaultiers, and decided to mail the ten-dollar gift certificate back to us: "They need every dollar they can get."

The hits kept coming. We were in and out of court, debating over every detail with Isetan, and, as if that wasn't enough, Bob and I got hauled into the Manhattan DA, who was having a poke around, too. (I sat for one interview and was never asked back.) We were negotiating with an employee's union, with a panel of our incensed creditors (some of whom began, in a panic, selling our debts to vulture funds), and fighting to focus on the bankruptcy proceedings at hand while Isetan, in a fury, was still trying to sue us personally for repayment of the loans we'd guaranteed ourselves. We were selling our stakes in most of the Pino Luongo restaurants. Fred's health continued to decline precipitously, as he watched the store he'd dedicated his life to slipping out of his grasp.

In May, I was blowing off some steam on the golf course in Westchester, or trying to. One of my partners that day was my friend Steve Florio, the CEO of Condé Nast. For whatever reason, Steve thought he should bring me an advance copy of the new *Vanity Fair*. He probably was trying to be nice.

Inside was the article by the reporter who had spent months tailing me. Over ten pages, she eviscerated Barneys, pointing out every misstep and wrong turn, and placing all the blame on one person: me. I was "bringing down Barneys," as the headline put it, and had "wreaked havoc on the family business—and on the family as well." Isetan's side of the story was taken as a given—there was good old Michio Jomori, happy to tell the magazine that we weren't to be trusted—and while Bob was "stodgy," "socially awkward," and without "the sensitivity to the product, or to people, that you have to have to be good at this business," this particular story had a public enemy number one, and his name was Gene. This reporter even tracked down Barney's widow, Isabel, who told her my grandfather was rolling in his grave.

We couldn't take any more. I didn't care about myself—OK, I didn't care about myself *much*—but I couldn't bear what this was doing to Fred. He was getting worse and worse; by this point, he was mostly confined to bed in Harrison. Through it all, he remained his gracious self. He believed we'd still turn it around. But he deserved an exit on a white horse—not this.

The lawyers had all told us to say nothing, to keep our heads down, not to argue our case in the press—why, when we could pay them hundreds of dollars an hour to argue it in court? But our silence was accomplishing nothing but letting the other side have the last word. That was the message from the crisis management guy we brought in, a heavyweight consultant named Michael Sitrick.

Sitrick advised us to start talking—fast. He knew an editor at *New York* magazine who he trusted to be fair, and recommended that we bare both our souls and our ledgers. We did. We spent hours with the guy, showing him as much paperwork as he could handle to prove that, while Isetan may have been right that we had fallen behind on our obligations and overrun our costs on the three major stores, we had kept them informed of all of that—the numbers had all been there on the page, and we sent them plenty of pages. They could yell all they wanted about not knowing, but—at least as far as what Bob showed the reporter—they could have, and should have, known it all. The press had been saying for months that we'd overexpanded, that the Barneys America stores weren't working, and that, in our hubris, we assumed everyone across America would want what Barneys shoppers in New York and Los Angeles wanted, just because we said so. But all of the Barneys America stores save one were profitable—we didn't only show those numbers to the magazine, we had to submit them to the creditors panel, too, with legal repercussions if they were found to be inaccurate. They weren't. Some of the Barneys America stores weren't making a *ton* of money, but every one except Short Hills, New Jersey, was in the black, and we closed that one that same year.

The article got in a few good digs at us—I was arrogant, Barneys was snooty—but it was fairer than most everything else that was out there, and a lot was. There were weeks when *Women's Wear Daily* would have two, three, or four Barneys stories. It felt good to get our side aired. As the article pointed out, there was speculation that Isetan was interpreting the numbers in a way slanted to its own benefit, too. We still thought—foolishly, perhaps, but we did—that this was a painful phase, but a phase nonetheless; we'd get through it, and continue on. The thought of not running Barneys was inconceivable to us, and we weren't the only ones who felt that way. "Observers indicated that the Pressmans are too integral to the operations of Barneys to push them out, and there is little chance that they could be separated from the company . . ." *WWD* reported in February. "I still feel like it's this exercise," I told the *New York* magazine guy about our ongoing litigation. "I don't know why we're doing it; why can't we just keep going?"

By the time that article came out, it looked like the exercise might be nearly over. "Barneys, Isetan May See Case Solved by Summer," headlines read. The whole dispute boiled down, essentially, to a real estate issue: It wasn't feasible for us to pay Isetan the rents we owed on the Madison, Beverly Hills, and Chicago stores. We had been pushing to restructure our deal with them for years—weren't they trying to be in the retail business, not the real estate business?—and were optimistic we would finally, if painfully, come to terms on how. There were two proposals being considered. We'd sweeten and lengthen their license in Asia, and they would either forgive the rent debt and accept a minority equity stake in lieu of future payments, or take no equity and continue as our landlord, but with renegotiated rents that would be $10 million annually, down from $24 million.

We weren't out of the woods yet, but I was hoping we were close. It had been a hellish few months as Public Enemy Number One, at the same time as I was going through the early stages of divorce, trying to be there for my kids, and, by the way, trying to keep a multimillion-dollar retail empire aloft, with all the attendant drama that entails. (Somewhere in the middle of all of this, Azzedine went ballistic because we were carrying Hervé Leger, a designer he was convinced was ripping him off. That problem, at least, was easy enough to solve: Bye-bye, Hervé.)

Any free moment I had, I spent at the Westchester Country Club. At least on the golf course, I could turn off my brain and focus on my swing. One day, I was playing with Al Pirro. Al was a local lawyer; his then-wife, Jeanine, was the district attorney for Westchester County. We socialized with them a bit, long before Jeanine's bizarre Fox News era—she had a habit of leaving parties just when they were getting fun, so as not to see anything a Westchester DA shouldn't.

We got to the tenth tee, right in front of the clubhouse where everyone was eating lunch. On cue, Al took out his flip phone—the first ones had been introduced that year—and answered it. I begged him to turn it off. Al went on and on and finally said, "He wants to speak to you." I told him, "I'm not talking to anyone. I'm playing golf." But he wouldn't take no for an answer. I took the phone.

Donald Trump was on the line. "Gene," he barked. "I understand things aren't looking good for you right now."

I said, "Donald, I can't talk to you now." But he wouldn't take no for an answer, either. "You gotta tell me something, you gotta tell me," he kept saying. He wouldn't get off the phone. Okay, I finally said to him, what do you want to know?

"How much debt do you guys have?"

I barely knew the guy. I was sure our lawyers wouldn't want us making small talk about it, but on the other hand, numbers were flying in every newspaper day in and day out. The truth was, if we didn't settle the Isetan dispute, or find a new investor to buy them out, we'd be in the red for hundreds of millions of dollars, between what Barneys owed and what we personally had guaranteed—which Isetan was still pressing for in state court, separate from the bankruptcy proceedings.

I sighed, and told him.

Trump just laughed. "Ah, that's nothing," he bragged. "I've got more."

I hung up the phone.

# 24

# THE BAND BREAKS UP

## 1996–1998

Sunday morning, July 14, 1996, Fred died. He was at home in Harrison, exactly where he wanted to be—no hospital at the end. His family was around him, and I got to see him one last time before he went, one last chance to tell him that I loved him and that I was so grateful for the perfect life he'd given me. Even with all the shit roiling us at that moment, I wouldn't have changed a thing. I remember it so clearly: Early that morning, I'd been sitting on my dock in Larchmont, trying to enjoy a rare minute of peace. There had been a storm—Hurricane Bertha, a category 2 hurricane made landfall in North Carolina two days before, sending heavy winds and rains all up the eastern seaboard—but it had passed, and out on the water, everything was calm and beautiful. That's when the call came to the house that Fred's last moments were near. It was as if Bertha had come to take her son home.

Sixteen months after his diagnosis, Fred's suffering was at an end. The greatest men's merchant of his generation was

Fred goofing around with Tom Kalenderian, one of his dearest
and longest-serving merchants, at Lock & Co. Hatters of London.

gone, at the age of seventy-three, a full twenty-three years younger than his father before him. Barney had been gone less than five years.

The papers the next day celebrated him as a hero of his industry. "Transformed Barneys into Designer Mecca," read the cover of *Women's Wear Daily*. His life's work had been to celebrate not only design, but designers—"The problem comes when manufacturers get hold of their ideas. The manufacturers water it down," he had said—and the designers paid him tribute. Even his competitors acknowledged his preeminence. Fred was "the gold standard" other retailers measure themselves by, the chairman of Bergdorf's said. In a prime window of the Madison store, Simon placed a tribute: a single mannequin wearing Fred's never-without Burberry raincoat.

Phyllis received beautiful letters from across the globe. "His enthusiasm for me and my work was crucial to my career, for which I will always be indebted to him," Giorgio wrote from Milan. "I am proud of knowing both of you, and honored," wrote Jean-Louis Dumas, the chairman and CEO of Hermès. "Fred will be remembered not only for his vision in the business world, but for his integrity, personal style, and wonderful generosity," from Ralph Lauren. Decades' worth of employees and collaborators, from Jack Byrne to store associates, wrote to her, too. The coordinator of Barneys' summer youth program, which gave neighborhood kids their first job for some twenty summers running, recalled the philanthropic side of Fred, one he rarely talked about—he just did it. In later years he made the participants a promise: If they graduated from high school, all they had to do was bring in their diploma, and Barneys would send them off with new clothes for college or their jobs.

At Central Synagogue in Manhattan, we celebrated Fred's life. If the measure of a man is what he leaves behind, Fred was a giant. A thousand people crowded in for his funeral service. Calvin and Donna. David Dinkins, the former mayor, and Robert Abrams, the former attorney general. The presidents and CEOs of Bergdorf's, Zegna, Brioni, and Condé Nast. Anna Wintour. Gabriella Forte, who twenty years before had dialed up Armani for the first time from a listing in the Milan phone book at Fred's behest, and went on to become one of Armani's most trusted lieutenants. Nancy spoke. Peter Rizzo, who'd spent eighteen years working as Fred's right hand, spoke. Fred's doctor, Moshe Shike, recalled his grace, remembering that when he was at his sickest, he managed to send handwritten notes to five of his physicians, thanking them for his care.

And I spoke. Of course I did. My concession to the occasion was a black suit, but my hair was down to my shoulders, and I kept my sunglasses on, so no one could see my tears. I eulogized him as a brilliant mentor and a best friend, whose greatest mission had not been to expand and improve on his father's store or to build his own legacy, but to ensure his family's happiness. "Maybe you and Barney can now open a branch upstairs," I said.

Back in Harrison, we sat shiva, where Jews greet guests for seven days after a burial. I barely remember it. We were all in a haze, sleepwalking through grief. Guests came, people ate. The one thing I do remember is Nancy's husband, Ken, the oncologist, going upstairs to speak to Phyllis, where she was resting, and then summoning the rest of the family. Three days before Fred's death, Phyllis had taken a few hours to go see her doctor. Right before the shiva, Ken had gotten a call. Phyllis had breast cancer.

"You are bringing her to me at Sloan-Kettering tomorrow," Ken told us. "The surgeon's already in place. It's out tomorrow."

When it rains, it pours.

. . .

Meanwhile, the Barneys battle raged on. For every step forward, there seemed to be an equivalent setback. We would agree to a two-month grace period to negotiate, we'd get nowhere, it would run out, we'd be back in court. Isetan won the right to pursue Bob and me personally for the guarantees we'd made, and did, with relish. Once it wrote down $33 million in debt in May of 1996—on top of $300 million in losses—the tenor changed. The back-and-forth in legal filings and the press got more vicious; Kosuge even got kicked off Isetan's board. (Or resigned, if you believe what you'd read in the papers.) I still believed we would set things right. The rose-colored glasses my charmed life always kept perched on my nose hadn't slipped yet, but they would.

Our debt was still trading on the vulture market, where companies would offer creditors pennies on the dollar in cash for their debt holdings, giving those owed money a choice: Accept less now without risk, or wait for a full payout that might never come. In an encouraging sign, the price for our debt was ticking up—the market was hopeful our situation might improve. We also were getting bites from potential buyers both at home and abroad. Some of these bidders may have just wanted to get a look at Barneys' books, which anyone with an even halfway serious claim of interest was entitled to do. We, who had always been a private company, who had barely ever let a non-Pressman look into the ledgers, were now open to anyone with a lawyer on retainer.

Saks was sniffing around, behind our backs and in partnership with Isetan, in a deal that came to naught. They were chasing Neiman's, *their* biggest competitor, and not only would Barneys help elevate their "dowdy" image (that was the press's word, not mine), but Saks and Barneys together would be about Neiman's-sized. Neiman's considered a bid, too.

The best option, as far as I was concerned, came from Dickson Poon, of the Hong Kong-based Dickson Concepts, which had made a fortune licensing European luxury brands in the Far East. He owned franchises and licenses for Hermès, Chopard, Ralph Lauren, and Escada, and in 1991, he bought Harvey Nichols and turned it around. Harvey Nicks sold many of the same labels as Barneys, and it had a history and legacy we liked. Dickson Concepts had also taken a stake in one of Isetan's Japanese competitors, which I didn't hate, either.

I could recognize some of myself in Dickson. He was one of the major players in Hong Kong. He was young, he was hungry, he liked the finer things—he'd been educated at English boarding schools, had a taste for fine wine, had been married to a former Miss Malaysia named Michelle Yeoh, the future movie star. I thought it could work. He was eager to get into the US market—he'd been interested in Bloomingdale's a few years earlier when its parent company went bankrupt—and he guaranteed the Pressmans' future involvement in the store, though what that involvement would look like was still to be hashed out. Was I naive enough to believe that? Didn't matter. When we began talking to him that horrible summer of 1996, he seemed like a sort of salvation. We were taking hits on all sides, and the Pressman name was getting dragged through the mud everywhere. Even Bonnie came in for it. As a Pressman, she was destined to be excommunicated, and she was demoted by Bunstine and whoever the highly paid turnaround expert of the moment was, despite her enormous impact on the store and its success. Peter Rizzo was promoted to oversee women's, at my suggestion. The powers that be wouldn't have even known who to appoint.

The months wore on. We were allowed to submit our own reorganization plan, and the court set a date for outside bids. The creditors—our creditors' committee, plus Isetan—would consider the options and make a decision. It would come in July of 1997, a year after Fred's death. That same month, we made the decision—I should say, the decision was made for us—to close Seventeenth Street. It wasn't the original America House, Barneys-by-Barney—the lease on that had finally expired in 1996, and in our crunch we gave it up to Loehmann's, which brought, once again, discount goods to Seventeenth Street. Now the beautiful store we had worked so hard to build in 1986 shut its doors. We closed a few other stores at that time—in Houston, in Dallas, in Troy—but none of those hurt the way that Seventeenth Street did, for us and for the neighborhood. We had been one of the cornerstones of Chelsea. Eulogies began appearing. "Those of you who thought Barneys New York was all about buying things—hah!" a woman wrote in the *Times* that summer. Barneys had been, she said, "the genesis of fashion as we know it today. . . . You philistines, you naysayers can have your Loehmann's. I still have my memories." The one street in New York I avoid when walking around is Seventh Avenue and Seventeenth Street. My girlfriend Christine—now my wife—says the only time she's ever seen me cry was when I had to hand over the keys.

When the buzzer for bids sounded, there were a few offers, the best of them being from Poon and from Saks. But neither of them valued Barneys as highly as both the Pressmans and the creditors thought it should be, or hoped it would be—at least $300 million. Saks bid $260 million, in cash and stock; Poon, $247 million, in cash and convertible notes against future equity or licensing. It came down to gut, not numbers, and we decided to proceed with Poon. Yes, we would be getting into bed with another international retailer, but Poon seemed to have the appetite for risk and the vision that Isetan's recent Mitsubishi-controlled operators did not. The stakes were truly existential, and we were tantalizingly close to pulling it off. Bob wasn't exaggerating when he told the *Times* we were "thrilled to death with this deal"—though what he meant was, we'd be dead without it.

Still, the numbers were lower than we might have wished. Dickson Concepts would pay $78 million for a 51 percent equity stake in

Barneys, and pump in $127 million of financing, to be converted into equity or repaid, plus an additional $42 million to be repaid by royalties from Isetan's use of the Barneys name in Asia.

Isetan had to accept it. Part of the bankruptcy negotiations prevented them from unilaterally squelching any bids, but that also put our fate in the hands of the creditors' board. And after months of negotiations, and a signed agreement, the board decided they couldn't stomach $247 million. In May of 1998, they vetoed the deal, offering an alternative plan—led by two distressed-assets firms that had bought up much of the debt—to take Barneys out of bankruptcy and assume control of it themselves, valuing it at around $290 million.

That May, the creditors' committee, the vulture funds, and Isetan agreed to their final deal. Isetan would accept $25.6 million, and the creditors would own 93.5 percent of Barneys in its new era. The outstanding debt would be converted to equity, and Isetan would be Barneys' landlord on the flagships; it received full control of the Japanese Barneys stores, and as part of the overall agreement, the debt we'd personally guaranteed was wiped out. But the Pressman family, which had once owned Barneys outright, would retain just a tiny fraction of our former treasure.

We had shot the moon, and ended up flying too close to the sun.

No single failing brought us to our predicament. We had been willfully blind, we had shown hubris, we had striven for excellence without considering that excellence comes at a cost. We had trusted that being the best was a business strategy unto itself, but business is more complicated than that. Once again, Bob and I had been the kids in the basement, me playing with the band onstage, Bob minding the cash box. I should have paid more attention to the money. He should have cared more about the art.

I knew that Barneys would rise from the ashes again. Whatever the finances were, however hamstrung we had been by unforeseen expenses and unexpected changes in the economy and in our partners' executive leadership, we had built something unbelievable. That was clear from the interest that it continued to generate. Everyone wanted a little bit of Barneys' magic mix, from the curious investors to the long succession of money men, turnaround "experts," bankruptcy specialists, and lawyers who volunteered themselves (at great expense, naturally) to cure what ailed us. They were ravenous for a little of Barneys' shine. And though few of them had any great ideas about what Barneys was and how to help it thrive, almost all of them found they loved rubbing elbows with Barneys' starry customer base and helping themselves to Barneys clothing allowances for Italian-made suits.

But as for me, I was exhausted. It had been a battering three years, and after Fred's death, I felt unmoored from Barneys and what we'd created. As part of the buyout deal, Bob and I stepped down from the company and accepted contract positions, as did Phyllis, Nancy, Liz, and Holly. But I was already drifting away. I had always been focused on moving forward, forward, forward, and it was clear that Barneys was going forward in a different direction. Tom Shull, who was made president in 1997, came from *Macy's*, for Christ's sake—by way of West Point, no less. "Adding a soupçon of business strategies from Macy's, where he was executive vice president for two years, Mr. Shull insists that none of the creativity will be hurt," wrote the *Times* in 1998—yeah, right. "The new mantra—'customers are guests in our home'—is borrowed not from Neiman Marcus, the leader in customer service among luxury retailers, but from Target."

. . .

Our consulting contracts, which on their face seemed generous, were in reality strategic on the part of Barneys' new owners. They barred us from doing or saying anything disparaging about the company and, what's more, from working for any Barneys competitor. Shull et al. knew that they couldn't dispense with our connections and our taste. For all the bad press that had spent years tarring us—me especially—as arrogant, many of the companies we'd worked with knew Barneys and the Pressmans to be synonymous. "We hope to continue to work with the Pressmans," the wholesale director of Hermès said at the time. "Maybe they had that little oops, but the franchise is so strong."

For years, we'd been trying to save the family's place in the institution at any cost: giving up equity, giving up majority equity, closing Seventeenth Street, anything and everything to survive. But we had finally come to accept that the Barneys we knew, or at least the place we had in it, was gone. It passed, in many ways, with Fred, even though he didn't live long enough to see the final resolution.

In a way, I was glad he died before knowing what would become of Barneys. He was always very hopeful, and I'm sure he figured it would come out OK. But then, his cup was always full. He taught me charm, and charm goes a long way.

The best of Barneys, the people who truly knew what made it special, had all been taught by Fred. Many of them, happily, stayed on, and stayed on for years. Peter Rizzo, for one, who had been his closest deputy. "We are all world-class merchants today, thanks to Fred, and we believe these qualities to be our treasure," he said at Fred's funeral. Tom Kalenderian, who had walked into the store in 1979 and never left—not until the bitter, bitter end much later, at which point he had served for forty years. Judy Collinson, who'd arrived as a little vintage-shop girl and went on to become the head of all women's buying. In contrast to the revolving door of executives, they were the heart and soul of Barneys. But those other trainees of Fred's—me,

Phyllis, Bonnie, the rest of the family—there just wasn't a place for us anymore. The spirit had changed. Those who stayed, like Simon, were tamped down. The winter of 1997, *WWD* ran an item about holiday windows, noting that "this year, Barneys New York has traded its trademark sarcasm and satire for *fashion*, of all things." When the humor went, the nail met the coffin.

Leaving Barneys was unimaginable. Yet it also represented a second chance, a new beginning. Since walking into the warehouse twenty-six years earlier, I had basically never had another job. Barneys had seen me through my twenties, my thirties, and most of my forties; marriage; two kids; the deaths of my grandfather and my father; more money than I could have imagined and more twists of fate than I'd wish on my worst enemy. Now my marriage was over, Barneys was in the rearview mirror, and I was knocking at the door of a very young fifty. Who knew what would come next?

If it was a sea-change moment in my life, it was also a sea-change moment in the culture. The internet, still basically in its infancy, would soon revolutionize everything from retail to personal communications. Remember, this is the moment when the digital era truly began. Even computers as we know them today were relatively new; Fabien Baron still chuckles remembering the single, enormous computer in the art department during his days there in the 1980s. Even into the '90s, the primary mode of sending orders was the fax machine, and there was a room in the basement where junior buyers would be tasked with typing out international orders on a machine known as a Telex, its hulking predecessor.

By 1998, floppy disks offering AOL subscriptions arrived regularly by mail, but less than half of American adults went online, even if that was about twice as many as two years earlier. The first iMac—the personal computer as design object and fashion statement, with its translucent plastic cover in pop colors—arrived in 1998. Two grad students in computer science founded a company called Google that same year.

The millennium was approaching—before long, everyone would be panicking about a phenomenon called "Y2K," when the computers would reportedly short-circuit and pandemonium would ensue—and I was gung ho on the possibilities of the digital age. I dreamed of a new kind of store, one where digital video would allow customers down the block or across the country to check out merchandise virtually and—with the digital camera as personal shopper—either order it remotely or come to the store to see it, a hybrid model. I tried to drum up investment from a large real-estate trust, to develop the shop in the still-virginal Meatpacking District, where it would be the anchor to a neighborhood I was sure would grow. But it never got off the ground. It would be years before online retail *really* took hold. Jeff Bezos may have been *Time* magazine's 1999 Person of the Year, but selling clothes online, much less designer clothes, was a riddle that would take much, much longer to unravel.

By November of 1998, my consulting contract was winding down. I was technically still at Barneys, but in name more than in reality. More people in the office were working away with no connection to me. There was no point in being there, and I certainly didn't want to sit around. I had an empty feeling in my gut. I had put so much time and effort into building that place from ground up with my father and grandfather. Now the ship was heading into uncharted waters and I didn't want to be on it.

Packing up my office was bizarre. My exit wasn't even an exit from the Seventh Avenue offices across from the store where we'd plotted so much of the company's growth and direction; by the time I left, we were in a Midtown office tower on Fifth Avenue, befitting our ever-more-corporatized status. The day I left for good, no one really knew.

No teary goodbyes, no champagne send-off. I just left. I had gone through the stages of grief—the anger, the guilt, the bargaining . . . three years of bargaining. Now I was running on empty, and there was very little emotion left. The biggest insult isn't anger, it's apathy, and I didn't—I couldn't—care anymore. The second I walked out that door, I thought: *Next.*

# GIVE PEOPLE WHAT THEY DON'T KNOW THEY WANT

Barneys had been a spectacular machine. And we had fucked it up.

But Barneys didn't end—not then. Released from bankruptcy, it went on, even if it seemed to be running on Pressman fumes. Barneys remained a status symbol, in many ways, even more of a status symbol, in the status-obsessed '90s and early aughts. When *Sex & the City* debuted in 1998, Sarah Jessica Parker's Carrie Bradshaw and all her girlfriends were constantly referencing Barneys, just as Sarah Jessica herself did—as she'd told the reporter for the *Vanity Fair* hit piece on me, "Barneys is like a decadent reward. If you're a decent person and you work hard, you get to go to Barneys."

Barneys had always been more than a store. People were proud of it, proud to be associated with it. Before we opened in Japan, on one of our trips, we saw a woman carrying a Barneys shopping bag—we couldn't figure out where it had come from. But when we got closer, we saw that it was a real Barneys bag that she had laminated. That's how much she wanted to keep it. It's telling that that's how people felt about being part of Barneys. Even after all the agita of our final years there, that feeling hung on. It had the energy, the sophistication, of the city itself. "Barneys seemed to me to be a symbol of New York," Jil Sander told me recently.

She wasn't the only one who felt that way. When, after the 9/11 attacks in 2001, New York's retail was hurting as much as its citizens, it was at Barneys that Rudy Giuliani—then its heroic mayor, long before his crackpot, hair-dye-dripping, conspiracy-spouting current era—chose to hold a press conference, to encourage shoppers to return to normalcy, for all of our sakes. Simon even did up a Rudy window, with a papier-mâché mayoral reindeer, "Rudolph the Right-on Reindeer."

"The spirit of New York City is not only alive and well, it's stronger than it was before September 11," Giuliani said from the floor. That spirit, the message was clear, was at Barneys.

.  .  .

Timing is everything. It seems uncanny, in retrospect, that we left Barneys just as another major change was engulfing the world. The internet was a huge shift, but it wasn't the only one. Fashion was changing. The city was changing, too.

You only had to look at Barneys' Seventh Avenue to get a sense of how far it had come in the store's lifetime. Barneys spanned nearly the entire twentieth century: older than Mickey Mouse, Bugs Bunny, the National Broadcasting Corporation, the Empire State Building, the Toll House cookie, and Memorial Day. The Old Homestead Steakhouse on Ninth Avenue, where Fred used to take staffers for dinner after working late, is still there, but Kaps' cafeteria, where Barneys' midcentury salesmen used to get coffee and sandwiches for lunch, had by 1998 turned into the trendy, capital-C Cafeteria, a twenty-four-hour hipster restaurant whose waiters wore Dolce & Gabbana. Chelsea became the new epicenter of the art world, as the galleries that had made SoHo SoHo in the '80s migrated north and west. Up around them sprang restaurants, bars, and clubs—not the seedy sex clubs that had defined the Meatpacking District for everyone but the meatpackers, but see-and-be-seen power spots like the French brasserie Pastis, which opened in 1999.

From Paris, warring titans of industry were building luxury conglomerates, hoovering up young designers to refresh their recently purchased heritage brands and sweetening the deals by investing in their designers' own. Bernard Arnault, who had bought a distressed Dior for a song in the 1980s, was building LVMH. He'd snapped up Kenzo and Loewe, Marc Jacobs, and eventually Fendi and Donna Karan, too. He tried to make a run at Gucci, which a young Tom Ford was then returning to its former glory. Arnault and Gucci waded into a protracted court fight and years of dueling plutocrats. All of that eventually led to the creation of a rival group, now called Kering, which came to acquire Yves Saint Laurent, Bottega Veneta, and Balenciaga.

No designer seemed able, let alone willing, to resist the lure of corporate contracts. A tide of new fashion talent had cropped up in the '90s, the way that Gaultier, Mugler, and Montana had in the '80s, punkish upstarts like John Galliano and Alexander McQueen. Soon they were flush with the corporate investment and seemingly desirable positions. Shortly before I left, Arnault bought a majority stake in Galliano's label, which Barneys had carried off and on for years, and placed him first at Givenchy, then at Dior. McQueen took over the spot he'd vacated at Givenchy, designed it for a few years, and jumped to Kering, which bought his own label. We'd been circling both Galliano and McQueen for years, supporting them when we could, buying small and early—even when they were doing their own production and the quality was not up to snuff. They were dreamers, alien to the cold business of logistics and reality.

Maybe having the backing of businessmen who could handle their logistics and fund their work would be good for them; after all, to some extent that was what Barneys had been doing for years, connecting talented designers with manufacturers and often prepaying small designers and companies for orders so they could actually get them made. "Both designers are young and talented creators and you can't fault a company for trying to stay current," I told *Women's Wear Daily* about the Galliano and McQueen appointments when they called. "Hopefully, they'll then nurture the designers along properly."

Not everyone was as glass-half-full. "The new trend," *The New York Times* wrote, "has seemed in many ways a dubious opportunity, forced on designers by disappearing financing and by the globalization of the fashion business." And whether they nurtured the designers along properly, I don't know. People got very, very rich—Arnault was, for a time, the richest man in Europe—but for the designers, success seemed to come at a cost. McQueen died by suicide in 2010, widely attributed, at least in part, to the punishing pace the conglomerate-led fashion system now demanded. Galliano descended into alcoholism and addiction, and nearly ruined his career with a drunken, antisemitic rant at a Paris bar in 2011.

Though it grew to become a corporation, Barneys had always been the antithesis of corporate—ultimately, it probably grew too large to maintain the charm that was the secret to its success. But the whole world was on a steady march toward corporatization, the fashion business no less than any other. Even the customers began to seem like corporate insiders. "I was surprised by how many women were familiar with even the linguistics of fashion and who the players were," Simon told the *Times* in 1995. "They talk like people who work in the fashion business."

Fashion was undergoing the latest in its long line of evolutions. In Barney Pressman's day, it was a commodity: the sea of sleeves, product to be bought as if by the pound. In Fred's, an art form: the rise of the designer-artist and the connoisseur-customer who understood his or her genius. (And the connoisseur-merchant who was the conduit between the two.) In my day, it turned into a global and globalized fascination, a lingua franca that could be spoken wordlessly between New York, Milan, Paris, London, Tokyo, and everywhere else: the mavens of Japan and of SoHo alike swanning around in their Comme des Garçons. Now, fashion was becoming a pop entertainment, a reality show of mass proportions. The runway shows that had been for industry insiders and trade papers went online, on a new website called Style.com, founded in 2000. (No one remembers now how hard most of the brands fought against this development.) Suddenly everyone seemed to know about the Bryant Park tents where New York Fashion Week was held, whether they had a ticket or not. *America's Next Top Model* began airing on TV in 2003, and *Project Runway* in 2004.

I was less interested in all that. I had done retail already; on to the next. I found other projects. Graydon Carter asked me to become a contributing editor for *Vanity Fair*. My old friend Steve Hanson hired me to help design a new hotel call The James he was opening in Chicago. Vera Wang, whose business Barneys helped to start, had me consult on expanding her line to include fragrance and homewares. And I cowrote my first book, based on the lessons of Barneys and the insight I picked up from the luminaries I met along the way. *Chasing Cool* is about what everybody does, and Barneys didn't—we focused on relevance, and that's what made it cool, not the other way around. It's now assigned reading at business schools across the country, not that it seems to have helped curtail the chase.

The chasers of the cool all had their crack at Barneys. The parade of executives who marched through, each with their own ideas as to how to make it work, seemed endless. They remade some of our mistakes for good measure—they tried, again, to open stores in new markets, like Boston and San Francisco and Las Vegas, and bigger ones at that. Owners would own it for a few years and then pass it off to the next. The vultures sold it to Jones Apparel Group, a very Seventh Avenue concern—they owned Nine West shoes and Anne Klein—in 2004. Within four years, they had sold it to Istithmar, the investment fund of the government of Dubai, for just under a billion dollars in 2007, more than doubling their investment. A few years after that, Istithmar sold a majority stake to a hedge fund zillionaire named Richard Perry in 2012, a stiff money guy with a "fashion designer" wife, Lisa, whose pop art-covered clothes magically appeared in Barneys not long after Perry Capital acquired the company.

The new overseers changed Barneys enormously. They dismissed most of the merchants who remembered the Pressman era, and set about uncharming Barneys. They stripped it of everything that had defined it and turned it into a robot's paradise. They began a major renovation—basically a demolition—of Madison in 2011, and the first thing they did was rip out the mosaics. If you needed a metaphor for the destruction of Barneys as it had been, there it was. "Gone was the glittering mosaic floor, replaced by slabs of cool gray stone. The place was already a more hard-core version of itself: luxury incarnate," *New York* magazine wrote.

The luxury groups, LVMH et al., had so taken over the industry that everyone was chasing their version of the world. Except, instead of needing stores like Barneys, the groups realized they could cut them out and develop their own stores instead. The department stores helped accelerate that by racing to discount merchandise to get it off their shelves; the holiday sale season crept up earlier and earlier every year, from what used to be a time set by gentleman's agreement to whenever the executives started to sweat. Once one store moved their sale, the rest had no choice but to follow, a vicious downward spiral. As the Mafia would tell you, war is bad for business, and these were war games that screwed the whole retail sector. The customer learned that there was no need to pay full price for anything, and the brands were powerless to stop it—except at their own stores, which they began opening like never before.

If you walk westward on Sixty-First Street, from Madison toward Fifth, you can still see a little sliver of the mosaic that endured: It's preserved, and visible from the street, a testament to the past like a mural in Pompeii. But that's about all you'll see of Barneys on Madison anymore. Retail had its hard years as well as its boom times—the 2008 crash and the subsequent recession took a toll—but whatever the cause, in 2019, once again, Barneys declared bankruptcy. Once again, there were public eulogies, and this time, a depressing, everything-must-go fire sale. Once again, excoriating in the press and lists of vendors owed millions. And once again, Barneys was sold, this time for a pittance, to a company called Authentic Brands Group, which bought up intellectual property and copyrights and licensed them out. If you've seen a T-shirt stamped with a likeness of Marilyn Monroe or Elvis Presley, you've seen an ABG. Flush with private-equity investment, they've lately been buying up truly authentic brands—Barneys, Brooks Brothers, Reebok—and licensing those out, too. That's how Barneys became, just in time for its centennial, little shop-in-shops in Saks Fifth Avenue. Years after their attempted takeover, Saks got Barneys at last.

· · ·

Barneys had a way of touching everyone who came into its orbit. The people who had worked there, the people who had shopped there, and even the people who never bought a thing but went to see and feel and learn and enjoy there. Its reach was enormous, and people to this day go goggle-eyed when they realize I am one of *those* Pressmans. Barneys was bigger than Barneys. "I'm still in mourning," Linda Evangelista told me recently. "It's hard to fathom New York without Barneys." Sandra Bernhard still does a joke in her shows about it: "Like the Dalai Lama said, the closing of Barneys is one of the greatest tragedies of mankind."

Barneys was the pinnacle of aspiration. We got dinged again and again for being expensive, for being elitist—but we weren't elitist. We were elite. That's a big difference. Where everything has now become democratized to the point of being a fucking bore, Barneys had a point of view. Fred's guiding belief was in the best, and he passed it down to me. When the fashion journalists used to ask me after the shows who my favorite designers of that season were, I would say, "Quality." Quality is the best designer, always.

Digging back through twenty-five years of history, I can see more clearly than ever what made Barneys great. The people did, for one. We hired the best people, who were often not the most obvious people. We trusted our guts. The Pressmans were the genius loci of Barneys, and we set the tone—Fred used to say all the time, "You can never stop giving direction"—but we couldn't do it alone. The greatest merchants of their generation came through Barneys, absorbing the magic mix. I used to tell my team, we've got to be our own Bauhaus, the German school from which so many of the great artists and designers emerged in the '20s and '30s. Simon never lets me forget the one time I got over-excited and told him what we needed was to create the Barneys Bathhouse. He roared. "No, that's slightly different, honey," he said.

We trusted them. We let them follow their own guts. We kept an eye on the sales, and certainly an eye on the margins, but we weren't slaves to the figures. You *have* to buy some things just because you believe in them. One of my longtime buyers remembered going to one of the most famous Comme des Garçons shows of all time, a collection where Rei showed outfits stuffed like lumpy pillowcases: The "lumps and bumps" collection for spring 1997. The real artists got it—Merce Cunningham did a whole dance performance with them—but they were not what you'd call salable. My poor buyer was trembling in his seat, wondering how the hell he was going to sell any of this stuff, and he looked to me to see if I'd forbid him from placing our usual order. But I only laughed. "Good luck," I told him, on the way out of the show. The other stores used to watch what we bought, wait for it to become successful, and then follow our lead, leaving us to take all the risk. They would literally tell our buyers that. We didn't care. We bought Hussein Chalayan's graduate collection, for god's sake, for which he literally buried his dresses like corpses and then dug them up again later. No one questioned it. Otherwise, it's just sleeves.

The pace has only gotten faster. Digital and social media have made everything accessible instantly, multiplying everything a zillion-fold. So many people who love fashion don't even see it in person anymore, they just click. One has to question how these new websites even make a dime, and the places that seemed eternal are teetering. Neiman Marcus declared bankruptcy in 2020, and Saks' owners swooped in and bought them in 2024. Early this year, they announced they'd close Neiman's downtown Dallas flagship, the one that's stood on Main Street for more than one hundred years. Could it be that Saks is next?

Online, everyone has an opinion, and no one's an expert. The only expert is data, and everyone follows the analytics. If something sells on day one, they buy a hundred more; if something doesn't, they never touch it again. But that's not merchandising. It's a recipe for a Stepford store where everyone will end up looking the same. Head-to-toe shit!

Analytics is a way of thinking big. Get the most information, comb it for patterns, maximize your sales, minimize your risks. That misses the point completely. You have to take risks. You don't give the customer what they want. You give them what they don't know they want yet. You've got to tell them the story behind it, and the story's gotta be true. They may not always know what they want, but they know what's bull, and they're not stupid. Tell them the truth, show them the things you love, and they're yours forever. It's a continual conversation. Some things took longer to bloom than others, but that's not a reason to give up. Even after it was a big store, Barneys didn't think big; it thought small. The small labels we searched for and ferreted out, the aspiring customer that could only buy a lipstick at a time, the personality and charm that comes from specificity. We might have been the size of a department store at the end, but we never were one. We had the soul of a specialty store. And the chip on our shoulder of a downtown runt, till the end.

# THE BARNEYS DIASPORA

One of the things I'm proudest of is how strong Barneys' influence remains today, and you don't have to take my word for it. "Every single retail person was influenced by what Barneys did," Vera Wang says. "Whenever I go to a store, I think, *Gene did this first*." It didn't just happen, and it wasn't just me. With the hindsight of history, it seems clearer than ever that the greatness of Barneys was its people and its customers. A store without a soul is just real estate—at best, it's a supermarket. But Barneys was the wonderland it was because of the people who passed through its doors.

The Barneys diaspora stretches far and wide. Barneys alums have bubbled out into the highest reaches of the fashion and retail industries, assuming high-level positions at Prada, Dior, Burberry, Zegna, and Thom Browne, to name a few. Many launched stores of their own. Others, creative agencies and PR firms that represent the best in the business. Our old art directors are the creative directors of the top magazines, the top ad campaigns. Now they've filtered out into the world, but when they were all together under our one roof, it was magic. They're the reason, as Marc Jacobs put it to me recently, that Barneys held the torch as the most prestigious address for designer brands. "I felt like I must be doing something right if Barneys wanted what I was doing," he said.

Writing this book, I spoke with many of them, often for the first time in years or even decades. Their memories informed and reinforced my understanding of what went on in those twenty-five years at Barneys, and this book would have been poorer without them. To all of them, I am grateful. And to the many more I didn't get to, know that your contributions also made Barneys what it was.

My first thanks go to my family. To Fred and Phyllis, Barney and Bertha in the big Barneys upstairs. I hope Fred would recognize his life's work in this book, and I wish I had had the chance to talk it all through with him again. In his absence, I relied on Mom's meticulously kept collection of letters and scrapbooks, documenting their lives together from their first dates. Mom herself was able to sit for several hours of interviews with me and my cowriter before she passed away in April 2024, at the age of ninety-five. My sister Nancy's giant collection of Barneys ads and photos helped color in many of the lines and jog many of my memories. I owe a huge debt of gratitude to my first wife, Bonnie Pressman, for sharing her own recollections of both our time together and her impact on the store.

Then, the merchants. Fred's men's merchants made, in many cases, commitments that lasted nearly a lifetime—that's how devoted they were to him, and to Barneys. Eddie Glantz died in 2004, but his wife, Gabriella Forte, shared wonderful memories of his and her experiences with Fred and Barney. Peter Rizzo, whom Fred considered almost a third son, arrived in 1972 and stayed until 1997. Roger Cohen, a gentleman. The furnishings gurus Tom (he'll always be Tommy to me) Kalenderian, who joined in 1979 and stayed for forty years, and Jody Kuss, his partner in crime, whose sentences he still finishes. Peter went on to become the president of Bergdorf Goodman (where he realized that Barneys uptown did as much business as hundred-year-old BG in its *first year*). Cohen ran Corneliani, the Italian suit maker. Jody took a top job at Coach. And Tommy became and remains the chairman of the Americas at Ermenegildo Zegna. Those are the kind of careers the School of Fred prepares you for. Thanks, too, to Gildo Zegna, who also shared his memories of Fred.

Michael Schreier—aka Michael Skidmore—was both a friend and a longtime colleague, and an irrepressible font of memories. Several of our other friends from the '70s shared their memories: Jeff Klein, Steve Hanson, Jeff Lowitz, Bob Beauchamp, Johnny Calvani. And several staffers from the store in the 1970s helped me remember that time better than I would have alone: Paul Buckter, John Overgaard, and Hal Davis. Pat Harrington and Caryle Duffy were present for the birth of Basco in the late '70s and remembered it fondly and well, though Lance Karesh, the designer who elevated it with me to the success it became, sadly died in 2018. Peter Guarraci, a riot who shared Fred's love of shoes, spoke with me before he died in February 2024.

Then there were those who didn't work at Barneys but worked *with* Barneys from their perches in the men's market. Jean de Noyer, whose boutique I used to shop at (and whose La Goulue restaurants I still eat at). Barry Wishnow. Paul Cavaco, who styled some of the early Barneys fashion shows, and introduced me to Bonnie. My friend Paul Corvino, who was Barneys' ad rep at *The New York Times*.

Among the women's merchants, both Louise Ohm and Barbara Warner are no longer with us. But Marion Greenberg, the Bendel's buyer who clued me in on women's, shared wonderful details, and I reconnected with several women's merchants from the 1970s and 1980s: Debbie (Bernstein) Martin, Kathy Walsh, Beverly Wilburn, and Phyllis Babila. Jayne Harkness, the queen of the Co-op, who came on board in the '80s and took Nancy under her wing. And many more women's merchants from the '80s and '90s. Judy Collinson, an import from Iowa, who had run Reminiscence, a kooky-cool downtown vintage shop, and eventually took over all of Barneys' women's buying. Sandra Constantine, a no-nonsense merchant with a sharp eye for accessories. Richard Lambertson, only at Barneys a short time but at a key moment as the women's store was getting off the ground. Jeffrey Kalinsky, who worked for Bonnie in shoes and later ran his own namesake boutique to great success in the aughts. Alex Koo and J. P. Correa, designer-buying partners in crime in the Barneys of the '90s. Terence Bogan, who succeeded Jayne at the Co-op. Lyssa Horn, who ran Barneys' Paris operation and remains one of the Barneys diaspora's central connecting nodes (ask her for *anyone*'s phone number). Vince Ehly, David Rubinstein, and Nick Wooster among the latter-day men's merchants. And Julie Gilhart, a displaced Texan who came to Barneys young and stayed on long after I left, eventually rising to become fashion director.

From operations, we were able to speak with Frank Ball, who worked with us in the '90s, though not, sadly, his late wife Anne, who ran Barneys America. John Wolohojian and Marina Crispo, who ran the downtown men's and women's stores with velvet-gloved iron fists, and Kevin Dyson, who ran several Barneys America locations and eventually much of Madison. Madison's top personal shopper, Louise Maniscalco. Thanks also to Betty Atkins, a long-serving veteran of the finance office.

Among the architects and designers, Jim Harb, who designed many of the Barneys America stores, and Jeff Hutchison gave us wonderful context. Andrée sadly passed away in 2013. Peter Marino, whose career Barneys all but made, wasn't able to make it to the phone.

Public relations was a huge part of Barneys' success, and we had some of the all-time great PRs. The formidable Mallory Andrews (who married her Barneys colleague, one of our top finance guys, Jesse de la Rama). Her team from over the years: Roman Alonso, Ellen Carey, and Gina Nanni. (And her friend and collaborator, Anne Livet, whose company, Livet Reichard, arranged many of Barneys' collaborations with artists, including the 1986 Levi's jean-jacket show.) All of them have memories like steel traps, and publicists' native discretion, despite my pleas to spill it all.

Advertising, too, played a huge role at Barneys, and this book gave us an opportunity to reach back decades to the greats of the past. Amil Gargano, still sharp as a tack. Tom Messner and Helayne Spivack, who worked on the Barneys account at Ally & Gargano, and Steve Horn (Lyssa's dad!), who directed the "You'll All Need Clothes" spot. SVA's Milton Glaser Archive had wonderful holdings of the Barneys work by Glaser's partner, Ed McCabe. We found great materials in the Indiana University Library's Moving Image Archives, as well as invaluable help from their curators and librarians, not to mention the archives of the New York Public Library and the library at the Fashion Institute of Technology. Our early art director, Marc Balet, who helped set the tone for Barneys' advertising in the modern era. Paula Greif, who directed some of the great 1980s ads. Fabien Baron, whom I hired from *New York Woman* magazine and went on to become one of the industry's great art directors, challenged only by his successor, Doug Lloyd. Ronnie Cooke Newhouse, whose '90s ads with Steven Meisel and Linda Evangelista are still being referenced today, often. Thanks also to Linda herself, who got on the phone to fondly remember those good old days. And a number of the other great ad campaign photographers and talent, like Timothy Greenfield-Sanders and Sandra Bernhard.

And windows! Few had as great an impact on Barneys as Simon Doonan did, and he remains its stalwart ambassador, even after its demise, though I am grateful as well to have reconnected with one of his longtime collaborators, Steven Johanknecht.

The modern Barneys we ushered in depended as much on the great fashion designers as it did on us merchants, and I am proud to say we started or supercharged many, many careers. It's no surprise that many of those designers remain close friends today, and generously shared their reminiscences. Azzedine passed away in 2017, though his former assistant, Sophie Théallet, shared many great stories from our times in his atelier. Giorgio Armani sent in wonderful memories. Calvin Klein. Tommy Hilfiger. Jean Touitou, now known for his own label, A.P.C., but whom I met first at Kenzo, and then at Agnès b. Paul Smith, who memorialized our first collaboration by gifting me a lovely little David Hockney drawing in 1977. One of Barneys' most treasured discoveries, Dries Van Noten. The inimitable Romeo Gigli. Martin Margiela, who has not given an interview in decades, kept up his streak, but his longtime comms maven, Patrick Scallon, gave great insight. The greatest designers of the '90s, Helmut Lang, Jil Sander, and Marc Jacobs, all chimed in about their own experiences. My dear friend Vera Wang. Jean-Michel Cazabat.

About the culture of fashion and the culture of New York and beyond in the '70s, '80s, and '90s, thanks to Adrian and Bob Leibowitz; Lisa and Eric Eisner; AREA's Serge Becker and Shawn Hausman; Dianne Brill; Browns' Robert Forrest; and my Paris driver and confidant, Eric de Vuyst. The things that guy has seen.

Jen Marshall and Jane von Mehren at ACM, with the kind of sharp eye and discriminating taste that would've made them excellent Barneys buyers, helped coax this book into being. At Viking Books and Penguin Random House, Rick Kot saw the early potential, and Patrick Nolan and Emma Dollar saw us through to the finish line. Gabriel Baumgaertner provided research support and double-checked some of the stickiest bits.

I am grateful to my coauthor-in-crime and good friend Matthew Schneier, who was instrumental in writing this book with me. He started out as the sweetest guy and ended up, for better or worse, just like me. To my patient wife Christine, for putting up with the long process of researching and writing this book, and for dealing gracefully with the ghosts of history. And to my children, Keith, who was instrumental in getting ancient footage digitized, my daughter, Wallis, and my young son, Fred, who's keeping his grandfather's name alive.

Gene at Mr. Chows. aw
for Basco 83

# PHOTO SOURCES AND CREDITS

Page v. From the collection of the author.

Page 3. Image by Fred R. Conrad, originally published in *The New York Times*, courtesy of Redux Pictures.

Page 14. From the collection of the author.

Page 18. From the collection of the author.

Page 18. From the collection of the author.

Page 25. From the collection of the author.

Page 30. From the collection of the author.

Page 42. From the collection of the author.

Page 43. From the collection of the author.

Page 49. From the collection of the author.

Page 60. From the collection of the author.

Page 72. Source: Barneys Advertisement.

Page 89. From the collection of the author.

Page 101. Source: Barneys Advertisement, 1976.

Page 117. From the collection of the author.

Page 117. From the collection of the author.

Page 117. From the collection of the author.

Page 132. From the collection of the author.

Page 160. Photo by Bob Kiss.

Page 164. From the collection of the author.

Page 173. From the collection of the author.

Page 181. From the collection of the author.

Page 181. From the collection of the author.

Page 182. From the collection of the author.

Page 182. From the collection of the author.

Page 187. Source: Barneys Advertisement, 1968.

Page 187. Source: Barneys Advertisement, 1970.

Page 203. From the collection of the author.

Page 211. © Dafydd Jones.

Page 222. Photograph by Frank Schramm, originally published in *New York* magazine/Vox Media, LLC.

Pages 228–29. Photograph by Harry Benson.

Page 236. Ron Galella/Getty Images

Page 250. From the collection of the author.

Page 267. © Steven Meisel.

Page 268. © Elliott Erwitt/Magnum Photos

Page 268. Portrait © by Timothy Greenfield-Sanders.

Page 275. By Annie Amante Photo.

Page 283. © Roxanne Lowit.

Page 288. Photo © Andrew Garn.

Page 292. © Stephanie Berger.

Page 293. © Stephanie Berger.

Page 294. © Roxanne Lowit.

Pages 298–99. © Peter Mauss/Esto.

Page 314. © Fred Licht, all rights reserved.

Page 314. © Fred Licht, all rights reserved.

Page 315. © Fred Licht, all rights reserved.

Page 324. Image by Kimberly Butler.

Page 324. Image by Kimberly Butler.

Page 329. 1994 cover/ *New York Daily News* / TCA.

Page 341. *Women's Wear Daily*, via Getty Images

Page 354. From the collection of the author.

Page 384. Photo by Arthur Elgort.

## *100 YEARS of PUBLISHING*

———◇———

Harold K. Guinzburg and George S. Oppenheimer founded Viking in 1925 with the intention of publishing books "with some claim to permanent importance rather than ephemeral popular interest." After merging with B. W. Huebsch, a small publisher with a distinguished catalog, Viking enjoyed almost fifty years of literary and commercial success before merging with Penguin Books in 1975.

Now an imprint of Penguin Random House, Viking specializes in bringing extraordinary works of fiction and nonfiction to a vast readership. In 2025, we celebrate one hundred years of excellence in publishing. Our centennial colophon features the original logo for Viking, created by the renowned American illustrator Rockwell Kent: a Viking ship that evokes enterprise, adventure, and exploration, ideas that inspired the imprint's name at its founding and continue to inspire us.

———◇———

For more information on Viking's history, authors, and books, please visit penguin.com/viking.